PENGUIN BOOKS

Cinema Bhojpuri

Avijit Ghosh graduated in history from St Xavier's College, Ranchi, and completed his Masters and M.Phil degrees from Jawaharlal Nehru University, New Delhi. Born in Agartala, Tripura, he grew up in the small towns of Bihar and Jharkhand—Dumka, Giridih, Arrah and Ranchi. He has been a journalist since 1991 and has worked with the Press Trust of India, *Pioneer* and *Telegraph*, and is now with the *Times of India*.

Ghosh writes regularly on cinema and sports, and is the author of the novel *Bandicoots in the Moonlight*, published by Penguin Books India. He lives in New Delhi with his mother, wife, and two naughty children, Abhishek and Diya.

Cinema
Bhojpuri

Avijit Ghosh

PENGUIN BOOKS

An imprint of Penguin Random House

PENGUIN BOOKS

USA | Canada | UK | Ireland | Australia
New Zealand | India | South Africa | China | Singapore

Penguin Books is part of the Penguin Random House group of companies
whose addresses can be found at global.penguinrandomhouse.com

Published by Penguin Random House India Pvt. Ltd
4th Floor, Capital Tower 1, MG Road,
Gurugram 122 002, Haryana, India

First published by Penguin Books India 2010

10 9 8 7 6 5 4 3 2

ISBN 9780143103783

Typeset in Sabon by Eleven Arts, New Delhi

Printed at Repro India Limited

www.penguin.co.in

For the cinema halls of Arrah—Rupam, Mohan, Sapna and Moti Mahal—where I fell in love with the movies.

Contents

THE EVOLUTION OF BHOJPURI FILM MUSIC

Preface

I spent most of my teenage years in Arrah, a small town in Bihar's Bhojpur district. In the 1970s, the price of a balcony ticket never exceeded Rs 3.70 in any of the theatres. But we preferred to watch Hindi films in the cheaper rear stalls, or, even the special student class that used to cost just Rs 1.05.

My first Bhojpuri movie was *Balam Pardesia* (1979). I enjoyed the family drama though I was addicted to the action films of Amitabh Bachchan, Dharmendra, Feroze Khan and Dara Singh. That's because I already knew the movie's songs by heart. A neighbourhood grocer owned a record player and used to play them over a loudspeaker throughout the day. Thanks to the grocer, I had developed a fondness for Bhojpuri film songs by the time we left Arrah.

The idea of writing this book first came to me in 2005 after I saw *Sasura Bada Paisewala* and *Panditji Bataeen Na Biyah Kab Hoee*. I started working on the book in fits and starts in 2006. The work gathered momentum in 2008 after I finished writing my first novel, *Bandicoots in the Moonlight*, which incidentally is located in Ganeshnagar, a fictional Bhojpuri-speaking town.

This book tells the story of Bhojpuri cinema since its inception in 1962. I have spoken to many people associated with the industry, including those who worked in the industry in the 1960s. Their narratives have hopefully given the book an up, close and personal view of the times. I have also referred to regional newspapers of the 1960s and 1980s. This will provide some insight into how Bhojpuri films impacted the intelligentsia in cities like Benares, especially in the 1960s.

With the help of my esteemed colleague Vinay Pandey, I have offered English translations of every Bhojpuri film named in the book, either in the filmography or in the text. This wasn't easy because the nuances, located in a particular cultural context, are often lost in translation. In some places, we have offered a flavour of the text rather than a literal translation. The responsibility of any error is, of course, only mine.

I sincerely hope that the book will be enjoyed both by Bhojpuri film buffs as well as anybody who enjoys cinema.

Many people have contributed to the shaping of this book. I am indebted to Munnu Prasad Pandey, veteran journalist who owns and edits *Rambha*, for letting me look at the old issues of this Benares-based weekly film newspaper. I am also grateful to Harmandir Singh 'Hamraaz', the famous collector of melodies, for helping me with the filmography. I will always be indebted to Ramesh Kumar Singh (*Pioneer*) for his generous help during my Benares visit in May 2008 and to Sushil Mishra for being my friend and guide on the same trip. I will never forget the motorbike ride on a searing summer afternoon to the *qasbah* cinema halls about twenty kilometres from Benares.

I am equally grateful to Subodh Verma, Manoj Mitta, Peggy Mohan, Vanaja Thekkat and S.P. Pachauri for their support.

I wish to record my appreciation for Kunal Singh, Rakesh Pandey, Ashok Bhatia, Sanjay Sharma, Anil Grover, Firoze Rangoonwalla, Shiv Viswanathan, Susmita Dasgupta, Imtiaz Ahmed, Bipan Chandra, Aditya and Mridula Mukherjee, Chandra Bhan Prasad, D. Shyam Babu, Ananth Srinivas and Jagdish Yadav.

I believe this is also a suitable occasion to say thanks to some friends and colleagues: Shishir Prashant, Deepika Sahu, Sidharth Gautam, Chitra Padmanabhan, Anuradha Raman, Namrata Joshi, Samita Bhatia, Amita Shah, Monobina Gupta, Anirban Das Mahapatra, Pradeep Thakur, Dhananjay Mahapatra, Syed Saud Akhtar, Shashi Prasad, Malini Sen, Asha Ramachandran, Renu Pachauri, Novy Kapadia, Diwakar, Nandita Sengupta, Meenakshi Sinha, Shreya Roy Chowdhury, Deepak Manki, Geetashree, Rakesh Batabyal, S. Anand, Shankar Raghuraman, Amit Bhattacharya, Nirmal Sharma, Neeraj Paul, Vijay Lokpalli, Yeshi Seli and Atul Tiwari.

I would also like to thank Udayan Mitra and Anupama Ramakrishnan at Penguin who edited the manuscript and hammered it into shape.

I must express my gratitude to my mother Anjali, sister Bani and my Jamai babu. And last, but not the least, this book wouldn't have been completed but for the support and help offered by my wife and first reader-editor, Rachna. My gratitude cannot be expressed in words.

PS: Abhishek and Diya, if you want to know more about Bhojpuri films after watching one of those VCDs kept in the study, you know what to do.

Introduction

Everybody knows of Rani Mukherjee. But few have heard of Rani Chatterjee. Just as Ms Mukherjee has reigned over Bollywood, Ms Chatterjee is a star in her own right in Bhojpuri films. Yet an overwhelming majority of the cosmopolitan multiplex audience is unaware of her existence.[1] Why? This book strives to answer that question by narrating the story of Cinema Bhojpuri.

In less than two years, Bhojpuri cinema will celebrate its golden jubilee. It has been a remarkable journey, involving men and women who may not have made it to the covers of glossy Bollywood film magazines, but who have contributed enormously to the making and shaping of this genre. It is a journey marked by highs and lows, a journey that encapsulates as well as maps the evolving social and political trajectories of the region in the larger context of a changing India.

For instance, back in the 1960s and 1970s, the audience of Bhojpuri films was largely confined to eastern Uttar Pradesh and Bihar. Now, due to migration, the genre's footprint has expanded significantly to include cities like Mumbai, Delhi, Calcutta, Ludhiana, Jalandhar, Amritsar and the various towns of Gujarat and Rajasthan.

1

Roughly speaking, Bhojpuri films can be divided into three phases. The first period (1962–68) begins with *Ganga Maiya Tohe Piyari Chadhaibo* (1962), followed by other high-quality movies such as *Bidesiya* (1963), *Laagi Nahin Chhute Ram* (1963) and *Hamaar Sansar* (1965).

Between 1969 and 1976, only one Bhojpuri film, *Dher Chalaaki Jin Kara* was released.[2] The comatose genre burst back into life with *Dangal* (1977), gathered momentum with superhits such as *Balam Pardesia* (1979) and *Ganga Kinare Mora Gaon* (1983) and continued with crests and troughs till 2001.

There is no gap between the second and the third phase, but the third phase marks the advent of a new, confident Bhojpuri cinema. In the five years between 2004 and 2008, over 275 Bhojpuri films have been produced. In 2006 alone, a whopping seventy-six Bhojpuri films were cleared by the censor board. The fledgling cottage industry of the 1960s has now become a bustling regional film industry. In all, between 1962–2008 at least 475 Bhojpuri films have been released.[3] By now, the figure would have easily crossed 500.

In the 2001 Census, about 3.3 crore Indians recorded Bhojpuri as their mother tongue, though the number of those who speak or simply understand the language must be several times higher.[4] In other words, in terms of geographical reach as well as population, the industry has plenty to play for.

Over the years, Bhojpuri films have become visually glossier than before. Gone are the days when films were canned in 16mm and blown up to 35mm. Now big-budget films are shot in CinemaScope and some have even been shot abroad in London, Mauritius and the Middle East.

Thematically, a majority of Bhojpuri films belong to the broad category of family dramas, with plenty of songs, dance, laughter and tears. Most superhits till the end of the 1980s fall in this category. With time, however, the percentage of action films has grown significantly in the genre.

There are a few mythologicals too, but these have generally flopped. Other categories are exceptions to the rule. *Bairi Kangna* (1992), *Piparwa Paar Ke Brahm* (2004), and *Naag Nagin* (2008) are rare supernatural movies in the genre.[5] *Tu Hamaar Haoo* (2007), which borrowed heavily from the Bollywood thriller, *Darr* (1993), is one of its kind. *Ho Jaye Da Naina Chaar* (1995), a remake of Bollywood film *Kohinoor* (1960), which starred Meena Kumari and Dilip Kumar, is a one-off costume drama with palaces, kings and swordfights.[6] There are some dacoit dramas too: *Saiyan Bedardi* (2002), *Ganga Jwala* (1987), *Dhartiputra* (2005) and *Hum Ta Ho Gaini Tohaar* (2005) to name a few. Half-hearted attempts to film Rabindranath Tagore's classic, *Nauka Doobi*, had a disappointing outcome: *Piya Bin Nahi Chain* (1991).

In recent years, the genre has attracted Bollywood biggies, actors as well as producers, leading to it gaining some prestige. Way back in 1984, Amitabh Bachchan made a special appearance in director Sujit Kumar's *Paan Khaye Saiyan Hamaar*. In recent years, he has played major roles in two big-budget films, *Ganga* (2006) and *Gangotri* (2007). And who in his wildest dreams would have foreseen six prints of *Spiderman 3* being dubbed in Bhojpuri and actor Ravi Kishan (also spelt as Ravi Kishen and Ravi Kissen) being the *desi* voice for Toby Maguire?[7]

The early whispers of the current aggressive stage could be heard in the moderate success of *Saiyan Hamaar* in 2002

Well-known novelist Amitav Ghosh watched Bhojpuri films like *Mai Jaisan Bhauji Hamaar* while doing research for the novel *Sea of Poppies*.[11]

and *Kanyadaan* in 2003. But this third wave became a tsunami with the blockbuster *Sasura Bada Paisewala* in 2004, which turned actor Manoj Tiwari into a superstar. Superhits such as *Panditji Bataeen Na Biyah Kab Hoee* (2005) and *Nirahua Rickshawala* (2007) ensured that the industry continued to enjoy the upward surge.

The going was too good to be true. In 2007, Cinema Bhojpuri became the target of sectarian violence aimed at migrants from Bihar and Uttar Pradesh. From Mumbai to Nashik to Ludhiana, cinema halls showing Bhojpuri films were attacked. Posters were torn, prints were burnt and the audience beaten up. In Punjab, the Sikh extremist group Babbar Khalsa was suspected to be involved in the blast in a cinema hall showing a Bhojpuri film.[8] In Mumbai, these attacks were allegedly carried out by Raj Thackeray's political outfit, the Maharashtra Navnirman Sena (MNS). Social scientists feel that the attacks are expressions of envy and resentment stemming from the politics of insecurity.[9] Political scientist Imtiaz Ahmed believes that in cities such as Mumbai and Ludhiana, Bhojpuri films had not only become synonymous with a particular social group but also symbolized its success,[10] an observation that highlights the enormous distance covered by the genre. Despite many such hiccups, however, the journey continues.

So let us get back to the beginning and find out how it all started.

PART I

THE
STORY OF
BHOJPURI CINEMA

I

Jai Ganga Maiya

**The making of *Ganga Maiya Tohe Piyari Chadhaibo*,
the first Bhojpuri feature film**

Some time in the latter half of the 1950s, character actor Nazir Hussain met the then President, Dr Rajendra Prasad, at a film awards function in Mumbai. Hussain, remembered among Hindi film lovers as the caring vicar who brings up Amitabh Bachchan in Bollywood blockbuster *Amar Akbar Anthony* (1977), was tall and fair. 'Are you a Punjabi?' the President asked Hussain. When the actor replied that he was from Ghazipur district in eastern Uttar Pradesh, it was a moment of serendipity for Rajendra babu. He immediately started talking to him in Bhojpuri—after all, India's first president was born in Jeeradei village in west Bihar's Bhojpuri-speaking Siwan district.

The conversation soon veered towards movies. Rajendra babu asked Hussain, 'Why don't you make a film in Bhojpuri?' The actor gently submitted that he was a mere character artiste and making a film required a lot of money. But Rajendra babu wasn't giving up and insisted, 'It is hard work for sure. You also require a lot of courage. But you can do it.'[1] The President, in fact, was articulating Nazir Hussain's own heartfelt desire.

A couple of precedents had also inspired the character actor who had already made a name for himself playing Dharamdas, the protagonist's faithful servant in director Bimal Roy's *Devdas* (1955), the story of a young man who becomes an alcoholic when his family does not allow him to marry the woman he loves.

The encouragement Hussain got from the President prompted him into action. He had already penned the story of *Ganga Maiya Tohe Piyari Chadhaibo* which roughly means, O Mother Ganga I'll offer you the yellow cloth. Yellow cloth is considered to be auspicious.

But Hussain, who was also working as director Bimal Roy's assistant, had handed over the script to the masterclass director of women-oriented films. *Ganga Maiya Tohe Piyari Chadhaibo* too had a similar subject. Roy had liked the story and probably wanted to film it. But now Hussain wanted his script back. 'He told Bimal *da* that he wanted to make the film in Bhojpuri. Roy was surprised. "Bhojpuri? What language?" he asked. Hussain replied, "It is the language of the President." He then took the script back.'[2]

Hussain had come to believe that if a critically acclaimed and commercially successful film like *Ganga Jamuna* (1961) could have some dialogues in Avadhi, then making a Bhojpuri movie wasn't just a pipe dream.

In fact, it is possible to argue that even the soul of Bimal Roy's *Do Bigha Zameen* (1953), which dealt with a migrant peasant's plight in Calcutta, had a distinctive Bhojpuri flavour, though the film was made in Hindi. One can easily visualise Balraj Sahni, who plays the farmer turned rickshaw-puller, speaking in Bhojpuri.

Incidentally, Hussain was not the only one thinking about making a Bhojpuri film. According to writer-director Govind Moonis, Hindi film actor Bhagwan Sinha was among those who nursed a similar dream. Sinha, who had played the villain in Chetan Anand's *House No. 44* (1955), was from Patna. He loved literature. 'Sinha had selected a story by Babu Shivpujan Sahay titled *Ek Kahani Ka Plot* and had engaged Kalim Rahi from Patna to write the film's screenplay. I was to direct that film. We had almost completed the script, which had shaped up well. Then Bhagwan Sinha started looking for a financier but it was very difficult to find one,' recalls Moonis, who later directed *Nadiya Ke Paar* (1982), the superhit Hindi film produced by Rajshri Productions.[3] Incidentally, Sinha also played a small role in *Ganga Maiya Tohe Piyari Chadhaibo*.

It is quite possible that several others like Sinha also wanted to make a film in the regional language around the same time. But a chance encounter between Nazir Hussain and Bishwanath Prasad Shahabadi, a rich businessman from west Bihar, set the ball rolling for Cinema Bhojpuri.

Born in Bandhuchhapra village, about sixteen miles from Bihar's Arrah town, Shahabadi was a prosperous owner of mica and coal mines with a flourishing liquor contract business to boot. He owned movie theatres in Dhanbad and Giridih and had some patriotic credentials too. Back in 1938, he had bought six yards of khadi from Rajendra Prasad at a special auction for Rs 15,000, which was his way of contributing to the cause of freedom.[4]

His son, Rajkumar Shahabadi, says that his father would have never produced a film but for a personal request made by Rajendra babu after he had become the President of India. 'In fact, our surname was Shah. On Rajendra babu's request, my father changed his surname to Shahabadi.'[5]

On a visit to Mumbai, Bishwanath Shahabadi went to a film studio with a friend to see the shooting of a Hindi film called *Paagal Premi*. Later, at a tea stall, he was discussing the shortcomings of what he had seen when Nazir Hussain overheard him.[6] Hussain was impressed by the arguments made by Shahabadi. Since both came from the Bhojpuri-speaking region, the two got talking. As the character actor had taken the script of his film back from Bimal Roy and was desperately looking for a producer, he immediately narrated the story's outline to 'the simple and humble businessman,' as a *Rambha* article says, and stated that he could make a Bhojpuri film provided someone was willing to invest Rs 1.5 lakh in it. Impressed with the story, Shahabadi readily agreed to the proposal and fished out Rs 10,000—all the cash he was carrying that day—from his pocket.[7]

Now it was all about putting the rest of the team together. Both wanted a director who understood the nuances of the script. They finally chose Kundan Kumar, a young, talented director from Benares. Kumar had already directed Hindi films such as *Bade Ghar Ki Bahu* (1960), starring Geeta Bali and Abhi Bhattacharya, and was then shooting *Aag Aur Paani* with Balraj Sahni and Nirupa Roy. Unfortunately, the second film was never completed.

The core team wanted Hindi film actress Kumkum to play the heroine's role, but it was not easy to get her to join the cast. She was the lead in the great director Mehboob Khan's much-hyped *Son of India* (1962). 'I was approached by Nazir Hussain. He convinced Mehboobsahib to allow me to do *Ganga Maiya Tohe Piyari Chadhaibo*,' says Kumkum, who had already made her mark in films like *Mother India* (1957) and *Kali Topi Laal Rumaal* (1959).[8]

Ashim Kumar was chosen to play the male lead. He had played the role of Paro's step-son in Bimal Roy's *Devdas* and Nazir Hussain knew him. Ashim was a Bengali, his surname being Bhattacharya, but he was born and brought up in Benares. 'He used to speak Bhojpuri like it was his mother tongue,' says Mumtaz Hussain.[9]

The film's *muhurat* (symbolic first shot) was conducted at Patna's Shaheed Smarak (a memorial for martyrs) on

16 February 1961 and the shooting began the following day.[10] The film was shot around Bihta, a qasbah about thirty kilometres from Patna, and in Benares.

Producer Shahabadi's initial experiences in the Mumbai film industry were far from pleasant. By his own admission, nobody paid much attention to what he said. 'I was only regarded as a *mota bakra* [a fat moneybag]. *Ganga Maiya Tohe Piyari Chadhaibo* was finally completed for Rs 5 lakh and not for Rs 1.5 lakh as promised.'[11] The first shot in *Ganga Maiya Tohe Piyari Chadhaibo* shows Shahabadi dedicating the first Bhojpuri film ever to India's first president, Dr Rajendra Prasad. The story, screenplay and dialogues are credited to Nazir Hussain. As the film proceeds, one realizes that the girl introduced as Kumari Padma is none other than Padma Khanna, who went on to become one of the most famous Bhojpuri heroines of all time, but not before making a name for herself as a dancer and character actress in Hindi films such as *Johnny Mera Naam* (1970), *Saudagar* (1973) and *Us Paar* (1974).

Ganga Maiya Tohe Piyari Chadhaibo is a classic rural north Indian tale of a rich boy, Shyam (Ashim Kumar), falling in love with a poor girl, Sumitri (Kumkum). The boy's money-lender father, however, wants to cash in on his son's marriage. At one point when the son objects to his plans, he says unabashedly, 'I educated you and raised your market price. Why shouldn't I look for a decent return as dowry?' Like Devdas, the son is unable to marry his lady love. And like him, he leaves home. By a twist of circumstance, the girl is forced to wed a sixty-year-old. Unfortunately, the groom dies even before he can consummate the marriage. Stereotypically, the in-laws ill-treat and conspire against the young widow. She attempts suicide but survives and ends up becoming a dancing girl. Her boyfriend, who has meanwhile left home after a showdown with his father, eventually finds her. Initially he is more angry than sympathetic at her plight, but soon reconciles to what has happened and is willing to take her back. But before he can do that, he gets injured in a fight and is nursed back to health by the girl. The boy's father then repents and takes both of them back to the village.

Barring the language, the story is not very different from numerous other rural family Hindi social dramas filmed in the 1950s and 60s. But that's completely missing the point, which is that *Ganga Maiya Tohe Piyari Chadhaibo*'s soul is one hundred per cent Bhojpuri.

Quietly flows the Ganga

Ganga is the most common word in Bhojpuri film titles. The river, which passes through several Bhojpuri-speaking districts in both Bihar and Uttar Pradesh, is venerated by millions, which is why the river is often equated with a goddess or a mother. Beginning with *Ganga Maiya Tohe Piyari Chadhaibo*, the name of the holy river, which flows through the Bhojpuri-speaking hinterland, has figured in at least twenty-five movies and the list is still growing: *Ganga Ghat, Ganga Saryu, Ganga Maiya Bhar Da Acharwa Hamaar, Ganga Kinare Mora Gaon, Ganga Maiya Tohar Kiriya, Dulha Ganga Paar Ke, Ganga Ki Beti, Ganga Hamaar Mai, Ganga Jaisan Bhauji Hamaar, Ganga Jwala, Ganga Aabad Rakhiha Sajanwa Ke, Ganga Maiya Kara Da Milanwa Hamaar, Ganga Aur Gouri, Ganga Ke Teere Teere, Ganga Maiya Bhar Da Godiya Hamaar, Ganga Se Nata Ba Hamaar, Ganga Jaisan Paawan Pirityaa Hamaar, Ganga Ke Paar Saiyan Hamaar, Aashish Ganga Maiya Ke, Ganga Mile Sagar Se, Ganga Tohar Pani Amrit, Ganga Maiya Tohe Chunri Chadhaibo, Ganga, Ganga Jamuna.*

Apart from the novelty of watching a film in their own language, what could have drawn the Bhojpuri-speaking audience is the movie's ability to recreate the sights and sounds of the region. From the ghats of Benares to Arrah railway station and Patna's landmark Gole Ghar, the movie has it all. The film also touches on the talking points of the time such as the importance of *chakbandi*, a land-reform measure that helped people create contiguous landholdings.

In one scene, the heroine takes food for her father toiling in the fields. The poor man's meal is *bajre ki roti* (millet rotis), *bathua ke saag* (a local dish) and chutney. On another occasion, the heroine's father is served *sattu* (roasted and pounded black gram). In a touching scene set in a *tadikhana*, the village drinking place, the heroine's father (played by Hussain) keeps staring at a glass of palm toddy. When asked why, he replies, '*Hum dekhatani ee kitna gahir ba. Ae ma hamra khet, ghar, bagiya sab doob gayil*' ('I am measuring its depth. I have lost my home, my fields and my garden to the bottle').

In the beginning of the film, the hero's father wants to organize a dance performance to celebrate the completion of his son's postgraduate studies. Finally he settles on *bidesiya*, an indigenous form of theatre. The performer is a fully-covered Helen who sings, *Poorab des gaeel more saiyan* ('My beloved has gone eastward').

Migrants who work in the cities are woven into the movie's plot. In one scene, the villagers discuss a community project for the local school. Someone suggests that those working in cities like Calcutta, Mumbai and *pardes* (not necessarily foreign—a place which is not your home) should be asked not to waste money on bioscopes, trams and tea, but should send money back home for the project. The film also dares to sail against the wind. It supports widow remarriage at a time when such a view was unimaginable in the boondocks of central Bihar and eastern Uttar Pradesh. But it also takes care not to shock the public—for example, despite her travails, the heroine remains a virgin till the end. *Ganga Maiya Tohe Piyari Chadhaibo* also examines the land question and the pauperization of the peasantry.

The narration of the film's story is mature. Unlike most Hindi socials of the 1960s made in the studios of south India, there is no parallel comedy track, no vulgarity and no over-the-top melodrama. The movie is enhanced by the understated performances of its lead characters, especially the heroine Kumkum. From an innocent village girl to a married woman and then a dancing girl, her role has several shades and she delivers a competent performance. The scene where she teases the hero in the field—*Shahar ke aadmi sukumar hola* ('City men are softies')—even as she fills water from the well has all the subtle elegance of the time when love was not expressed in words but through gestures.

'I vividly remember an incident which happened when I was working on the film. Although I come from Bihar, I was not very fluent in Bhojpuri. My first shot was with Nazirsahib. It was an outdoor scene and a very emotional one between the father and the daughter. When the scene was over, I was surprised to see tears in the eyes of unit members and the general public watching the shoot. That gave me immense confidence,' remembers Kumkum.[12]

But the movie's real stars were its songs with lyrics by Shailendra, the well-known Hindi film lyricist, and music by Chitragupta, the Bollywood composer from Bihar. Every song is catchy. Simplicity was always the hallmark of Shailendra's song writing and in *Ganga Maiya Tohe Piyari Chadhaibo*, he forges a perfect combination with Chitragupta. Even in the mid-1970s, the songs of the film were played often on All

India Radio's Patna station. The dances in the film also display a harmony of grace and movement.

Mumtaz Hussain recalls watching a trial showing of the movie when he was a boy at the Bombay Film Laboratory, where the film was being processed. Many years later, his father recounted an incident which took place the same day. The story goes that Tarachand Barjatya of Rajshri Productions, who was also the film's distributor in Mumbai, saw the film and commented, 'The subject is very dry.' Hussain retorted, '*Aap* [subject] *samjhe nahin*' ('You have not grasped the subject').[13]

The film was specially shown to Rajendra Prasad who later called up Nazir Hussain and discussed it with him. He wanted to know why the heroine had to go to the *kotha* (brothel). 'Is there no other option for her?' he wanted to know. Hussain pointed out that it is only because her husband's family throws her out that she ends up becoming a dancing girl. He also explained that since the girl is illiterate, she has fewer choices before her. In this way, the audience is also exhorted to educate the girl child![14]

Ganga Maiya Tohe Piyari Chadhaibo was released on 5 February 1962 at Prakash Talkies, Benares,[15] and people thronged to see it from the surrounding hinterland. Madhuri Mishra, daughter of veteran character actress Leela Mishra, was about twenty years old then. 'I remember I was on a *vrat* [fast]. But since we got the tickets after a lot of effort, I decided to go for the film. I still remember the huge crowd outside the hall. Some of them had spread out sheets and were sitting on the ground. I enjoyed the movie though I felt hungry during the show. Kumkum's work was superb. In fact, I ended up seeing the movie three times,' says Mishra, who has acted in more than fifty Bhojpuri films herself.[16]

A silver jubilee hit, *Ganga Maiya Tohe Piyari Chadhaibo* ended up grossing Rs 75 lakh.[17] 'The film ran for six weeks in Bombay's Imperial theatre. It also had a glitzy premiere in Delhi's Golcha theatre where top political personalities such as Lal Bahadur Shastri and Jagjivan Ram were among the guests,' recalls Rajkumar Shahabadi.[18]

'There was a buzz about the movie. It had great songs,' says Kirit Desai, who runs Delhi's Moti cinema which screens Bhojpuri films regularly these days.[19]

Soon *Ganga Maiya Tohe Piyari Chadhaibo* became a symbol of regional pride, a positive expression of identity for those who spoke Bhojpuri. In 1965, a newspaper article stated, 'A few years ago the rest of the country considered Bhojpuri as the language of the rustic people of east Indian villages. In Bombay, it was known as the language of the '*bhaiya*s'. In Calcutta and other cities, it was known as the language of labourers of north India and Bihar. Against this backdrop, the announcement of a Bhojpuri film [*Ganga Maiya Tohe Piyari Chadhaibo*] must have been laughable [for many]. One would have required plenty of courage, commitment and patience to make the film for which [producer] Bishwanath babu must be congratulated.'[20]

'The Bhojpur region has abundant folk songs. Although these tunes and songs have been used in Hindi films from time to time, they are never described as Bhojpuri songs. But the songs of *Ganga Maiya Tohe Piyari Chadhaibo*, bathed in the colours of fellow Bhojpur*wasi* Chitraguptaji, have popularized Bhojpuri.

'The film's commercial success has raised the significance and value of Bhojpuri. Like a shining diamond, it has attracted every class in society: political, literary and the trader class. Bhojpuri magazines, Bhojpuri literary conferences, Bhojpuri film festivals, plus many new organizations and cultural programmes have created a new awareness in the Bhojpuri belt. Like many regional languages, Bhojpuri has also become a respected language and those in Bhojpur who know the language feel pride in writing and speaking it.'[21]

As film historian Firoze Rangoonwalla wrote, 'The novelty of its language and folk music made it such a sensational hit that it let loose a flood of films in its sister dialects.'[22] Indeed, history had been made.

Now, nearly five decades later, the movie continues to inspire Bhojpuri film-makers. Babloo Soni, director of Bhojpuri films *Banke Bihari MLA* (2007) and *Bihari Mafia* (2009), says the film had a delicate rhythm that is impossible to create these days. He says, 'The day I make a movie like *Ganga Maiya Tohe Piyari Chadhaibo*, I will be at peace with myself.'[23]

2

High Noon

The first wave after *Ganga Maiya Tohe Piyari Chadhaibo*

The success of *Ganga Maiya Tohe Piyari Chadhaibo* (O Mother Ganga I'll offer you the yellow cloth, 1962) unleashed a wave of films in the regional genre. Between 1962 and 1966, a total of nineteen Bhojpuri films were released, most of which were family dramas, while a few were mythologicals. These films were culturally located in the Bhojpuri-speaking area and directors took pains to illustrate the region's customs, rituals and traditions in detail. Scenes of weddings or even a tadikhana or drinking place as in *Ganga Maiya Tohe Piyari Chadhaibo* carried a degree of authenticity. They gave the target audience a sense of watching their own lives in a way Hindi films could never manage. No wonder the first three Bhojpuri films—*Ganga Maiya Tohe Piyari Chadhaibo*, *Bidesiya* (1963) and *Laagi Nahin Chhute Ram* (1963)—were all well received.

Their success caused a feverish rush among producers to make Bhojpuri films. Going by reports in the regional film newspapers of the 1960s, at least fifty such movies were left incomplete. Some never progressed beyond the muhurat or the recording of a few songs; others perished after a few reels were shot. At least four movies of this period—*Ganga Maiya Tohe Piyari Chadhaibo*, *Bidesiya*, *Laagi Nahin Chhute Ram* and *Hamaar Sansar* (1965)—can easily make it to the all time top twenty list of Bhojpuri films (all these films are now available in digital form). This was also the golden era of Bhojpuri film music.

* * *

Like *Ganga Maiya Tohe Piyari Chadhaibo*, *Bidesiya* is also a wonderfully rooted film and its folk music is delightfully authentic. The term bidesiya is generally used to indicate a person who has left his land to work in a faraway place. Often, he is perceived as a deserter because he leaves his wife and family behind.

Flavoured with the sights and sounds of the hinterland, it is a love story between an upper-caste thakur and a low-caste girl, something unimaginable in the 1960s. The film was produced by Bachubhai Shah, a Gujarati, and well-known composer, S.N. Tripathi, was the director. Many Hindi film lovers remember him as the music director of hit mythologicals. Who can forget *Binaca Geet Mala*'s No. 1 song of 1957, *Zara saamne to aao chhaliye* from the Hindi film *Janam Janam Ke Phere* (1957)? He also composed music for historicals like *Lal Qila* (1960), and came up with memorable experimental compositions such as *Na kisi ki aankh ka noor hoon* and *Lagta nahin hai dil mera*. In all, Tripathi composed music for over ninety Hindi and Bhojpuri films and acted in at least thirty of them.

Bidesiya's second major contributor was Rammurti Chaturvedi, who wrote its story, screenplay, dialogue and lyrics. Chaturvedi was a well-respected man of letters with deep knowledge of local customs and traditions, and his influence shows in the film. The dialogues are peppered with sparkling proverbs and repartee—'*Bhookha na jaane baasi bhat, neend na jaane tooti khat, preet na jaane jaat kujaat*' ('Hunger knows no stale rice, sleeps knows no broken cot, love knows no caste').

The story of *Bidesiya* goes like this: the protagonist Bidesi Thakur (Sujit Kumar) is the son of a reformist upper-caste zamindar who gave away most of his land to the low-caste families of the village before his death. Much of the remaining land is usurped by his lascivious uncle (played by Jeevan) who is also desperate to seduce Parbatiya (played by Naaz), a poor low-caste girl who works on his fields. Bidesi, who sells paan for a living, and Parbatiya fall in love. But taunted by the zamindar's henchmen about his daughter's love affair, Parbatiya's father pleads with Bidesi to leave the village to save his honour. Bidesi leaves for Benares where he drives an *ikka* (horse-cart) for a living. But when Parbatiya's father falls ill, he is asked to return home. Before dying, Parbatiya's father accepts his daughter's relationship and this angers the zamindar, who creates more hurdles for the lovers. In the climax, he shoots at Bidesi Thakur, but Parbatiya comes in the way and dies.

The film does not confront the caste question. It preaches the Gandhian line of changing oneself to change society. When a thakur's henchman stops low-caste women from filling water from a well, a well-meaning elderly woman in the family does not hit out at the henchman; instead, she offers water from her own well.

By settling for an unconsummated love affair, the film steers clear of offending the socially conservative. To be fair, the film has its heart in the right place and needs to be appreciated for at least engaging with the caste question. It begins with the song—*Koi chhota nahi, koi bada nahi, koi oonch nahi, koi neecha* ('No one is small, no one is big, no one is superior, no one is inferior')—making a clear statement of intent. It may sound rather tame today, but nearly five decades ago, such an assertion was quite radical in the Hindi hinterland.

Actor Sujit Kumar's maturity, heroine Naaz's spunk and effervescence—their love scenes crackle with electricity—and Padma Khanna as the feisty but well-meaning wife of the zamindar, are all memorable. The great poet of the region, Bhikhari Thakur, makes an appearance in a scene, reciting his own poetry and S.N. Tripathi plays the *daroga* (police sub-inspector who mans the local police station). Even the dances are wonderful to watch—Bela Bose, Helen and Naaz provide perfect moves for the folksy music. It is no surprise then that *Bidesiya* became a superhit and ran for twenty-five weeks in Benares.[1]

* * *

Laagi Nahi Chhute Ram (Love never goes away), released the same year, was another box-office success. Veteran character actor Ramayan Tiwari was the film's producer and he opted for the same team that worked in *Ganga Maiya Tohe Piyari Chadhaibo*, including music director Chitragupta, who composed a rich, expressive score for the film.

Laagi Nahi Chhute Ram may not have risen to the artistic levels of *Ganga Maiya Tohe Piyari Chadhaibo*, but it is quite a watchable film. Clearly defined images of rural central Bihar in the 1960s abound—tongas, cattle-fairs, a cow suckling its calf, goats in the field, potters at their wheels, farmers who really look like farmers, ram fights. These images remind you of the time when the Indian film-maker was not ashamed to show his own landscape.

The film is an unlikely love story between a *nautanki bai* (dancing girl) and the son of a well-off priest. It begins with Chanda (played by Kumkum) getting down from a train with her *kaka* (uncle) at the Bihta railway station (incidentally, producer Tiwari was from the same qasbah). She gets into a spat with the ticket collector and then with a *tangewallah* (horse-cart puller) who demands what she thinks is an exorbitant charge. Enter Suraj (hero Ashim Kumar), who gives her a free ride and falls in love with her when he watches her perform at the *nautanki* (village dance show).

But Ashim Kumar is not the only one attracted to her. A lustful thakur, who rides on an elephant and enjoys getting massaged even as he watches a nautanki, is fascinated by her. His underling Firangiya (played by Anwar Hussain, actor Nargis' brother and a famous villain in his time) gets her uncle drunk and kidnaps her. But Kumkum is saved by the hero who chases the horse carriage, overtakes it and beats up Firangiya.

After this incident, the heroine falls in love with the hero. The hero's father is enraged because no respectable family can even think of bringing home a dancing girl as daughter-in-law. Plenty of twists and turns follow—Panditji (the priest-father) overcomes his class prejudices and the lovers are reunited.

The film is too one-dimensional, but two features—unforgettable songs and the lead pair's uncluttered acting—make the film worth a watch. Kumkum's performance, especially, is the glue that holds the film together.

Interestingly, Hindi film comedian Mehmood plays a small role of a nautanki owner in the film and along with Helen, even dances in an item number: *Moohwa se bola kanakhiya na maara, Patna ke babu jawaniya sambhara* ('Speak, don't wink, o gentleman from Patna, don't go astray').

Two of Chitragupta's compositions—both duets sung by Talat Mehmood and Lata Mangeshkar—are outstanding. The title track is a piece of art: perfect words, catchy tune, proficient singing and uncomplicated picturization. *Lal lal onthhwa se barse lalaiya ho ke ras chooela, jaise aamwa ke mojara se raas chooela* ('Your red lips drip with juice, like the mango's pollen') is another great tune. With Talat's quivering voice and Lata's perfect accompaniment, the song is an all-time classic.

* * *

The success of *Ganga Maiya Tohe Piyari Chadhaibo, Bidesiya* and *Laagi Nahi Chhute Ram* spurred the great Cinema Bhojpuri rush. In fact, 1964 saw a whopping seven films being released. (This record was broken only in 1983 when eleven movies, including the superhit *Ganga Kinare Mora Gaon*, were released.) By this time, several well-known non-Bhojpuri-speaking producers and directors had jumped into the fray.

Among the more famous names who tried their luck was Bollywood producer Shakti Samanta, who had already made Hindi film hits like the thrillers *Howrah Bridge* (1958) and *China Town* (1962), but was still some years away from attaining his legendary director status with *Aradhana* (1969).

He produced the Bhojpuri film *Ayeel Basant Bahar* (The spring has come, 1965), a tragic social drama about the inequities of the caste system. Devendra, who had directed the flop Hindi historical *Razia Sultana* (1961) and the Bhojpuri *Naihar Chhutal Jaiye* (Leaving my parent's home, 1964), was the director. The film's story, dialogue and songs were written by Rammurti Chaturvedi, who had proved his mettle in *Bidesiya*.

Shakti Samanta said he decided to make the regional film because a distributor had suggested that it would be a good idea to do so. Samanta did not know the language but director Devendra did. The film was shot near Benares and barely managed to recover money.[2] However, at least one newspaper said it was a huge hit.[3] Chaturvedi's work came in for praise in *Ayeel Basant Bahar* and character actor Chandrashekhar's performance was also acclaimed by the Benares press. But critics felt that the film's music by Hemant Kumar was unsatisfactory.[4]

Few know that P.L. Santoshi, father of Hindi film director and producer Raj Kumar Santoshi, also directed a Bhojpuri film: *Saiyan Se Bhaile Milanwa* (When I met my lover, 1965). Starring Sujit Kumar and Saeeda Khan in lead roles—the duo was also paired in the Hindi suspense film, *Ek Saal Pehle* (1965)—the movie is about a dutiful and self-sacrificing heroine who nurses her husband back to health after he suffers memory loss. The film, just like *Ayeel Basant Bahar*, was full of Calcutta-based actors in supporting roles—Sabita Chatterjee, Tarun Kumar and Jahar Rai—and the music was composed by Robin Chatterjee. Indeed, in the 1960s, the Bhojpuri film industry had strong links with Calcutta's Tollywood, which provided both technicians as well as actors for the genre. Films were processed in laboratories in Calcutta and even the sound recordings were conducted there. A few exceptions aside, that link has weakened over the decades.[5] Santoshi, the director of famous films such as *Shehnai* (1947) and *Barsaat Ki Raat* (1960), also recorded seven songs with composer C. Ramachandra for an incomplete Bhojpuri film, *Angna Bhayeel Bides*.[6]

Slowly, Bhojpuri films started looking beyond social dramas and a new sub-genre made its advent: the mythological. In 1964, two such films were released, *Naag Panchami* and *Sita Maiya*, both directed by the redoubtable S.N. Tripathi. Before *Sita Maiya* was released, Tripathi told an audience in a function at the Kashi Nagri Pracharini Sabha building that 'This is the first experiment of its kind. Ram *katha* [the story of Lord Ram] has never failed in the past and it will not fail now.'[7] Unfortunately, it did.

By late 1964, after a few movies flopped, a degree of uncertainty and angst set in. The tendency was to blame the 'outsider' producer for most of the ills plaguing the fledgling Bhojpuri film industry. Speaking at a gathering at the Varanasi (Benares) Film Club on 1 December 1964, Sheel Kumar, the hero of *Naag Panchami*, said, 'Some people are treating Bhojpuri films like a golden goose. That's why they are flopping one after the other. The producers are not paying enough attention to the region's culture, lifestyle and music.'[8]

The anxiety over flops continued into the next year. 'These are fragile times. Due to films crashing at the box-office, even in the areas regarded as strongholds of the genre, cinema owners are hesitant to exhibit Bhojpuri films,' said a report.[9]

Yet another contemporary newspaper article pointed out that over a hundred Bhojpuri films were announced between the years 1962 and 1965, and in 1965, at least two dozen films were under production. 'Encouraged by the success of Bhojpuri films, producers are making films in several other regional north Indian dialects: Braj, Avadhi, Maghi, Maithili, Chhattisgarhi.'[10] Now, after the success of *Sasura Bada Paisewala* (Father-in-law has pots of money, 2004) and *Panditji Bataeen Na Biyah Kab Hoee* (Tell me panditji, when will we I get married?, 2005), several producers from southern India, especially from Hyderabad, have made films in Bhojpuri. How history repeats itself!

'The long queue to produce Bhojpuri films,' wrote Bansidhar Raju in Benares-based weekly film newspaper *Rambha* in 1965, 'is rooted in the *ek lagawein, chaar pawein* [Invest one, get four] motto of producers. Since Bhojpuri films cost less and a successful one grosses profits three to four times the investment, it has prompted several producers to announce their films. And yet many of them seem to have lost the enthusiasm to complete these films following a string of flops.'[11]

He added, 'The producers who had come to ride the gravy train, hoping to make some easy money like investing in a good firm in the stock market, had to quit midway as the financiers would have backed out of further investments. Many films have been aborted midway, yet, the number of films that have been completed and released is substantially higher.'[12]

In the same article, Raju pointed out that the critics as well as the audience of Bhojpuri films wanted to watch the same antiquated themes—by which he meant rural family dramas. Then he asked, 'The question is, are we the same people as before? If Bhojpuri films are influenced by twentieth-century happenings, they are criticized. But the truth is, today people of the Bhojpuri-speaking region are also educated. They wear coats, pants and ties. Young women wear salwar kameezes and skirts. Their style of living has changed. Yet critics and audiences want to see the same old village, the broken *madai* [hut], poverty, dhoti-kurta and torn blouses. There is nothing surprising if we adopt and adjust our customs and traditions, and style of living according to [the present] time and era. Critics and the audience should think about these issues seriously.'[13]

* * *

The same year, 1965, saw the release of films like Nazir Hussain's *Hamaar Sansar* (My/Our world) and Kundan Kumar's *Bhauji* (Elder brother's wife). The promos described *Hamaar Sansar* in the following words: '*Bhojpuri bhasha ki yugantari tasvir. Jisme aapko Bharat ki atma—gramya vatavaran ke khet khalihan, kisan wa uske jeevan ki sachchi jhalak dekhne ko milegi* ('A ground-breaking Bhojpuri film where you'll see India's soul—the village environment, the fields, a glimpse of the real life of a farmer'). The advertisement indicates that for a traditional film-maker like Hussain, rural life was the soul of India and his artistic pre-occupation lay in effectively portraying the farmers' condition. Hussain's son, Mumtaz, feels that *Hamaar Sansar* was the finest film that his father wrote and produced.[14] The film was directed by Naseem who had earlier directed *Raat Ke Rahi* (1959), a flop Hindi film starring Shammi Kapoor. Ashim Kumar and Lily Chakraborty,[15] the well-known actress from Calcutta, formed the lead pair.

In the first half, *Hamaar Sansar* recreates 'village' life authentically. The scene of action shifts to the city in the second half, and has shades of *Do Bigha Zameen*. Like Balraj Sahni in the film, Nazir Hussain too becomes a rickshaw-puller in Calcutta.

The movie received glowing reviews in newspapers. An article in *Dainik Aaj*, Benares, commented, 'This is probably the first Bhojpuri film that holds its own against the best realist films in any language.' *Poorvi Times*, Gorakhpur, stated, '*Hamaar Sansar vastav mein hamaar aansar hai*' ('*Hamaar Sansar* means "our world", the film is truly our world'). *Dainik Gandiv*, Benares, wrote, 'It is the finest among the Hindi and Bhojpuri films made so far.'

Even the English press was floored. The *Pioneer*, published only from Lucknow then, said, 'Among the problems dealt with in the film are the gradual break-up of the joint-family system and consequent division of land, appalling illiteracy, child marriage, lack of modern amenities in villages and the steady migration of peasants from villages to big cities in search of menial jobs. All these burning problems are dealt with most naturally in *Hamaar Sansar*.'[16]

Another article says, 'In *Hamaar Sansar*, Nazir Hussain graphically and beautifully depicts the social realities of the region such as [the] low level of female education, shortage of hospitals, and farmers migrating to cities for jobs. With a beautiful story, *Hamaar Sansar* is a true Bhojpuri film. We need to make such films. But it is important that producers come from [the] Bhojpur region.'[17]

Indeed, the importance of having Bhojpuri-speaking producers is one of the driving intellectual concerns of these reviews. There is also a propensity to pin the blame for badly-made films on the greedy and ignorant 'outsider' producers.

Interestingly, the newspaper advertisements of this period bring to light a peculiar problem: people demanding free passes to watch a movie. It prompted advertisements of *Hamaar Sansar* brought out in *Rambha* to emphasize: 'No free pass or concession for the next six weeks.'[18] The advertisement did not say that handing out free passes is 'wrong', but only pleads that free passes be stopped in the first six weeks. Similar advertisements were also brought out by the producers of *Bhauji*.[19]

Hamaar Sansar was declared tax-free in Uttar Pradesh, a factor that played a crucial role in its success. There is a story about how the film got its tax-free certificate. According to veteran film journalist Munnu Prasad Pandey, Chandrabhanu Gupta was the kingmaker in Uttar Pradesh politics in those days. 'After watching the film, he requested Sucheta Kriplani, the then chief minister of Uttar Pradesh, to declare the film tax-free because it highlighted the problems of farmers. Nobody objected.'[20]

In 1965, Shahabadi produced his second film, *Solaho Singaar Kare Dulhiniya* (The bride decks up). The film, largely shot in Benares, was among the last movies in which the legendary Motilal acted. No prints of this film remain. 'Unfortunately, the film's negative was ruined in the laboratory. The print could not be salvaged. We cannot even make a 16 mm print,' says Rajkumar Shahabadi.[21]

The first Bhojpuri Film Awards were presented in 1965. From 23 to 27 April, the Bhojpuri Film Samaroh Samiti organized special screenings of the best Bhojpuri-Magadhi films till date at the India Film Laboratories, Calcutta, to decide on the awards. The jury was headed by film-maker Mrinal Sen, while other members of the jury included director Tarun Mazumdar, B.C. Agarwal, editor of *Cine Advance*, Rajendra Prasad Singh, poet and critic, and Rajendra Prasad, editor of *Lokpath*, Patna.[22]

On 27 April, awards in thirteen categories were presented at the Ananda Bazaar Patrika Bhavan, Calcutta. Since these were joint Bhojpuri-Magadhi awards, some of them also went to Magadhi films, but *Ganga Maiya Tohe Piyari Chadhaibo* walked away with the most honours.

The best film award went to *Ganga Maiya Tohe Piyari Chadhaibo*; best actor, Sujit Kumar (*Bidesiya*); best actress, Kumkum (*Ganga Maiya Tohe Piyari Chadhaibo*); best supporting actor (male), Nazir Hussain (*Ganga Maiya Tohe Piyari Chadhaibo*); best music, S.N. Tripathi (*Bidesiya*); best lyrics, Shailendra (*Ganga Maiya Tohe Piyari Chadhaibo*); best story, *Ganga Maiya Tohe Piyari Chadhaibo*; and best singer (male), Mohammed Rafi (*Sonwa ke pinjra mein* ['In the golden cage']).

When *Bhauji*, directed by Kundan Kumar, was released a few months later, the film's promos took a cue from the awards and described Sujit Kumar and Kumkum as the best actors of their time. Music by Chitragupta was one of the film's highlights, and the popular folk song in the film, *Chanda mama aare* ('Come, o moon') became a roaring hit, even topping the charts of the popular weekly radio show, *Binaca Geet Mala*.[23]

Another interesting film from this period, *Mitwa* (Lover, 1966), was directed by Govind Moonis, who later directed the successful Hindi film *Nadiya Ke Paar* (often mistaken as a Bhojpuri film). Moonis also wrote the dialogues and screenplay of the superhit Rajshri Productions' film, *Dosti* (1964). Moonis recounts the experience of making *Mitwa*:

Character actor Bhagwan Sinha (*Ganga Maiya Tohe Piyari Chadhaibo, Sita Maiya*) had wanted to make a Bhojpuri film for very long. Sinha finally found a financier, Jagmohan Mattu. Bhagwan came to me and we met Mattu. We then decided on a story to be made into a film called *Mitwa*. Sinha was to be the producer, but then finally Mattu gave his own name as the producer and credited Bhagwan as associate producer.[24]

Mitwa was largely shot at Filmistan Studio, but some scenes were filmed at Kandarpada, a suburb of Mumbai, and a few reels were also shot in and around Patna. Shooting for the film was completed in around five months. 'I am not exactly aware of the amount it cost, but I think it was completed in about Rs 3.5 lakhs,' says Moonis.[25] As a debutant director, Moonis was paid a miserable Rs 2,500. 'I did not even get all of it. But I had the satisfaction of making a good film,' he says.

Like *Ganga Maiya Tohe Piyari Chadhaibo*, the film discusses widow remarriage. There is a dialogue in the film, which roughly translated into English means, 'If enslaved India could stop sati, then why can't independent India give a widow the right to live?' C. Ramchandra, a Maharashtrian, was the film's music director and according to Moonis, he was Mattu's choice for the job. 'Lyricist Shailendra promised to suggest folk tunes, which he did,' says Moonis.

Moonis adds, 'The film's hero Shekhar was not a "serious" actor and he took things very lightly. He also had some difficulty with Bhojpuri dialogue. But Mattu sahib had chosen them [Shekhar and heroine Ameeta] saying that he is recreating the hit pair of Mahesh Kaul's Hindi film, *Abhimaan* (1957). Ameeta was a very sincere artiste and she did full justice to the role.'[26]

Mitwa was not properly distributed because the Bhojpuri film market had collapsed after a series of mediocre films. 'But the film recovered its costs and I think it made marginal profit. It earned praise and was exempted from entertainment tax for six weeks in both Uttar Pradesh and Bihar.'[27]

In the same year, the popular radio play, *Loha Singh*, was filmed and released as a feature film. Partly shot in Hazaribagh, it starred Sujit Kumar, Vijaya Chowdhury and Professor Rameshwar Singh Kashyap, who had written the play for All India Radio. Kashyap's colourful expressions such as *Khaderan ke mother* (Khaderan's mother) are part of regional lore. The film, about a jovial retired army man, was directed by Kundan Kumar, the director of *Bhauji*.

* * *

What Bhojpuri films stood for and their possible role in shaping society were the subjects of discussion in the mid-1960s. A newspaper article commented, 'Bhojpuri films can play a crucial role in highlighting the social evils of the region. It would be great if good Bhojpuri films are made—films that project the area in a proper light and help eradicate the social evils of this region.'[28] Casteism, dowry and female infanticide were some such ills. The article also said, 'The success of regional films depends on their accurate portrayal of the life and times of the region. For example, Bengali, Marathi and Gujarati films are successfully able to project the dilemmas and social evils of their respective regions.'[29]

The writer, Shankar Dutt Dubey, praised films like *Laagi Nahin Chhute Ram* and *Bidesiya* for their effective use of folk tunes. But he was sharply critical of 'outsider producers' who 'just think that Bhojpuri people are backward and want to exploit them commercially. It is good that some of these films have flopped because they have stopped making Bhojpuri films now.'[30]

For all practical purposes, the first phase of Bhojpuri films was over by 1966. Between 1967 and 1976, only two little-known films were released: *Vidhana Naach Nachave* (Fate makes you dance, 1968) starring Mumtaz and Sujit Kumar, and *Dher Chalaaki Jin Kara* (Don't act too smart, 1971), which was made in Marathi too.

Long is beautiful

Like the Nasir Hussain films of the 1950s and 1960s (*Tum Sa Nahin Dekha* [1957], *Dil De Ke Dekho* [1959], *Jab Pyaar Kisi Se Hota Hai* [1961], *Phir Wohi Dil Laya Hoon* [1963]), Bhojpuri films often have long, lively titles beginning with *Ganga Maiya Tohe Piyari Chadhaibo*. Sample some others: *Jekra Charanwa Mein Lagle Paranwa* (At whose feet lies my heart), *Panditji Bataeen Na Biyah Kab Hoee, Ho Gayeel Ba Pyaar Odhaniya Wali Se* (I have fallen in love with a girl wearing a stole), *Ego Chumma De Da Rajaji* (Give me a kiss my love).

3

Life after Death

The second phase of Bhojpuri films, 1977–2001

*D*angal (The Bout, 1977), the first Bhojpuri film made in colour, heralds the beginning of the genre's second phase. Much credit for infusing fresh life into this dormant regional film industry goes to Bachubhai Shah, who had also produced *Bidesiya* (1963). At a time when everyone seemed to have washed their hands off Bhojpuri films, the Gujarati producer took a bold gamble—and it paid off.

The other film that injected vigour into and shaped a productive phase in Bhojpuri cinema was Nazir Hussain's *Balam Pardesia* (1979), which roughly translates as the foreigner/outsider lover. It needs to be understood that in the social context of the Bhojpuri-speaking region, a *pardesi* isn't just someone from a foreign land; a stranger from a nearby town can also be a pardesi.

Over twenty-five years, between 1977 and 2001, about 150 Bhojpuri films were produced—an average of six every year. During the years 1986–89, a whopping fifty-one films were released and it was during this time that the more popular movies were made. The genre peaked in 1986 when nineteen films were certified by the censors. The Bhojpuri movies of the 1990s were largely mediocre, barring a few exceptions—they neither entertained the public nor impressed the critics.

Apart from *Dangal* and *Balam Pardesia,* some other successful movies in the second phase were *Dharti Maiya* (Mother Earth, 1981),[1] *Hamaar Bhauji* (My elder brother's wife, 1983), *Ganga Kinare Mora Gaon* (My village is on the banks of the Ganga, 1983), *Bhaiya Dooj* (1984), *Naihar Ki Chunri* (The stole from my parents' home, 1985), *Piya Ke Gaon* (My lover's village, 1985), *Dulha Ganga Paar Ke* (The groom from across the Ganga, 1986), *Ram Jaisan Bhaiya Hamaar* (My brother is like Ram, 1986) and *Mai* (Mother, 1989). Barring *Dangal*, all of them were family dramas. In fact, a good tear-jerker seemed to be the safest way to box-office glory in Bhojpuri films during the 1980s.

With Sujit Kumar and Prema Narayan, a former beauty queen, in the lead roles, *Dangal* can be roughly categorized as a rustic masala entertainer. It has plenty of desi-style fights with henchmen carrying sticks as was the common practice in eastern Uttar Pradesh of the 1970s. One extremely interesting scene is a duel between rams, which was promoted as the film's highlight, and of course, as the title suggests, the film also shows a dangal (a wrestling bout) in an *akhara*—the traditional mud pit.

At a superficial level, the film has plenty of similarities with *Bidesiya*. In both films, the hero is an upper-caste thakur going through hard times due to the machinations of his close relatives (actor Iftikhar in *Dangal* and Jeevan in *Bidesiya*). In both films, he falls in love with a 'low-caste' girl (Prema Narayan in *Dangal* and Naaz in *Bidesiya*). From here on, the films progress on slightly different lines though. In *Bidesiya*, the zamindar covets the heroine; in *Dangal*, it is the zamindar's henchman (played by Ram Singh who was from eastern Uttar Pradesh's Deoria district) who craves for the leading lady. *Bidesiya* dealt with the inter-caste love affair as a serious social issue, while *Dangal* is more of an action-entertainer.

The change in the treatment can be attributed to the emergence of a new kind of hero in Hindi films. Amitabh Bachchan's portrayal of the angry young man in *Zanjeer* (1973) had further crystallized in *Deewar* (1975). This change could have impacted the mindset of regional producers and financiers who perhaps wanted to incorporate more action scenes in their films. Subsequent Bhojpuri hits, however, indicate that the regional genre was more attuned to socials or family dramas.

Dangal was directed by Rati Kumar and written by Rajpati Rahi, who was from eastern Uttar Pradesh's Jaunpur district. Rahi's dialogues are peppered with plenty of local proverbs such as '*Badakwa ke agari aur ghora ke pichhari se bach ke rahe chahin*' ('Stay away from the front door of the rich and influential and the backside of a horse'). At one juncture in the film, the heroine named Badamiya (again a very local name) says, '*Badamiya kouno kohra ke batiya naikhe ke oongli dekh ke murjhai jai*' ('I am not a baby pumpkin that withers when a finger is pointed towards it'), echoing the commonly-held belief in many parts of eastern India that a pumpkin will wither if anyone points a finger at it.

Rajpati, who went on to direct films like *Mai K Lal* (Apple of mom's eye, 1979) and *Ganga Ghat* (Ganga banks, 1981), also wrote the chartbuster '*Kashi hile, Patna hile, Kalkatta hile la*' ('Kashi shakes, Patna shakes, Calcutta shakes', sung by Manna Dey) a take-off from the famous folk song, *Arrah hile, Chhapra hile, Baliya hile la* ('Arrah shakes, Chhapra shakes, Balia shakes').

Dangal's hit music was composed by Nadeem-Shravan, the pair still some years away from becoming famous in Hindi films. The mandatory *mujra* (dance) number was performed by Laxmi Chhaya (who would be called an 'item' girl today), an artiste forever embossed in the memory of film lovers for her *Maar diya jai ke chhodh diya jai* act in Raj Khosla's Hindi film, *Mera Gaon Mera Desh* (1971).

Dangal proved to be a box-office success. Amazingly, the film was re-released in Mumbai in 2005 in Jawahar cinema, Mulund, and collected Rs 40,000 in its first week, before it was shifted to Moti cinema for another one-week run.

* * *

Two years later, Nazir Hussain made his directorial debut with *Balam Pardesia*. In spite of the film's unimaginative script, it celebrated its silver jubilee in Benares, Gorakhpur and Patna. The movie also ran for sixteen weeks in Mumbai in a theatre called Ganga Jamuna (which no longer exists) according to its hero, Rakesh Pandey (his Hindi films include *Sara Akash* and *Andolan*).[2] Pandey was shooting for Gemini's Hindi film, *Ek Gaon Ki Kahani* (1975), when Nazir Hussain, who was playing his father, offered him a role in a Bhojpuri film he wanted to make. 'I respect seniors. So I said yes, though till then I was only doing Hindi films,' he recalls.[3]

However, Pandey did not realize how serious Nazir Hussain really was about the offer. The actor says, 'One day in 1977, he came home and said, "I am ready with the script!"'[4]

But there is a twist to the tale. Pandey did not know how to speak the language: 'He must have thought that I was from Bihar or Uttar Pradesh because of my surname. But I grew up in Himachal Pradesh and didn't know Bhojpuri at all.'[5]

'Hussain sahib said he was ready to work on my diction. So I thought to myself, if someone elderly is willing to work hard, then I shouldn't be creating a fuss. But I wasn't too enthusiastic about doing a regional film. And to be honest, till the very end I had no idea that the film would do so well,' he admits.[6]

The film begins as a commentary on the poverty-stricken life of rural musicians, in this case a *shehnai* (wind instrument) player portrayed by Hussain himself. But the film soon lapses into a lost-and-found drama, staple Bollywood fare of the 1970s. Hussain's son (Rakesh Pandey) gets separated from the family and is brought up by a single woman in a nearby village. He grows up learning to play the *dafli* (tambourine, an instrument popularized by Raj Kapoor in the 1950s and 60s and Rishi Kapoor in *Sargam* [1979]) and falls in love with a poor girl (Padma Khanna), who again, rather stereotypically, is coveted by the local zamindar's henchman.

Balam Pardesia is not a classic, but makes for easy viewing. Pandey's light-hearted banter with heroine Padma Khanna and her friends evokes an amused response from the audience, when, for instance, he tells the heroine, *'Je hasal, se phasal'* ('One who laughs at you has actually flipped for you').

Another scene in the film preaches family planning, a much-dreaded word in the mid-1970s. Barring a couple of stray examples like this, Bhojpuri films in this phase were spectacularly indifferent to any sort of political talk. The genre seemed to be living in a cocoon. However, when depicting the details of the local culture, Hussain, as usual, is spot on. For example, the heroine wears her sari a little above her heel, as many village women did in those days.

The film stands out for Pandey's acting. The scene where Pandey teases the heroine—just like Dilip Kumar behaves with co-star Vyjayanthimala in *Paigham* (1959) and Amitabh Bachchan with Zeenat Aman in *Dostana* (1980)—is hilarious. 'He worked hard and picked up the language,' recalls Nazir

Hussain's son, Mumtaz, who wrote and produced the film.[7] Pandey is also first-rate as a dancer in the song, *Jaagat raha bhaiya* ('Stay awake, brother').

Parts of the film were shot near Buxar in Bihar. Pandey remembers that on one occasion the crowd that had gathered to see the shooting went berserk and began pelting stones. 'The location had to be shifted. For certain scenes, Nazir Hussain used a local artiste to act as a body double for Padma Khanna. Some of her shots were later filmed in a Mumbai studio and cleverly interspersed. In the film, you can never tell the difference between the two locations.'[8]

Balam Pardesia was filmed in bits and pieces. 'Five days of shooting was followed by a few months' gap; then again we would shoot for seven days. That's how films were made in those days,' recalls Pandey. Mumtaz says that his father shot the film at a languid pace. 'He used to say movie-making is creative work, not a factory job.'[9]

But the movie would have never worked without Chitragupta's irresistible music. When Nazir Hussain went to sign him for the film, the well-known music director of *Bhabhi* and *Akashdeep* was going through a bad patch due to health problems. Assistant directors and friends advised the director against taking him on, but Nazir Hussain is said to have replied, '*Hing ke dabbe se hing ud bhi jaye, khushboo rehti hai.* [The smell of asafoetida stays even after it has evaporated.] He will always be a good composer.' The success of *Balam Pardesia*'s songs gave a second lease of life to Chitragupta's career.

Mumtaz Hussain recalls that his father was not satisfied with the film and expressed his displeasure on seeing the rushes of the song *Gorki patarki re* ('O slim, fair woman'). 'But when he saw the audience shouting and screaming in the theatre, he laughed and said, "*Zamana badal gayeel ba*"

[The times have changed].'[10] Plenty of broken bangles were apparently found outside the movie ticket counters in Benares, suggesting that women too were jostling for tickets.[11]

'After the success of *Balam Pardesia*, the regional genre [again] became the playground of dozens of wannabe producers. Moneybags wanting to make easy money rushed to make Bhojpuri films,' says veteran film journalist Munnu Prasad Pandey.[12] But the effect of this was seen only in the 1980s.

* * *

The only other film released in 1979 was *Mai K Lal*. An action drama on the lines of *Dangal*, the movie is staple masala fare with a famous ikka race and wrestler's fight. But the film is momentous for other reasons. *Mai K Lal* was distributed by the Jains—Ashokchand and Mohanchand—who later went on to produce films like *Dharti Maiya* and *Ganga Kinare Mora Gaon*. Till then, Bhojpuri films seldom made it beyond Bihar and eastern Uttar Pradesh—but the Jains released this film in Lucknow in central Uttar Pradesh, thereby expanding the genre's territory.

Mohanchand Jain, who became well known as the actor J. Mohan through films like *Dharti Maiya*, *Ganga Kinare Mora Gaon* and *Dulhin* (Bride, 1986), recalls, 'The positive feedback encouraged us to release the film in Hardoi, a non-Bhojpuri-speaking belt. People said they did not understand the dialogues completely, but really enjoyed the movie. This encouraged us to show *Mai K Lal* all over central and western Uttar Pradesh, including in Kanpur, Etawah, Shahjahanpur, Ghaziabad, Agra, Nainital, Faizabad, Firozabad, Aligarh, Haridwar, Rishikesh, Moradabad, Haldwani, Saharanpur, Hathras, Khurja, Muzaffarnagar and Meerut. Some of these areas are now part of Uttarakhand. The film was also exhibited in Delhi's Majestic cinema, though only in morning shows.'[13]

Mai K Lal was among the first Bhojpuri films to adopt innovative and aggressive marketing practices. The publicity material was published in Bhojpuri. The stars were also made integral to the film's promotional campaigns and during the intervals, the actors were presented before the audience in various towns.

In Gorakhpur's Vijay Talkies, heroine Prema Narayan wore a *ghaghra-choli* (long skirt and blouse) specially gifted by the theatre owner. Jain also brought out full-page advertisements in *Aaj*, the popular regional Hindi newspaper. 'Every other week or so, I would ensure an article or two was published in local newspapers and magazines,' he says.[14]

According to Mohanchand Jain, *Mai K Lal* was made for Rs 8 lakh and grossed about Rs 25 lakh in Delhi and Uttar Pradesh where it was declared tax-free. But the movie did not fare well in Bihar.

By now, the Bhojpuri film industry was up and running again. Right through the 1980s, there was a steady stream of movies. In 1980, three Bhojpuri films were released—the highest since 1965. Two of these were directed by veterans of the genre. Nazir Hussain made the moderately successful *Roos Gayeele Saiyan Hamaar* (My lover is sulking, 1980) with the same lead pair as *Balam Pardesia* (Rakesh Pandey and Padma Khanna). S.N. Tripathi repeated the *Dangal* pair (Sujit Kumar and Prema Narayan) in *Jaagal Bhag Hamaar* (My stars are rising). The third film was *Baaje Shehnaai Hamaar Anganaa* (The shehnai plays in my courtyard).

1981 saw five movies hit the screens. One of them, *Chanwa Ke Taake Chakor* (The chakor bird looks at the moon), featured Rakesh Pandey and Hina Kausar in the lead roles. This movie, directed by Nazir Hussain, is about a love affair between a boy who grows up in a temple and a child widow. The story starts out quite radically by questioning class as well as social barriers. But in the end, the film loses its spunk as the hero, rather conveniently, turns out to be the long-lost son of a rich woman. The film's highlights are the love scenes between Pandey and Kauser—intimate and tender without being physical, these scenes are some of the finest in Bhojpuri films.

But it is *Dharti Maiya* (1981), produced by Ashokchand Jain, which became the most-talked-about film of the year. With the passage of time, Ashokchand, Mohanchand's elder brother, became one of the most successful producers of Bhojpuri films. The Jain brothers were known to have helped the makers of *Dangal*, a fact which is acknowledged in the credits. Born in Arrah, businessman Ashokchand Jain entered Bhojpuri film distribution with *Mai K Lal* and became a producer with *Dharti Maiya*.

Approximately ninety-five per cent of the film was shot in rural areas near Benares. He said in a 1983 interview, 'We tried to bring alive the sound of Bhojpuri. We tried to provide a glimpse of small day-to-day problems that common people face in the villages.'[15]

Later Ashokchand Jain also produced *Ganga Kinare Mora Gaon* (1983) and directed *Dulhin* (1986), where his brother J. Mohan was the hero and Kanan Kaushal (of *Jai Santoshi Ma*) was the heroine.

In its broad framework, though not exactly in its storyline, *Dharti Maiya* is Bhojpuri cinema's *Mother India*. Leading lady Padma Khanna goes through life and much of its vicissitudes as Nargis did in Mehboob Khan's 1957 masterpiece. Pandey, already a star in the genre, plays Padma Khanna's husband who is killed in the thirty-seventh minute of the film by an evil money-lender. He leaves behind a pregnant wife and a son from his previous marriage. How

Padma Khanna brings up the two children under tough circumstances (that includes ploughing the field without bullocks) makes up for much of this engrossing tale.

Right from the film's first shot, director Qamar Narvi (who went on to direct Hindi films such as *Kaun Hai Woh* [1983], starring Raj Kiran, Mazhar Khan and Madhavi, and *Rahemdil Jallad* [1985] with Mazhar Khan and Zubeida) never loses his grip on the narrative. Taut and engrossing, *Dharti Maiya* never lapses into a maudlin melodrama. And most of the ensemble, barring Hari Shukla in the role of a barber, is controlled. The film celebrated its silver jubilee in at least six towns.[16]

Rakesh Pandey is excellent in the role of a young farmer who marries a second time because he wants a mother for his son. In the *suhaag raat* (wedding night) scene, Padma Khanna rushes to touch her husband's feet as Nargis had done for her husband played by Rajkumar in *Mother India*. As a heroine who makes a transition from a young *bahu* (daughter-in-law) to an aging mother, the film rests on Khanna's attractive shoulders. And she carries it with aplomb, even though her make-up as an older woman varies from scene to scene. After her husband dies, she fends for the family, fetches fuel, feeds the buffaloes and even makes cowdung cakes. Nothing stops her. Not even the poisoning of her bullocks, Hira and Moti.

The second generation walks into the movie after nearly an hour. The roles played by Rajendra Kumar and Sunil Dutt in *Mother India* are performed by Srigopal as the mature elder brother Ram and Kunal Singh as the flamboyant but error-prone younger Lakhan.

The film rightly gives top billing to Padma Khanna. Rakesh Pandey is credited with a 'guest appearance' though his role is more like a 'special appearance'. The film has lyrics and dialogues by Laxman Shahabadi, a talented lyricist-cum-composer who later wrote the music and lyrics for the hit, *Dulha Ganga Paar Ke* (1986).

Dharti Maiya has some of Chitragupta's most popular compositions. His sons, composers Anand-Milind, were his assistants for the film. The opening track, *Jaldi jaldi chala re kahara* ('Hurry up, o palanquin bearer'), is a great *doli* song that can match the best Hindi film numbers in the genre such as *Chalo re doli uthao kahar* ('Pick up the bridal cart, o bearer' in *Jaani Dushman* [1979]).

The film also has the first Bhojpuri song by Kishore Kumar—*Hum to ho gaili tohaar* ('I have become yours')—which was a superhit. In fact, *Dharti Maiya* was advertised as the first Bhojpuri film with a song by Kishore Kumar and the last Bhojpuri film for which Mohammed Rafi sang. The song, *Aare aare ee ka tu kare la sanwariya* ('What are you doing my love'), is picturized on the vivacious Meena Singh who plays Rakesh Pandey's sister in the film. Singh, who dances with verve in the track, is now married to Anand, Chitragupta's son.

The film was the first home production of the Jains. According to J. Mohan, *Dharti Maiya* was made for about Rs 12.5 lakh and ended up grossing Rs 1.5 crore. 'Before the day of the film's release, we took out a mock wedding procession through the streets of Benares carrying the film's prints to the cinema hall. It was an innovative way of attracting the public,' he says.[17] The film did good business in Punjab too. Says J. Mohan, 'In 1980, I had booked Ludhiana's Chand cinema hall for *Balam Pardesia*. The film ran for three weeks and collected about Rs 2 lakhs. *Dharti Maiya* was sold in the Punjab circuit for Rs 75,000 and pocketed around Rs 3 lakh.'[18]

Two years after *Dharti Maiya*, the Jain brothers released *Ganga Kinare Mora Gaon* (1983). Ashokchand Jain was again the producer, but had a new director-writer, Dilip Bose, who went on to become one of the most successful and respected directors in the genre.

Dilip Bose's son, Dipankar, recalls that producer Ashokchand did not like any of the stories initially narrated to him. 'My father,' says Dipankar, 'also had the story of *Ganga Kinare Mora Gaon* with him. But as the plot revolved around a small boy, he felt that the subject would not work. No Bhojpuri film had been made on such a theme before. But when he finally narrated the story to Ashokchand Jain, he liked it a lot and insisted it was worth filming.'[19]

Ashokchand was one of the few producers who sat with the director and discussed film-making, says Dipankar Bose, who assisted his father. He now makes low-budget Bhojpuri films. 'He used to wake my father up late at night and say, "Dada, let's discuss the movie,"' says Dipankar Bose.[20]

Ganga Kinare Mora Gaon turned out to be the biggest blockbuster of the 1980s. The movie celebrated its sixty-week-long run in Benares and, according to Jain, enjoyed a twenty-five-week-long run in Mirzapur, Jaunpur, Ghazipur, Balia, Allahabad, Kanpur and Lucknow. It was reported that during a show of *Ganga Kinare Mora Gaon* on 10 April 1984, in Mirzapur town in Uttar Pradesh, women formed ninety per cent of the audience.[21] In fact, it was during a show of the same movie that a black-marketeer was caught and thrashed by women outside Kanhaiya Chitra Mandir, Benares.[22]

In terms of artistic merit, the film is hardly in the same class as *Ganga Maiya Tohe Piyari Chadhaibo* or *Bidesiya*. In fact, it is laden with stereotypical characters: the evil *chachi* (aunt), the helpless mother, the lascivious village rowdy and the beggar who wants to gouge out the boy's eyes to make him beg.

Unlike the nuanced films of the 1960s, *Ganga Kinare Mora Gaon* is an unapologetic melodrama. In the best tradition of social dramas, the film relentlessly tugs at one's heartstrings. One of the songs says, '*Ansuan se apni ansuan ponchhni*' ('I wiped tears with my tears')—many in the audience must have felt the same way!

The film tells the story of a poor boy who is forced to stay away from his mother and lives with his wicked aunt and her henpecked husband. Having had enough of their ill treatment, he runs away and is adopted by a good samaritan. He grows up in an ashram and becomes a manager in a sugarcane mill. An employee's daughter falls for him and he gradually responds to her overtures, but the village baddies plot to make things difficult for him. How he gets reunited with his family forms the rest of the story.

This film took an interesting commercial risk because the hero (Kunal Singh) enters the frame sixty minutes after the film begins. Interestingly, Kunal Singh resembles Bollywood star and veteran of over two hundred films, Jeetendra, from several angles and J. Mohan, playing his brother in the film, looks a bit like Arun Govil, who starred in several Hindi films such as *Saawan Ko Aaane Do* (1979), and later, as Ram in the hugely popular *Ramayan* television series.

Kunal narrates a dramatic incident that occurred during the film's shooting. In a scene where he had to rescue his mother from a raging bull, the actor recalls that the animal in the shot had actually gone berserk due to the reflectors' glare. 'Quite literally, I had to take the bull by the horns. But I soon realized that I wouldn't be able to control the angry animal. The bull's owner was dead drunk and unable to intervene. So I asked Naaz [the heroine] to run fast. I knew if I let the animal go, she would get knocked down by the beast.'[23] He adds, 'After she had run to safety, I released the animal and climbed over a wall. But the bull knocked over the reflectors. Even director Dilip Bose was hurt trying to escape from the bull.'[24]

When watching the movie, it is pretty clear that the story is not apocryphal.

Ganga Kinare Mora Gaon also shows that Bhojpuri films were willing to experiment. Disco numbers were already a huge craze in Hindi films after Nazia Hassan's rendition of the superhit song *Aap jaisa koi* in producer-actor Feroz Khan's *Qurbani* (1980). *Ganga Kinare Mora Gaon* has an interesting track where disco beats blend with Bengali folk and Punjabi bhangra music.

The movie also presents the changing face of the Bhojpuri heroine. Lajo, the film's heroine played by Gouri Khurana, leaves her mark as the romantically aggressive gypsy girl. She even feigns drowning to entice the man she is attracted to. Dressed in a sleeveless blouse and translucent ghaghra-choli, she gets drenched in the rain in the song *Tanik humka odha da chadariya barsela saawan* ('Please cover me with the sheet as it rains')—a sequence that is gently titillating without being vulgar. But this shows that the genre was leaving its conservative roots behind. The film has aged badly, but in its time, it was loved by the audience and holds nostalgic value even today.

Hamaar Bhauji (1983) is another silver jubilee hit of this period. Directed by Kalpataru, the film was produced by Mohanji Prasad, now a top director of Bhojpuri films in his own right. The film was full of non-Bhojpuri speaking actors such as Tanuja, Sachin and Dr Shreeram Lagoo. 'But nobody really had any problems with the dialogues,' says Prasad.[25]

The success of *Ganga Kinare Mora Gaon* and *Hamaar Bhauji* drew comments in regional newspapers. An editorial in *Rambha* said that these films 'have again put Bhojpuri films in competition with Hindi films. They have revived the audience's interest in Bhojpuri films. Both are doing great business in Benares. The two films are being enjoyed by the rural and the city audience alike, especially the women and the middle-class. *Ganga Kinare Mora Gaon* causes [an] emotional upheaval in the hearts of the audience and urges them to change their attitude towards widows. *Hamaar Bhauji* espouses the cause of joint families. *Ganga Kinare Mora Gaon* also gave the opportunity to act to many local artistes.'[26]

* * *

By this time, the multi-starrer craze had reached its peak in Hindi films. Bhojpuri films soon followed this trend. Director Radhakant's Bhojpuri film, *Saiyan Magan Pahelwani Mein* (My lover is busy wrestling, 1984), joined the party with Rakesh Pandey, Sujit Kumar, Padma Khanna and Jayshree T. in leading roles. But neither the formidable star cast nor the amusing title could lure the audience to the theatres.

The film that the audience thronged to see was *Naihar Ki Chunri* (1985), the surprise superhit of this phase. A low-budget family social drama with young actors Meera Madhuri, Lalitesh, Kewal Krishna and Madhuri Mishra, the movie's success took everybody by surprise. Back in Benares, people still remember the movie with fondness.

Produced by Lalji Gupta, the film was directed and photographed by Hasmukh Rajput. Gupta, who idolizes Tarachand Barjatya of Rajshri Productions, followed his mentor's style of making clean, low-budget superhits with newcomers in lead roles. 'I belong to Uttar Pradesh's Mirzapur district but was born and brought up in Mumbai. I still own a sweetshop in Borivili and a travel agency in Colaba,' he says.[27]

Gupta had an interesting way of making films. He would take the entire unit to his native village Adalpura near Benares. Everyone, including the hero and the heroine, would be given a place to stay either at his residence or in village homes. He would also employ a cook to prepare food for the unit. There was no electricity in those days, so a generator was hired for the night. The films were shot in the cheaper 16mm and then blown up to 35 mm.

Gupta went to Mumbai's Siddharth College but never got down to academics. He entered film journalism briefly, but soon developed an interest in film-making. He recorded a few songs for a Hindi film titled *Surajmukhi*, but the idea was hastily dropped. 'I was inexperienced and some people tried to take advantage of me,' he says.[28]

At the same time, he became friendly with Ganesh Shelar, an award-winning make-up man. Shelar introduced him to director Dilip Bose and in turn, Bose took him to music director Ravindra Jain. The three teamed up to make *Ganga Maiya Bhar De Acharwa Hamaar* (O Mother Ganga, bless me [with a child], 1982). Gupta was only thirty-three years old then. The film, starring Narayan Bhandari and Madhu Mishra in leading roles, cost exactly Rs 5.34 lakh to make and grossed around Rs 10 lakh, making it a moderate success.

Hasmukh Rajput, the director of *Naihar Ki Chunri*, was born and brought up in Mumbai, where his family ran a laundry business. 'But I was fond of photography and interested in films. I was given a chance to work as an assistant cameraman by producer B.D. Kapoor, who had made low-budget suspense-thrillers *Teesra Kaun* and *CID 909*, both with Feroz Khan in the lead,' he remembers.[29]

Then luck came his way. Producer Lalji Gupta fell out with Bose after *Ganga Maiya Bhar De Acharwa Hamaar* and the director left with his story. Since he had already booked the entire unit's train ticket to Benares, Gupta was left without a director or a script. He offered the director's job to Rajput, the film's cameraman. 'We had only twelve days to get the story and the script in place,' recalls Rajput.[30]

Rajput took Gupta to the famous Gujarati writer, Keshav Rathod, who already had a string of Gujarati hits under his belt. 'He narrated a story to us. I was so impressed that I told the director, forget the script, let us start shooting,' says Gupta.[31]

A Gujarati himself, Rajput did not know Bhojpuri, but worked hard on understanding the nuances of local customs. 'I visited plenty of marriages at night. When people came to know that I was a film director, they allowed me to have a closer view of the rituals. I was helped in my efforts by Leela Mishra's daughter, Madhuri,' he recollects.[32]

Shooting for *Naihar Ki Chunri* began in November 1984 and the film was released in March 1985. Gupta's tight control ensured that the film' production was completed in a mere Rs 5.39 lakh. Released with nine prints, the film turned out to be the Bhojpuri equivalent of Rajshri's Hindi superhit, *Nadiya Ke Paar*, and earned about ten times more than its cost. 'I never believed in big stars. I always opted for new actors and technicians. I still believe that irrespective of the cast, a good story always works,' Gupta maintains.[33]

The film became a huge favourite among hinterland women who arrived in hordes at the mofussil cinema halls. 'They would leave their homes early in the morning and arrive by 9 a.m. for the 12 o'clock noon show. At Tamkuhi Road, Deoria, the morning show began at 9 a.m. Some men would even sleep outside the cinema hall after the late night show,' he says.[34]

When the film celebrated its hundred days' run, producer Gupta gave a huge bonus to the employees of Benares' Bhagwati cinema. Even the *mahant* (head priest) of Sankatmochan temple, Pandit Veerbhadra Mishra, liked *Naihar Ki Chunri*. Character actress Leela Mishra observed, 'It is a great clean family movie. Movies like these which point out the evils of the dowry system and the trials and tribulations of a daughter-in-law unable to bear a child can go a long way in eradicating these problems.'[35]

The movie's success prompted the film weekly newspaper *Rambha* to comment, 'Producers trying to make Bhojpuri films on the lines of Hindi movies will always be losers at the box-office. *Naihar Ki Chunri* has proved that you don't need big stars and a big budget. For creating a team of artistes from Poorvanchal, producer Lalji Gupta must be congratulated. If only the hundreds of producers making films in Bhojpuri use local artistes rather than *Bambaiyya* stars.'[36]

* * *

In 1985, Shatrughan Sinha, Bihar's most successful Bollywood hero also stepped into the genre with a home production: *Bihari Babu*. The film did well at the box-office primarily because it had a popular hero (Sinha himself), a top director (Dilip Bose), a great music director (Chitragupta) and two very famous 'item' girls—Tina Munim and Anita Raj.

Playing a character reminiscent of his title role in Devendra Goel's successful Hindi film *Aadmi Sadak Ka* (1977), Shatrughan Sinha enacted the part of a good samaritan who pummels evil money-lenders and helps the poor; the twist in the tale comes when his own sister becomes a dowry victim.

Apart from Dilip Bose and Hasmukh Rajput, the second phase of Bhojpuri cinema saw a host of other non-Bhojpuri-speaking directors working in the regional film industry. The period also saw Arti Bhattacharya, wife of actor Kunal Singh, become the first female director of Bhojpuri films with *Dagabaaz Balma* (Cheater lover, 1988).

By the mid-1980s, working in Bhojpuri films had become a craze in the region. Reports say that Benares was flooded with fake producers who fooled young actors and actresses into paying them big amounts of money by promising them

Comedian Asit Sen played a servant who speaks Bhojpuri in *Woh Koi Aur Hoga* (1967), a Bollywood thriller starring Feroz Khan and Mumtaz. The film was written by Qamar Narvi who went on to direct Bhojpuri superhit, *Dharti Maiya*.

a break in movies. Then they would vanish without a trace. A 1985 *Rambha* article says, 'Today such producers can be found in every nook and corner of Benares.'[37]

The genre's success even attracted producers from abroad. Few know that *Mai Ke Anchra (*Mother's aanchal), a film made in the late 1980s but never released, was produced by a gentleman from Holland. Character actors Vijay Khare and Dev Malhotra confirm having acted in the film. 'It was an extremely well-made film. Rama Vij played the heroine. The producer had invested a decent amount, but unfortunately, the film never got released,' says Malhotra.[38]

Director Hasmukh Rajput's second film *Bahina Tohre Khatir* (For you my sister, 1986) was also born out of a similar situation: a rookie producer driven by the desire to make a film. The movie was produced by Gyanendra Srivastav, a doctor from Benares. 'During the shooting of *Naihar Ki Chunri*, a metal stand fell on my hand. I was attended to by Dr Srivastav. Later he told me that he wanted to produce a movie,' says Rajput.[39] Rajput ended up directing the film, which was shot in Mumbai and in the areas around Gorakhpur. 'Critics found the sad ending unsuitable. After that, we also filmed a happy ending. There was real confusion about the climax. The collections suffered because Dr Srivastav had no idea how to distribute the film,' he says.[40] Indeed, the Bhojpuri film industry is full of such producers who were seduced by glamour and were sorely disappointed in the end.

* * *

Yet the regional film industry, much like Bollywood, is also a catalogue of men and women who came without experience or knowledge of film-making but eventually found their feet. The careers of Adarsh Jain and Rajkumar Sharma, two directors of this phase, provide interesting insights into such journeys.

Jain, the son of a bookshop owner, entered Bhojpuri films in the 1980s. He was born and educated in Kishanganj, a small town in north-eastern Bihar. Burning with a desire to be in the movies, he went to Mumbai with a friend's letter of recommendation to actor Dilip Sinha who had worked in *Dangal*. The effort did not lead to any result, but Jain struck a friendship with director Rajat Rakshit, who shared an apartment with Sinha.

Rakshit, who later made two interesting comedies with actor-producer Amol Palekar—the mildly successful Hindi comedy *Damaad* (1978) and the flop, *Meri Biwi Ki Shaadi* (1979)—was a Bengali. 'His Hindi wasn't up to the mark. All his assistants too were rather weak in the language. Since I was good at Hindi, it became my strength and I became his eighth assistant.'[41]

But Adarsh Jain could't get a break as a director in Hindi films, which is why he turned to the regional genre. In 1986, he directed the tacky, family tear-jerker *Ram Jaisan Bhaiya Hamaar* with Kunal Singh, Meera Madhuri and Hari Shukla in the leading roles. Playing a handicapped person in the manner of Sunil Dutt in the Hindi film *Khandaan* (1965), Kunal's role as a virtuous elder brother who spends his youth trying to raise his younger brother is memorable.

But the film almost missed seeing the light of day. Jain recalls that after the shooting was complete, some unit members were packed off in a bus and arrangements were made to send the negatives with them. Then, in one of those spur-of-the-moment decisions that can only be described as providential, Jain decided to carry the negatives himself. 'The bus met with an accident and fell into water. Some unit members were hurt. All our work would have been wasted because the negatives would have been destroyed,' says Jain.[42] The film, made for Rs 12 lakh, raked in double the amount.

Jain's next film *Dulha* (Groom, 1991) was a comedy and featured Attlee Brar as the hero. Diehard Hindi movie fans might recall Brar's debut as the villainous Shammi in Dev Anand's *Hum Naujawan* (1986), which was also actress Tabu's first Hindi film. At the time, gossip magazines were rife with stories on Brar's alleged bad behaviour. But Jain says he had no complaints either with Brar or his performance.[43] *Dulha* was shot in Hajipur and Mumbai, but the film did not do well at the box-office and Jain never directed another Bhojpuri movie. He moved on to film distribution and telefilms.

Unike Jain, Rajkumar Sharma, a Punjabi from the north Indian town of Haridwar, did not arrive in Mumbai to make a career in films. Far from it—he was a radio mechanic who came to hone his craft in the mid-1970s. Sharma happened to meet the well-known film writer Pandit Priyadarshi, who had penned the blockbuster *Jai Santoshi Ma* (1975). Panditji took him to the (now defunct) Basant Studio. When the studio's sound recordist Z. Haq found out that he was a radio engineer, he asked Sharma to join him as an assistant.

Later, in 1981, Sharma travelled to Bihar for the first time. He was part of the unit of *Jwala Dahej Ki* (1983), a Hindi film starring Arun Govil and Shoma Anand, which was shot in Rajgir and Dehri-on-Sone. 'This was my first exposure to the culture and language of the place,' he says.[44]

In 1983, he also worked as sound recordist on *Ganga Kinare Mora Gaon*. When Shahabadi, the lyricist of the film, decided to turn producer, he offered Sharma the director's job. 'Everyone questioned his decision. After all, I was just a sound recordist. But he said I know what this man is capable of,' recalls Sharma.[45]

Sharma, then forty years old, on his part encouraged Shahabadi to compose the music of his own film. 'He was a good lyricist and he had very good knowledge of folk tunes. He was initially hesitant but I told him, "You can do it." Shahabadi also wrote the film's dialogues. Being a poet, he knew economy of expression,' says Sharma, who has also directed several hit Nepali films.[46]

Dulha Ganga Paar Ke (The groom from across the Ganga, 1986) was a family drama with religious shades. Shot in Bihar's Sitamarhi and Hajipur districts, it celebrated its silver jubilee in Benares. The film also had a song penned by the renowned poet of the region, Bhikhari Thakur. Sharda Sinha, the famous folk singer, also sang a number in the film.

With *Mai* (1989), Sharma delivered his second silver jubilee hit in a row. Unlike *Dulha Ganga Paar Ke*, which was made for a mere Rs 13 lakh, *Mai* cost about Rs 24 lakh. In Sharma's own words, the movie had elements of *Mother India* and *Tapasya* (1975), the Rajshri superhit which became Hindi film actress Rakhee Gulzar's comeback movie. As in *Tapasya*, the protagonist in *Mai* was a self-sacrificing *bhabhi*.

Padma Khanna played the title role of a suffering mother and bhabhi. 'She charged only Rs 45,000 for the film. It was a great role. Padmaji was very happy about the way her role shaped up. She told me that she felt she had done her best Bhojpuri role,' says Sharma.[47] The hero of the film was Pankaj Sharma, a relative of the director. 'He was from Bareilly and was a chemical engineer by training. He was a good dancer. In one of the songs, he even dressed up as a woman and sang

Umariya bhayeeli mori raseeli ["My age has become juicy"].'[48]
The song was one of the highpoints of this successful film.

Sharma's third film, *Ho Jaye Da Naina Chaar* (Let our eyes
meet, 1995) was a rare costume drama in Bhojpuri—replete
with kings, palaces and swordfights—but it wasn't successful
at the box-office.

In fact, few Bhojpuri films have attempted to break away
from the familiar matrix of family dramas. *Bairi Kangna* (The
rival bracelet, 1992), a Kunal Singh-Meera Madhuri starrer,
was one such film. Directed by Nihal Singh, the silver jubilee
hit told the story of a young bride who is killed by her in-
laws, but returns from the grave to claim revenge. 'You could
call it a horror-emotional,' says Kunal.[49]

There were some dacoit films too such as *Ganga Jwala*
(1987) based on the life of the bandit Phoolan Devi. The film
tells the story of a young girl who is raped and goes on to
become a dacoit to avenge her dishonour.

By 1995, the audience seemed to be gradually losing
interest in Bhojpuri movies. Kunal, who witnessed the entire
phase first-hand, says that the period saw the rise of cheap
sex films in Hindi (many were dubbed) as well as vulgar
private album songs. 'This made families stay away from
cinema halls,' he says.[50] The actor also points out that during
this period, a fixed tax was levied on all cinema halls in Bihar
by the state government.[51] This further added to the problem,
creating a situation where the genre seemed to be meandering
aimlessly. Most Bhojpuri films made between the years 1995
and 2001 failed to make any kind of impact. As they say, it is
darkest before dawn.

4

The Third Wave

2002 onwards

When *Sasura Bada Paisewala* (Father-in-law has pots of money) was released in May 2004, few noticed it. This absence of enthusiasm was understandable. Of late, Bhojpuri cinema had shown little art or enterprise. After its gallant birth in the 1960s, the regional genre had enjoyed a boom from the late 1970s to the early 1990s and between 1983 and 1992, a total of ninety-eight Bhojpuri films were certified by the censors. But over the following nine years, 1993 to 2001, the number dipped drastically to thirty-three. The decline was not just in quantity, for from almost all accounts, most of the films from this period are unwatchable.

Broadly speaking, 2002 marks the beginning of a new phase because seven films were released that year—the highest since 1992. The year also produced a rare moderate success: Mohanji Prasad's *Saiyan Hamaar* (My beloved, 2002), which starred Ravi Kishan and Arpita Pal. Mohanji Prasad also produced *Kanyadaan* (2003), again with Kishan as the hero, which also fared reasonably well.

Then the unthinkable happened. At a time when most mainstream Hindi films were failing miserably at the box-office, the rustic tale of a young man's battle for self-respect against a rich and scheming father-in-law touched a chord with audiences in Bihar and eastern Uttar Pradesh. The genre had suddenly burst into life.[1]

The dusty 'House Full' boards were cleaned and hung outside cinema halls again. When the film was declared tax-free in Uttar Pradesh after twelve weeks, its success only intensified. *Sasura Bada Paisewala* (2004) brought the word 'jubilee' back into the Bhojpuri film business.

Shimmering banners proclaimed the film's completion of a fifty-week-run in Benares. In four other Uttar Pradesh towns—Gorakhpur, Deoria, Kanpur and Lucknow—the movie ran to packed houses for over twenty-five weeks. 'No film had celebrated its silver jubilee in Deoria before,' says the film's co-producer Sudhakar Pandey.[2] Adds Alok Kumar Dubey of Anand Mandir in Benares, '*Sasura Bada Paisewala* ran for thirty-one weeks in Anand. We gave them the film's entire production cost, which was around Rs 30 lakhs. The film ran for fifty weeks without a break in the city.'[3]

In Bihar too the film reached the silver jubilee mark in small town Hajipur. The tin-roofed cinema halls of mofussil towns, where men often stripped down to their underwear during summer matinee shows, were overflowing. The long queues before the ticket counters reminded old-timers of the mythological *Jai Santoshi Ma*, the freak 1975 superhit.

Made on a shoestring budget of Rs 30 lakhs, *Sasura Bada Paisewala* ended up grossing at least Rs 9 crore. No Hindi film could boast of a higher percentage of profit in 2004. Simply put, *Sasura Bada Paisewala* was the *Sholay* of Bhojpuri films. Manoj Tiwari, a folk singer of *kajri*s (folk songs associated with the rainy season), *chaita*s (folk songs associated with summer) and *purabiya*s ('songs of the east') from Benares, played the male lead in the film. He recalls, 'When director Ajay Sinha first approached me, I said I didn't have time.'[4] Tiwari wasn't bluffing. He was already a popular singer all over the Bhojpuri-speaking belt.

The actor-singer recalls listening to the film's story on a drive from Benares to Gorakhpur in his SUV. 'I liked the story and agreed to do the film. I was first offered Rs 1.11 lakh, but I asked for Rs 2.22 lakh and got it,' recalls Tiwari.[5] After the film's unprecedented success, his price went up to Rs 40 lakh.

But few know that the making of the movie itself was a miracle. Two days before the film's shooting began in November 2003, director Ajay Sinha began vomiting blood. Years later, Sinha is still not sure what exactly happened. 'Maybe I had chewed a shard of glass with my *tandoori roti*,' he ventures.[6] The effect of his unlikely ailment was damaging. The director was immediately admitted to a Gorakhpur hospital.

'The doctor told me two things: take rest and don't talk,' the director recalls.[7] Sinha had never heard a more depressing sentence in his life. The unit had already reached its outdoor location, Shamshabad village in the adjoining Mau district, and everyone was waiting for the cameras to roll.

For debutant co-producer Pandey, calamity had struck. He had to make a choice: either go ahead with the schedule or cancel the shoot. 'If I had taken the unit back,' says Pandey reconstructing those tension-filled days, 'the film would never have been made.' Finally after much deliberation, he took the choreographer's advice to shoot the songs first.[8]

On the other hand, Sinha was determined to direct the film. 'I told the doctor, "*Mere paas khone ke liye sirf jaan hai aur pane ke liye saara jahan hai*" ['I have nothing more to lose than my life and the world to gain'],' he says.[9] Contrary to the doctor's advice, he left the hospital within a few days

---

and joined the unit. Initially, he wrote his suggestions on pieces of paper, but obviously, that was not enough. As a director, he needed to give orders. Since he was also playing the role of the aggressive *sasur* (father-in-law), he needed to speak loudly as well. He would still bleed occasionally, but Sinha stuck to the job. 'Despite the risk, I did not hesitate either to scream or shout,' he says.[10]

Shooting was completed in only twenty days. After post-production work, *Sasura Bada Paisewala* was ready for viewing by March 2004. Unfortunately, national politics came in the way—with the Lok Sabha elections set to be held in April and May, Pandey felt the release needed to be postponed. 'In Uttar Pradesh and Bihar, elections are like festivals. Everyone is involved. So I decided to delay the release,' says Pandey, a former customs trading agent.[11] The decision was also prompted by the lukewarm response to the film's previews. One distributor from Gorakhpur wanted to be generous with his praise and told Pandey that it would run for at least a week.[12]

Even Tiwari had not imagined the film would strike gold. 'When the film became successful, I was presented with a Honda City car.'[13] He also praises the director. 'Despite being hospitalized before the shoot, director: Ajay Sinha was confident that the film would work. It was his project and he completed it successfully.'[14]

The first half of *Sasura Bada Paisewala* is about a hate-turned-love story between an educated city-returned village youth, Raja (played by Manoj Tiwari), and a rude city girl Rani (played by Rani Chatterjee, though the credits mention only 'Rani').

The second half details the evil machinations of Rani's rich father who gets his daughter married to Raja but ensures that the latter becomes a *ghar jamai*, that is, a husband who

Bollywood actress and item girl Rakhi Sawant performed a sizzling dance number in *Ram Balram* (2007), a Ravi Kishan-Rambha starrer.

stays with his wife's family, and this splits the hero's family. Being a ghar jamai is considered socially inappropriate and undignified. Raja swears he will not touch his bride until they go back to his house together.

Perhaps the movie worked because it had adjusted to the changing mood of the times. The hero is no village simpleton in a dhoti-kurta. In the film's opening shot, he is dressed in a bright yellow shirt and white trousers, with a pair of sunglasses positioned over his forehead—looking every inch a city slicker.

The beauty of *Sasura Bada Paisewala* is that it is not condescending and does not talk down to its core audience. Rather, it celebrates clichés that the qasbah and small-town audience enjoys: the rich-poor conflict, urban-rural differences, tradition-modernity contradictions, a good-as-gold brother-bhabhi relationship, lustful villains, stupid comedians and a class-conscious father-in-law.

The film often takes potshots at westernized Indians who are contemptuous of rural India. When Rani abuses Raja's porter-friend in English for dropping her heavy bag, the hero retorts in the same language: 'Hey you shut up. On getting a little education do you think that other people are insects? Madam, education enhances the power of civilization. But you people have degraded the culture of society [sic].' The audience claps uproariously at this point since the scene is a fantasy fulfiller, acting out a deep-felt desire to cut westernized Indians to size.[15] However, at another point, the heroine tells her mother: 'If I had been raped, I would have had no option but to give up my life'—no doubt a dubious message to the millions of women who watched the film in Bihar and Uttar Pradesh.

The final scene includes a fiery exchange between the son-in-law and his sasur. Dialogues such as, '*Hamaar sasur ke izzat izzat kahe ke hamaar sasur bada paisawala hawein. Aur hamaar izzat kotha ke randi, ke jekar man aawe nanga karke chal jaawe*' ('Your self-respect is important because you are rich and my self-respect is like a whore who can be stripped any time because she is poor'), also earned plenty of whistles and cheers from the audience.

In the end, the villain, who had earlier tried to rape the heroine, tries to kidnap her and shoots at the father-in-law, but Raja takes the bullet on his own shoulder. Rani prays to Lord Shiva to save his life even as doctors operate upon him. All's well that ends well and the lovers finally get to enjoy their much-delayed wedding night.

Shot in Uttar Pradesh's Mau district, the film's setting is suitably bucolic. At least geographically, the film is true to its soul. The movie progresses at a leisurely pace, with the songs being part of the narrative. In fact, without its twelve songs, the film would have been almost an hour shorter. From all accounts, Lal Sinha's music and Vinay Bihari's lyrics played a huge role in the film's success.

The songs of *Sasura Bada Paisewala* became trendsetters and a new form of foot-tapping tunes laced with a dash of ribald lyrics became the template for Bhojpuri film songs.

* * *

Perhaps the ground for the third coming of Bhojpuri films was prepared by a folk music revolution in Bihar and Uttar Pradesh. Singers such as Sharda Sinha, who also acted in the film *Mai* (1989), played an important role in popularizing Bhojpuri folk music.

By the 1990s, T-Series had already become a big player in the north Indian entertainment industry. It gave breaks to hundreds of small-time singers, some of whom became big names later, such as Manoj Tiwari. Certain genres such as *bhajan*s (devotional songs) became major money spinners and cassettes of these songs were sold out in regional languages too. Chandresh Yadav of Shubham Cassettes, Benares, says that the revival of the private Bhojpuri song album set the market for *Sasura Bada Paisewala*.[16]

'The bustling song industry moved to another level with the rise of the music video industry. A bunch of folk performers such as Manoj Tiwari became well-known faces much before their first films were released,' says Brijesh Tripathi, one of the top character actors in Bhojpuri cinema.[17] Adds *Sasura*'s music director Lal Sinha, 'Before *Sasura Bada Paisewala*, there was huge demand for raunchy Bhojpuri songs. It created the groundwork for a similar kind of cinema.'[18] Yet trade pundits were unwilling to accept *Sasura Bada Paisewala*'s success as anything more than a fluke. One swallow does not make a summer, they said.

Confirmation of Bhojpuri cinema's revival arrived with *Panditji Bataeen Na Biyah Kab Hoee* in 2005. The film starred Ravi Kishan, the son of a Jaunpur priest and a graduate from Benares Hindu University. Till then, Kishan had survived in Bollywood's backwaters, doing bit parts in movies like *Tere Naam* (2003) and *Army* (1996). The heroine of this film was Nagma, who had failed as a Bollywood heroine. 'But she was a well-known star down south. And I had to literally plead with her to do a Bhojpuri film,' recalls Kishan.[19]

Nobody seemed interested in the movie though. To create some buzz around it, Kishan hit upon an idea. Borrowing from Marilyn Monroe's famous skirt-flying scene in *The Seven Year Itch* (1955)—also redone by Kelly Le Brock in *The*

Woman in Red (1984) and Pooja Bedi in Bollywood's *Jo Jeeta Wohi Sikander* (1992)—he conjured a similar scene for the song *Lehnga utha deb remote se* ('I will lift your skirt with a remote'). 'The gimmick attracted media attention and created a much-needed hype around the film,' says Kishan, now a well-known star whose smart-talk in the reality TV show, *Bigg Boss* (a desi version of *Big Brother*), widened his mass appeal.[20]

Interestingly, the film's lyricist, Vinay Bihari, reveals that director Mohanji Prasad initially wanted to cast Manoj Tiwari as the hero. 'We had a meeting with Mohanji. The signing amount was paid. But later due to differences over the actor's fees, Tiwari moved out of the film. When Mohanji asked me to write the film's lyrics, I said, "I promise you the songs will make the film a musical hit." He said, "If the film does well, I will give you Rs 2 lakh more than your fees." The film did celebrate its silver jubilee and he did give me an extra Rs 2 lakhs,' Bihari says.[21]

Industry sources estimate that the film, made for Rs 60 lakh, ended up grossing at least ten times more. In Patna alone the film collected more than four times the Bollywood hit *Bunty Aur Babli*, a movie about small-town yearnings. 'With *Panditji*, we hit the jackpot,' says Kishan.[22]

The Hindi film industry was stunned. A second superhit, again from the boondocks of central India, was hard to ignore. Two more Manoj Tiwari movies were released that year: *Bandhan Toote Na* (The ties shouldn't break, 2005) and *Daroga Babu I Love You* (2005). Both became box-office biggies, making a hat-trick of successful releases for Tiwari. With the success of these movies, Bhojpuri cinema was suddenly hot and happening on a large scale. What followed was the great Bhojpuri rush by Bollywood bigwigs.

Singer Udit Narayan produced *Kab Kahbu Tu I Love You* (2007), *Ee Rishta Anmol Ba* (2008) and the national-award-winning *Kab Hoi Gawna Hamaar* (2005). Inder Kumar and Ashok Thakeria, makers of Bollywood superhits such as *Dil* (1990), *Beta* (1992) and *Raja* (1995), made *Sab Golmaal Ha* (2007). G.P. Sippy Enterprises was involved in the production of *Mai Ta Bas Mai Baadi* (2008) and N.R. Pachisia, who made the Bollywood film *Ziddi* (1997) and *Jo Bole So Nihal* (2005), produced *Dehati Babu* (2006) starring Manoj Tiwari.[23] Most of these films were box-office duds.

The genre also attracted corporates. To name a few, Balaji Telefilms co-produced *Hum Bal Brahmachari Tu Kanya Kunwari* (2006) and *Gabbar Singh*; Mumbai Mantra, a company backed by the Mahindra group, co-produced *Hum Bahubali* (2008).

The 1960s Bollywood heart-throb Saira Banu also produced a Bhojpuri film: *Ab Ta Ban Ja Sajanwa Hamaar* (2006). And the genre provided employment to ex-Miss World, Yukta Mukhi, who danced in an item number for *Kab Kahbu Tu I Love You*, while Miss India Worldwide 2007, Fareisa Joemmanbaks, an Indian from Surinam, acted in *Saiyan Chitchor* in 2008.

Some films are also being shot abroad now, such as *Kab Hoi Gawna Hamaar, Pyaar Ke Bandhan* and *Janam Janam Ke Saath* (2007), showing the genre's desire for upward mobility.

Further, who would have ever foreseen Bollywood stars such as Ajay Devgan (*Dharti Kahe Pukaar Ke*, 2006), Hema Malini (*Ganga*, 2006), Jeetendra (*Gabbar Singh*, 2008), Mithun Chakraborty (*Bhole Shankar*, 2008), and Raj Babbar (*Babul Pyaare*, 2006) acting in Bhojpuri films?

Statistics reveal the story. In 2004, a total of twenty-one films were cleared by censors and in 2005, the number had doubled to forty-five. In 2006, it was a staggering seventy-six, and sixty-seven the year after.

Joginder Mahajan, who distributes Bhojpuri films in Delhi and Uttar Pradesh, succinctly sums up this phenomenon: 'It is like a non-vegetarian restaurant doing well, followed by others springing up in the neighbourhood.'[24] Delhi-based distributor Sanjay Mehta describes the scenario more politically. He calls it 'the Laloo phenomenon of cinema'.[25]

The phenomenon finally reached its logical conclusion when Dinesh Lal Yadav 'Nirahua' emerged on the scene. *Nirahua Rickshawala* (2007), the story of an upright rickshaw-puller falling in love—and kissing—an MLA's sister set new box-office records. 'We had initially approached Ravi Kishan for the lead role. But he had no dates [to give],' recalls director K.D. (Dinkar Kapoor).[26]

With several other hits under his belt such as *Nirahua Chalal Sasural* (Nirahua goes to his in-laws', 2008), *Lagal Raha Ae Rajaji* (Carry on my love, 2008), *Pratigya* (Vow, 2008) and more, Nirahua is now the hottest star, delivering big hits with unfailing regularity. The slightly-built actor, who grew up in Calcutta, is also a fine singer of *birha*, a genre of folk song. A karate expert, his action scenes are a cut above the rest. A fine dancer too, Nirahua is a dream package for any producer. So it is no surprise that he commanded a fee of Rs 50 lakh for every film in 2009.

Like the success of a Shah Rukh Khan movie or an Akshay Kumar film that often spreads disproportionate cheer in Bollywood, Nirahua's successes too have kept Bhojwood happy and afloat.

5

Widening Horizons

The impact of success

Success creates visibility—and Bhojpuri films are no exception. Compared to the past, the genre has begun to get more space in film trade magazines, newspapers and even on television channels.

In 2007, the international satellite television channels Star and Sahara showed Bhojpuri films. When Sahara premiered *Ganga*, Ravi Kishan anchored the screening. Ajay Vidyasagar, the then president (content and new media) of Star India explained, 'By airing these films we hope to enhance the audience base.'[1]

Before 2004, Bhojpuri films barely occupied one or two columns of Bollywood trade magazines. By 2006, the industry had grown to huge proportions and on occasion, magazines devoted as many as three pages to Bhojpuri films under production. Right through 2007, *Film Information*, the well-known film trade magazine, carried under-production reports of ten to fifteen Bhojpuri films in many of its weekly issues. Now, Bhojpuri films are regularly reviewed, almost at par with Bollywood films.[2]

With Bhojpuri films showing plenty of market potential, the Amitabh Bachhan-hit *Namak Halal* (1982) was dubbed in Bhojpuri and released as *Dadua Khiladi, Babua Anari.* Some Mithun Chakraborty films were also dubbed and released in Bhojpuri.[3]

'The scenario has changed completely from the days when we started out. Now we have film parties, premieres and awards. We get interviewed like Bollywood actors do,' says Brijesh Tripathi, a character actor who has been working in Bhojpuri films for over two decades.[4]

In the new millennium, Bhojpuri films have also expanded their geographical boundaries. Back in the 1960s, and even in the 1980s, an overwhelming number of such films were shot either in eastern Uttar Pradesh or in different parts of mid-west and central Bihar. Most Bhojpuri films are still shot in Uttar Pradesh and Bihar. For example, *Maiya Rakhiha Senurva Aabad* had a month-long shooting schedule in Hajipur and Sasaram, small towns of Bihar. *Yashoda Mai Jaisan Bhauji Hamaar* was filmed in Motihari, another small town. *Saiyan Tohare Pe Naaz Ba* was shot in Benares, Ghazipur, Patna and Balia.[5] Other instances include *Jhulaniya Lai Da Rajaji*, which was filmed for eighteen days in Buxar,[6] *Pujiha Charan Mai Baap Ke*, which was shot in twenty-five days at Gorakhpur[7] and a large part of *Piya Tohse Naina Laage* was shot in Kushinagar.[8]

But with larger budgets, a growing number of film-makers are willing to shoot outside these standard areas. *Balma Bada Nadaan* (2004), directed by veteran Bhojpuri hero Sujit Kumar, was shot in Uttar Pradesh's Modi Nagar, Mussourie and Rishikesh. *Pyaar Ke Bandhan* (2006) was shot in Rajpipla, Khandala, central London, Windsor and Reading, while parts of *Balma 420* (2006) were filmed in central London, Piccadilly Circus and Leicester Square.[9]

'Although the audience in Bihar's main film-watching towns do not like films shot in western locales, I shot my first Bhojpuri venture in London and Mauritius,' says London-based Rajendra Patel, who has produced films in Hindi and Gujarati.[10]

Many films are shot in Rajpipla, Gujarat. Bhojpuri film-makers prefer travelling to this small erstwhile princely state rather than to eastern India. The reason for its popularity, is firstly, its proximity to Mumbai, where post-production is carried out. The availability of relatively better boarding and lodging facilities at budget prices has also helped.

The new Bhojpuri film often moves beyond the village family saga. On many occasions, the hero is a crook or a cop or a non-resident Indian (NRI) just as it is in Hindi films. For instance, in *Kab Hoi Gawna Hamaar* (2005), the leading character becomes a filmstar and goes to Mauritius for a shoot. In *Janam Janam Ke Saath* (2007), a multi-starrer shot in Mauritius, the hero goes to an African nation to attend to family business. In *Purab Aur Paschim* (2007), simpleton hero Ravi Kishan lands up in Dubai in search of a job.

It is no surprise then that there are movies with titles such as *Londonwali Se Neha Lagauli* (I have fallen for a girl from London, 2007) or that a Ukrainian actress named Tanya acted in *Firangi Dulhaniya* (2005). At one level, the geographical widening of locations can be attributed to expanding storylines. At another level, it also shows the genre's growing confidence in stepping out of its comfort zone and experimenting with the larger world, a phenomenon that has blurred the distinct identity of the regional film.

Several new Bhojpuri films are direct copies of Hindi ones. *Saiyan Se Solah Singaar* (2006) is a rehash of *Judaai*

(1997, starring Anil Kapoor, Sridevi and Urmila Matondkar, where a wife takes money from a woman to share her husband with her).[11] *Pandav* (2007) is inspired by the 1980s Bollywood hit, *Hum Paanch* (1981),[12] while *Didi Tor Dewar Deewana* (2006) is said to be a rip-off of many old films including *Hum Aapke Hain Koun . . .!* (1994). *Gabbar Singh* (2008) is *Sholay* (1975) revisited. Even *Panditji Bataeen Na Biyah Kab Hoee* (2005) borrows from *Sholay*'s basic plot about an individual whose family is wiped out by a ruffian, who then enlists two young men to carry out revenge.

The changes in the regional political milieu occasionally find reflection in the storylines. Take *Pandit* (2006), which is a regular revenge drama of an underdog Brahmin (named Pandit) against a *bahubali* (named Khan), a strongman with hordes of henchmen. When a whistle-blower tries to unite people to free thirty bighas of land forcibly occupied by the bahubali for a distillery, he is thrown off a parapet and fed to a crocodile. Most people in Uttar Pradesh would know of at least one well-known politician who used to have a pond full of crocodiles in his backyard.

The film has a pronounced pro-Brahmin tinge. At one point, the hero says, '*Pandit ke kamjor na samajhiha, je pandit biyah karavela, oo shradho karvawela*' ('Don't think the pandit is weak. The pandit conducts both marriages and the rituals of death'). *Pandit* was released at a time when Brahmins were going through a low phase in Uttar Pradesh politics, with the pro-Yadav Samajwadi Party holding state power. Since both the Congress and the Bharatiya Janata Party (BJP) lost power in Uttar Pradesh, Brahmins appeared to be a caste in search of a party. Things have changed now with the Bahujan Samaj Party (BSP) that currently governs Uttar Pradesh actively wooing them.

A majority of the films of the ongoing third phase have hackneyed storylines with equally stereotypical treatment. By and large, neo-realist fare is absent in new Bhojpuri films. Issues like Naxalism and the problems of migrant labourers or the peasantry are largely ignored.

Films focus mainly on individual and familial concerns; social problems are touched upon in a rather facile way. In *Hamaar Gharwali* (2006), the rich heroine rejects her would-be husband because he is less educated than she is. The rejected groom then becomes a manager in her house and wins her heart. *Rangli Chunariya Tohre Naam* (2006) is a family drama about a scheming uncle who gets two brothers to fight over family property. *Hamri Bhi Aawegi Baraat* (2006) is a convoluted story of a woman who is abused and almost murdered by her mother-in-law, but still believes that her life is with the family she has married into,[13] while *Balma 420* (2006) is about two crooks who help a mother meet her lost sons.[14]

In *Londonwali Se Neha Lagauli* (2007), hero Krishna Abhishek plays the dafli and sings songs praising Bharat in the same way actor Manoj Kumar did in the patriotic Hindi film *Purab Aur Paschim* (1970). The Bhojpuri film also has a gay character who tries to seduce the object of his ardour by saying, 'You give me the red card and I will get you the green card. *Chabhi bhi khush aur tala bhi khush* [The key is happy and so is the lock].' Now, that's straight talking.

Raja Thakur (2006), played by Shatrughan Sinha, is 'the story of a Robin Hood who can go to any length to set matters right.'[15] *Kab Aibu Aganwa Hamaar* (2007) is about a village singer who is spurned by his girlfriend. He leaves the village, becomes famous in the city and then comes back to claim his love.[16] *Suraj Bihari* (2006) is a story of how faith and prayers cure cancer.[17] Two cousins—one of them honest, the other crooked—fight over family property in *Sajanwa Anadi, Sajania Khiladi* (2007), while *Hanuman Bhakt Havaldar* (2007) is about two brothers who avenge their father's death. The *seedha-saadha* (good and honest) brother switches roles with his crooked brother in a plot that brings together two Hindi films, *Jaise to Taisa* (1973) and *Gopi-Kishan* (1994).

However, within the matrix of commercial cinema, some films do try to deal with social issues. *Saiyan Sipahiya* (2006), based on the true but little-known story of Zalim Singh Sipahiya who fell in love with a low-caste girl, raises questions about the caste system; *Kanyadaan* (2003) deals with female foeticide; *Dulha Babu* (2006) explores the phenomenon of shotgun weddings in rural north Bihar. Since the 1980s, potential grooms are often kidnapped and forced to get married to particular girls.

Pyaar Ke Bandhan (2006) shows the son of a *mochi* (cobbler) falling in love and marrying the daughter of a thakur. In *Pandit* (2006), when a Gandhian goes to claim his land, he discovers that the official record books list him as a dead person, which in reality is an infamous method of robbing innocent people of their land in Uttar Pradesh and Bihar, and the topic of dozens of newspaper articles.

In *Preet Na Jaane Reet* (2005), a dark-complexioned girl tries to commit suicide because her parents are unable to get her married. The film also touches on the practice of fooling a groom and his family by showing them one girl and marrying off another. Such a practice, though uncommon, does take place in the Bhojpuri-speaking areas.

* * *

Between 2004 and 2008, about 285 Bhojpuri films were made. Industry sources say over eighty per cent would have lost money in greater or lesser amounts and dozens of films hibernated in the cans without attracting distributors. Some managed a limited release in one or two territories, but others failed to get a theatrical release and were eventually sold as VCDs.[18] 'A huge majority of Bhojpuri films don't get distributors. The producer has to distribute his film himself,' says Alok Dubey of Anand Mandir, Benares.[19]

What then is the secret of Bhojpuri cinema's endurance? The fact remains that if ninety per cent of Hindi films also flop—that has never stopped Bollywood—why should the regional genre be affected? But to go beyond rhetoric, it is simply a question of economics. A host of macro-factors ensure a steady stream of fresh producers.

An average Bollywood masala movie costs about Rs 10 crore. In comparison, a Bhojpuri film can be made for around Rs 60–70 lakh (add another Rs 40–50 lakh if top stars like Tiwari, Kishan or Nirahua are involved). A low-budget film could cost as little as Rs 30 lakh. Despite the high percentage of films that are flops, the losses are too low to deter men with bagfuls of cash, especially in an era of abundant black money.

This is why the genre has also attracted producers from south India. Nasir Jamal burnt his fingers with *Raksha Bandhan-Aego Bachan* (2006). Sridhar Shetty made *Hamra Se Biyah Karba* (2006) and Ramesh Rao made *Banke Bihari MLA* (2007), starring Ravi Kishan and Rambha for an estimated Rs 1.5 crore. 'I made a film in Bhojpuri because there is a huge resurgent market for films in this dialect. What's encouraging is that this market is growing nationally and internationally,' says Shetty.[20]

As in Bollywood, a couple of big hits every year ensure that the interest of the producer is sustained. Everybody keeps chasing the box-office success Holy Grail, which is why there is a long list of first-time producers making flop films. Rajesh Kumar Singh, a Mumbai distributor of Bhojpuri films, talks about a doctor from Hajipur in Bihar: 'He came with Rs 20 lakh and wanted to make a Bhojpuri film. He recorded some songs and spent about Rs 2 lakh before realizing that he was getting into a business he knew nothing about. He quietly packed his bags and left. He was lucky. His losses could have been much more. *Sabko guru dakhshina dena padta hai* [Everybody has to pay the dues].'[21]

The financier of the big flop, *Baklol Dulha* (2007), Bir Singh Gujjar, deals in real estate. When asked why he invested in a Bhojpuri film, he had a simple answer: 'It is a good market.'[22]

Old-timers believe that too many Bhojpuri films are being made right now. Director Hasmukh Rajput, whose low-budget social *Naihar Ki Chunri* became a superhit in 1985 says, 'There is an overkill of such movies.' Even Delhi-based distributor Sanjay Mehta believes that the genre is suffering from overexposure. 'Every week a new release means there is over-production,' he says.[23]

But with the high percentage of flops, the genre is making use of every possible commercial trick to have as much money on the table as possible. In-film advertising is one such medium. *Kab Aibu Aganwa Hamaar* (2007) has two scenes peddling a brand of detergent powder rather overtly. In one scene, the shopkeeper asks heroine Shweta Tiwari, 'Why do you buy this detergent powder? Is it because it is cheap?' She replies, holding a packet in her hand like models do, 'Why should something be bad only because it is cheap?' In the next scene, she is shown holding the packet at home and talking about the merits of the detergent powder.

Similarly, in *Ganga*, Ravi Kishan eulogizes the virtues of a well-known brand of tooth powder.

Several other avenues of revenue generation have also helped producers bring down losses and even make profits. In August 2008, Bhojpuri movies got a huge fillip with the lanching of Mahua channel, India's first twenty-four-hour free-to-air general entertainment Bhojpuri channel. The channel initially bagged the satellite rights of 175 films, which meant another major source of income for producers. Several other such channels are said to be in the pipeline and have bought rights to many films to create movie banks. 'The satellite rights as well as the VCD/DVD rights are like oxygen for the producers,' says director Anand Ghatraj known for his film *Kab Hoi Gawna Hamaar* (2005).[24]

Back in 2005, a hit Bhojpuri film could fetch Rs 20 lakhs in the video market.[25] T-Series is still the big daddy of Bhojpuri films and has bought the VCD/DVD rights of many movies. Bhagtu Motwani, Delhi-based owner of TimeNTune Video, has also bought the VCD/DVD rights for about fifty Bhojpuri films, including superhits such as *Balam Pardesia, Dharti Maiya* and *Ganga Kinare Mora Gaon*.[26] 'We started buying video rights of Bhojpuri movies in the mid-1980s. Those were the VCR days. We bought the rights of *Ganga Kinare Mora Gaon* for Rs 20,000 and since then we have been renewing the rights every eleven years. In 1996, we renewed it for Rs 50,000 and again in 2007 for Rs 1 lakh,' says Motwani.[27]

He says the average rate for the rights of old films is around Rs 1 lakh. New films cost anything between Rs 5 and 7 lakh, with successful films selling for anything between Rs 8 and 15 lakh. 'The market is down in the dumps these days for a couple of reasons. The stars are overpriced and the producers are unprofessional. In 2006, we used to launch Bhojpuri film VCDs with about 50,000 copies. Now it is down to 20,000,' says Motwani.[28]

* * *

The market abroad also has tremendous possibilities. In the nineteenth and early twentieth centuries, thousands of labourers from Bihar and eastern Uttar Pradesh were shipped off to different parts of the globe to work on sugarcane plantations. Now, in countries like Mauritius, Fiji, Surinam, Guyana and Trinidad, they form the well-heeled Bhojpuri-speaking diaspora.[29]

The situation, however, is not as simple as it seems. Sheela Sahtoe, a Holland-based academic, says that there are no cinema halls left in Surinam. 'But now we have five Indian TV channels showing only Bollywood Hindi movies. Indian people also watch Hindi films on DVD. Bhojpuri films are not watched by Indian people or shown on television. Neither are they available on DVD,' she says.[30]

Similarly, Visham Bhimull, a Trinidad-based doctor with a great passion for Bhojpuri of the Caribbean variety, says that no Bhojpuri films are shown in Trinidad and neither are they available on VCDs or DVDs. 'The Bhojpuri-understanding and speaking population has no clue that Bhojpuri films exist,' he says.[31]

In Mauritius and Fiji, the Uttar Pradesh and Bihari disapora still speak and understand the language and croon folk songs that have filtered down the generations. Actor-singer Dinesh Lal Yadav 'Nirahua' was surprised to find many Fijians of Indian origin singing songs from his non-filmi album, *Nirahua Satal Rahe,* roughly translated as 'Nirahua

Clings'. But he too did not find any Bhojpuri film VCDs or DVDs there.[32]

Kab Hoi Gawna Hamaar was shot partly in Port Louis, Mauritius. 'While shooting in Mauritius, we felt we were in India. We met many Bhojpuri-speaking people,' says director Ghatraj, who is also brother-in-law of singer Udit Narayan, the film's producer.[33]

In *Ee Rishta Anmol Ba* (2008), Ghatraj worked with Nikhil Upreti and Rekha Thapa, two stars from Nepal. 'The idea is to attract the Madhesiya [the plains people across the Terai areas] population there because they understand the language. We have also tied up with top Nepali producers, Udhav and Ujjwal Paudel. Nepal can be a big territory for Bhojpuri films,' he says.[34]

* * *

Such possibilities notwithstanding, well-known Bhojpuri film producers like Sudhakar Pandey feel that unless the industry tailors its budget to the size of the market, the percentage of flops will not decrease. Blockbuster *Sasura Bada Paisewala* ended up grossing over Rs 8 crore but the film was made for a mere Rs 30 lakh. 'Any film with a budget of over Rs 65 lakhs is risky,' says Pandey, who is also the producer of *Daroga Babu I Love You*.[35] Other producers point out that while top actors are being paid vast amounts, the producers themselves are losing money on most ventures.[36]

But as top producer Abhay Sinha points out, 'The hero may be overpriced but why should they cut down their rates when they have producers queuing up outside their door?'[37]

It appears there is a wide gap between what the audience wants and what the producer-director-financiers provide.

Alok Dubey illustrates the point with an example: 'Former Miss World Yukta Mukhi was used as an item girl in a Bhojpuri film. The producers obviously thought she was a catch. But the question is: how many of those who watch Bhojpuri films know her?'[38]

6

The Diaspora Within

The ongoing third phase of Bhojpuri films has also seen a massive expansion in terms of the regions they are exhibited in. Back in the 1960s and 1970s, the regional genre's footprint was limited to eastern Uttar Pradesh and Bihar. But now it is viewed across most of Uttar Pradesh. That apart, Bhojpuri films are regularly shown in Mumbai and its suburbs and nearby towns like Bhiwandi and Malegaon. The regional film industry has also carved out a decent territory in Punjab, Delhi and Calcutta and can be viewed in towns that are home to substantial migrant populations in Rajasthan and Gujarat.

Rajesh Kumar Singh, a Mumbai-based distributor of Bhojpuri films, estimates that Bihar accounts roughly for about fifty per cent of Bhojpuri cinema's monetary collections. This is followed by Delhi/Uttar Pradesh (twenty per cent), Mumbai (fifteen per cent), Punjab (ten per cent), Bengal (three per cent) and others (two per cent). Some Bhojpuri films are also shown in Nepal.[1]

Kirit Desai's family has been managing the Moti cinema hall in Delhi's bustling Chandni Chowk area since 1938. He started screening Bhojpuri films in September 2004 with *Sasura Bada Paisewala*. Desai explains how screening such regional films became a part of his regular repertoire. 'I was unsure initially about screening them. But my staff told me that thousands of labourers from Bihar and Uttar Pradesh worked in Chandni Chowk. So I decided to take a chance with *Sasura Bada Paisewala*,' says Desai.[2]

The film grossed about Rs 3.40 lakh in its two-week run. 'It was very good business compared to our regular collections those days,' he says.[3]

In the five years since, Moti has screened at least fifteen to twenty Bhojpuri movies every year. The films which enjoyed a good run at his theatre are *Ganga Ke Paar Saiyan Hamaar, Daroga Babu I Love You, Bandhan Toote Na, Panditji Bataeen Na Biyah Kab Hoee* and *Damadji*. In 2009, Dinesh Lal Yadav 'Nirahua's *Pratigya* did very well, collecting Rs 2.5 lakh at the cash counters in just one week. At a time when single-screen theatres are shutting down all over the country, Desai admits that the regional movies have helped him sustain his business.

Delhi-based distributor Joginder Mahajan, who has been distributing Bhojpuri films in the capital for five years now, admits that the viewership of Bhojpuri films has grown significantly in the National Capital Region, which includes Delhi and neighbouring urban settlements Noida, Gurgaon, Ghaziabad and Faridabad. 'Three decades ago, even a superhit like *Balam Pardesia* ran only in morning shows in the national capital. In contrast, *Sasura Bada Paisewala* was shown in ten cinema halls with a record five prints,' he says.[4] It ran for twelve weeks in Sangam cinema near western Uttar Pradesh's Loni border—longer than any movie with Bollywood superstars Shah Rukh, Salman or Aamir.

The Delhi-based distributor points out that some theatre owners are averse to screening Bhojpuri films because they feel it will affect the image of the cinema hall adversely, in that the underclass Bhojpuri film audience 'doesn't have the purchasing power to boost canteen sales.'[5]

The theory, however, is partly erroneous. In places like Delhi and Mumbai, there is a sizeable potential middle-class audience—'gentry' in business parlance—which either speaks or understands Bhojpuri and a decent Bhojpuri film in a respectable theatre might attract them. The real question is whether the movies being made suit their cinematic sensibilities.

Bhojpuri films best indicate of the regions of India to which labourers from Bihar and Uttar Pradesh migrate. The films are shown across India, even in towns of the western states Gujarat, Maharashtra and Rajasthan, and the northern state of Uttarakhand. *Dharti Kahe Pukaar Ke* (2006) was screened for one week in Ajmer, Rajasthan. In Gujarat, *Ganga* ran for one week in regular shows in Rajkot at Deluxe and in morning shows at Girnar; *Sasurari Zindabad* (2006) ran for one week in Navsari's Prakash Talkies.[6] *Pandit* was screened even in far out Rajasthan's Sri Ganganagar town.[7]

The reach of Bhojpuri films extends to several other larger cities and towns with a significant migrant population from the Bhojpuri-speaking belt. *Raghupati Raghav Rajaram*, a low budget movie, opened at eight Calcutta theatres: Crown, Mayur, Jagat, Liberty, Indira, Vaishali, Liluah and Narayani.[8] *Sasura Bada Paisewala* drew big crowds at Moti Mahal cinema in Jaipur even on its second run. 'The audience included people from Uttar Pradesh, Biharis as well as Rajasthanis. A few months earlier, the same film was released at Milan cinema in Vishwakarma Colony, where the film raked in Rs 1.5 lakh within a week.'[9]

By 2006, Bhojpuri films ruled the roost in the smaller suburban theatres of Mumbai. According to *Film Information* (16 December 2006), six Bhojpuri films were playing in Mumbai the week before the magazine's December issue was released: *Bairi Piya*, *Chacha Bhatija*, *Ganga*, *Jhulaniya Lai Da Rajaji*, *Ho Gayeel Ba Pyaar Odhaniyawali Se* (all 2006) and *Ganga Ke Paar Saiyan Hamaar* (2004). The popularity of Bhojpuri films can be gauged by the fact that even a low-budget film like *UP Bihar Bambai Express* (2007) grossed Rs 7.11 lakh in the metropolis in its first week of release.[10]

Trade collections show that Ravi Kishan's *Pandit* (2005) earned Rs 13.13 lakh in its first two weeks in Mumbai[11] and *Nirahua Chalal Sasural* (2008) grossed Rs 9.17 lakh from six cinemas in its first week in Mumbai.[12] That's a staggering figure, especially since Mumbai is a relatively small territory for the genre.

These collections were no mere flashes in the pan. In its first week in Mumbai, *Kahan Jaiba Raja Najariya Ladaike* (2007) with Dinesh Lal Yadav 'Nirahua' collected a whopping Rs 13.28 lakh from five prints in its first week. From Thane, it mopped up another Rs 5.90 lakh from three cinema halls.[13] *Hanuman Bhakt Havaldar* (2007) opened with ten prints in Mumbai in Dreamland, Palace, Nandi, Navrang, Anupam, Mayor, Ajanta, Bharat, Natraj and Shri Krishna theatres.

In its first week alone, *Pyaar Ke Bandhan* (2006) collected Rs 12.76 lakh from nine cinemas in Mumbai and raked in another Rs 3.61 lakh on four prints in the second week.[14] *Bandhan Toote Na* (2005) even completed showing for a hundred days in Mumbai.[15]

In Bhiwandi, located about sixty kilometres north-east of Mumbai, Bhojpuri films have a sizeable audience of migrant labourers from Uttar Pradesh and Bihar working in the textile industries there. According to *businessofcinema.com*, 'Bhiwandi has fourteen cinemas of which eight screen mostly Bhojpuri films. Ratan, which accommodates 1,225 people and has a capacity of registering Rs 5.52 lakh in twenty-eight shows [was] screening *Hamra Se Biyah Karba* (2006).'[16]

Other theatres such as Apsara, Jhankar, Nazrana, Payal and Bharat also screen Bhojpuri films in Bhiwandi.[17]

Towns such as Ludhiana in Punjab, which has a huge migrant population working in its industrial units, have also become significant markets for Bhojpuri films. 'It's [on] the belt along the Grand Trunk Road where the Bihari migrant labourers have settled down,' reasons Delhi-based film distributor, Sanjay Mehta.[18]

Though Bhojpuri films were occasionally released in Punjab even in the 1980s, it became a lucrative territory after the success of *Sasura Bada Paisewala,* which ran for at least eight house full weeks in Ludhiana's Chand cinema hall.

Local distributors point out that Bhojpuri films were initially shown only in two Ludhiana movie halls: Swarn and Nirmal. Now they are also screened in theatres like Arora Palace, Basant, Society, Shingar, Deepak and many others. Naulakha theatre, which earlier showed foreign films, strategically shifted to Bhojpuri films in 2007. 'It has helped increase their footfall. For several single screen cinema halls on the verge of closure, Bhojpuri films have acted like oxygen,' says film distributor Ajay Bhanot.[19]

In 2007, Dinesh Lal Yadav's film *Nirahua Rickshawala* became the genre's biggest grosser ever in Punjab, overtaking the superhits *Sasura Bada Paisewala* and *Panditji Bataaen Na Biyah Kab Hoee*. Distributors estimate that the movie collected over Rs 30 lakh from this territory alone.[20] The movie ran to packed houses in three theatres in Ludhiana, besides being screened in three cinemas in Jalandhar and Bathinda. Theatres in Amritsar and Mohali also show Bhojpuri films.

In fact, such is the demand for Bhojpuri films that distributors have begun comparing the profits of Hindi films with Bhojpuri ones. In several areas, these films are more popular than Hindi ones. According to a 2007 newspaper report, 'If there is a toss between the Bollywood flick, *Cheeni Kum*, and any other Bhojpuri film, the latter will win hands down in Punjab. Surprised? Don't be, as Bhojpuri film, *Gawanva Le Ja Rajaji*, is running to packed houses in Jalandhar!'[21]

Unlike Bollywood blockbusters screened in multiplexes, Bhojpuri films are shown in cheaper theatres where tickets are available for Rs 15 or Rs 20. 'As the migrant labourers from Uttar Pradesh and Bihar cannot afford to watch films in multiplexes, Bhojpuri films have become popular among them,' says Rakesh Sabarwal, member of the Northern India Film Distributors' Association. Living away from their families, who usually stay back in villages, Bhojpuri films fill the cultural and emotional void migrants experience in Punjab.[22]

But what about Punjab's own film industry? Comedian Jaspal Bhatti, who has produced three Punjabi films, says that instead of assimilating with the culture of the state, the migrant population is decimating Punjabi culture and cinema. Bhatti blames Punjabi film producers for not coming up with watchable films. He adds that this is the worst phase ever for Punjabi cinema as local producers are incurring heavy losses. He, however, welcomes the fact that Bhojpuri cinema had managed to carve a niche for itself in Punjab.[23]

Distributors point out that Bihar and eastern Uttar Pradesh's migrant labour population is the primary audience for these films, but Bhanot, who distributes Bhojpuri films in Punjab, estimates that about five per cent of the genre's audience is Punjabi. He says, 'Some are young Punjabis who watch these films for fun. Another section is Punjabi labourers who interact with the migrant population and develop a familiarity with the language.'[24]

Bhanot believes that the audience in Punjab prefers a different kind of Bhojpuri movie: 'Back in Bihar and eastern

Uttar Pradesh, the core Bhojpuri audience wants clean family socials. But the audience here largely consists of young, single men who prefer spicier stuff.'[25]

* * *

In 2007, Bhojpuri films became victims of political ire in many areas in India. From Thane and Nashik in Maharashtra to Ludhiana in Punjab, cinema halls showing Bhojpuri films were targets of sectarian violence aimed at scaring off migrants from Bihar and eastern Uttar Pradesh. On 15 October 2007, a bomb blast in Ludhiana's Shingar cinema during the screening of *Janam Janam Ke Saath* left six dead. Terrorist group Babbar Khalsa was allegedly involved in the blast.[26]

On 1 February 2008, a print of *Kaise Kahi Tohra Se Pyar Ho Gaeel* (2008) was burnt at Nashik's Madhukar cinema, allegedly by activists of the Maharashtra Navnirman Sena (MNS), a political party that runs a belligerent campaign against north Indians.[27]

Again, on 3 February 2008, a print of *Saiyan Se Solah Singaar* (2006), was burnt at Thane's Pratap Talkies and the audience, mostly migrant north Indians, were roughed up.[28]

The next attack took place on 1 July 2008, when Deepak Talkies in Lower Parel in Mumbai was attacked, again allegedly by MNS workers. The theatre, which regularly screens Bhojpuri films, was showing *Banke Bihari MLA* when the activists barged into the theatre around 3 p.m., just before the film was about to start, and demonstrated vociferously against the film.[29]

'Shoots for Bhojpuri films in and around the city were often ambushed by the MNS. Things once became so bad that we had to cancel the shooting of our film *Hum Hai Khalnayak* in Satara and relocate to Ahmedabad in Gujarat to save our sets and equipment from MNS vandalism,' says producer Abhay Sinha.[30]

The reasons for the rise of the MNS lie in recent political developments in Maharashtra. Social commentators point out that after MNS leader Raj Thackeray disassociated himself from the Shiv Sena and ventured out on his own, he positioned himself as the new aggressive voice against 'outsiders'/north Indians in Maharashtra at a time when the Shiv Sena had become more accommodating of outsiders. For instance, the entire cast and crew of *Kab Hoi Gawna Hamaar* was felicitated at a grand function in suburban Mumbai by Shiv Sena MLA Subhash Desai.[31]

Social scientists feel that attacks on cinema halls showing Bhojpuri films are expressions of envy and resentment. 'The cinema halls are specifically targeted because that is where the community can be easily identified, found in large numbers and attacked,' says political scientist Imtiaz Ahmed.[32] He adds that in Mumbai, a section of the population fears getting 'swamped' by the migrants and groups such as the MNS hope to cash in on this sentiment.

Sociologist Yogendra Singh sums up the issue: 'It is a strategy where the aggressor believes that the denial of pluralism can be politically advantageous.'[33]

The fallout of the anti-north Indian agitation by the MNS has had its effect on the content of Bhojpuri films. *Bhole Shankar*, a 2008 film, showed actor Mithun Chakraborty saving his screen brother from Marathi-speaking hooligans and saying, '*Ek Bihari sau par bhari*' ('One Bihari is enough to tackle a hundred others'). The movie became a raging hit in Bihar and raked in Rs 30 lakh in the first week of its release. The film's success left even its makers completely surprised, considering that parts of Bihar were reeling under floods caused by the Kosi river changing its course.[34] The film was written and directed by journalist-turned-director Pankaj Shukla, which perhaps explains why the movie was in tune with the times.

The MNS-led anti-north Indian agitation had some unintended positive fallouts too. Over the decades, no Bihar or Uttar Pradesh politician had paid any serious attention to setting up infrastructure facilities for films in either of the two states. Magazine articles published during the first two phases of Bhojpuri cinema indicate that there was plenty of talk on the subject in the past, especially in Uttar Pradesh. But nothing really came of it.[35] For example, during a seminar organized on 8 May 1985, intellectuals, litterateurs and film-makers of the region lamented the absence of government assistance to the Bhojpuri film industry. It was pointed out that though film-makers were entitled to a grant of Rs 1 lakh for shooting at least eighty per cent of the film in Uttar Pradesh state, this sum is rarely released due to corruption.[36] That few talk about the need for government grants to make films these days illustrates how far the Bhojpuri film industry has progressed.

Now the anti-north Indian agitation has suddenly made Bhojpuri films a subject of interest for politicians. Politicians from Bihar such as Laloo Prasad Yadav and Nitish Kumar have been trying to outdo each other in their sympathy for migrants. In this political imbroglio, Bhojpuri films have also become a matter of prestige for top Bihar politicians.

So, for the first time, the issue of setting up a studio in Bihar seems to have been taken up with a degree of earnestness. At least, that seemed to be the state of affairs in November 2008 when Manoj Tiwari claimed that Bihar chief minister Nitish Kumar had informed him that a studio would be built on 200 acres of land on Rajgir Road, about forty kilometres from Patna. The estimated cost of this project is around Rs 200 crore. Says Tiwari, 'A committee will be set up to monitor the process of studio construction. An IAS officer will be made the CEO of the studio. The studio will have facilities for shooting, dubbing, editing, mixing, previews, and make-up. It will also house offices of producers, directors and actors.'[37] Whether all this will finally see the light of day remains to be seen.

Get shorty

Udhed Bun (2007), a 20-minute short film in Bhojpuri made by a Film and Television Institute of India student, Siddharth Sinha, won the best short film in the competition category at the Berlin Film Festival in 2008. Interestingly, Sinha is from Ghazipur in eastern Uttar Pradesh. *Udhed Bun* is about a teenage boy and the two women in his life—his lover, a married woman who waits for her husband to return from the city, and his mother, who is ill.[38]

7

Deciphering
Bhojpuri Cinema

Trying to explain the spectacular resurgence of the
Bhojpuri film industry is not an easy task. The reasons
are both multi-layered and complex. Part economics, part
sociology, brought together in the circumstances of a rapidly
changing nation. It would be erroneous to try and understand
the phenomenon as a series of causes and effects. One should
rather view it as a process with various interweaving strands,
which at certain points are complementary and, on other
occasions, contrast with each other.

At one level, the resurgence of Bhojpuri films could be
construed as a reaction to the way Bollywood refashioned its
cinematic language and landscape after the arrival of satellite
television in 1991. With the growth of the dollar-rich NRI
market and multiplexes becoming urban India's new temples
of entertainment, young gel-and-cologne film-makers with
Hollywood sensibilities found a formula to bypass 'India
Unhappening'. Soon, Hindi commercial cinema's alienation
from vast swathes of middle India was complete.

The phenomenon caused an explosion of feel-good urban
cinema. These films were marked by a sensibility and style

of narrative that the underclass—who viewed films in ramshackle single-screen theatres—was unable to identify with. It was this fissure in aesthetics that the region-specific Bhojpuri cinema adroitly filled.

From Bollywood's first talkie *Alam Ara* in 1931, popular Hindi cinema was a cinema of mass sensibility that cut across most classes and regions of India. An Amitabh Bachchan-starrer such as *Ganga Ki Saugandh* (1978) could reach out to urban, small-town and rural audiences alike. But this scenario was completely transformed in the last decade of the twentieth century. Bollywood films such as Karan Johar's *Kuch Kuch Hota Hai* (1998) and Farhan Akhtar's *Dil Chahta Hai* (2001) are good examples of such new trends in Hindi cinema.[1] Feel-good, upper class, urban-centric cinema took over and the rural, the aging and the underprivileged were all eased out of the frame.[2]

The years between 2004 and 2006 are marked by a thinly-veiled contempt for non-urban themes in most top-of-the-line Hindi movies. Even the traditional Bollywood style of story-telling, laced with songs and dances, has gone through distinct changes. Now driven by Hollywood sensibilities, many mainstream films are either songless (contrary to the earlier style of including at least eight to ten songs in a film) or have only two or three tracks. Several movies emerging from the 'school' of producer-director Ram Gopal Varma, such as *Company* (2002), *Ek Hasina Thi* (2004) and *Ab Tak Chhappan* (2004), as well as other alternative movies like *Bheja Fry* (2007) are examples of such overtly urban films.

There suddenly seemed to be no need to woo the economically underprivileged audience of the single-screen theatres where a balcony ticket could be bought for Rs 15. Significantly, millions of migrant labourers across north India, whose movie sensibilities are woven around songs and dance, and drama and action, were now ignored as an audience for Hindi cinema.

Part of Bhojpuri cinema's revival is a reaction to this factor. The genre's audience, wherever it is, seems to be telling mainstream Bollywood that it wants its own sights and sounds in the movies. The audience does not want heroines with toned bodies and size zero figures. They want their women big and fleshy, with oversized breasts accentuated by colourful cholis. Regional cinema provides alternative aesthetics to cater to regional sensibilities.

That is why in Bhojpuri films there are songs even on *litti-chokha*, a popular dish of the Bhojpuri-speaking region. In *Pyaar Ke Bandhan* (2006), the hero sings, '*Duniya ke number ek cycle sawari, eker aage phel ba Bolero-Safari*' ('The cycle is the number one vehicle in the world, it's better than Bolero and Safari')—the sort of song that the Hindi film hero had stopped singing by the 1990s. That is one of the reasons why, just as the Mandal Commission recommendations stratified politics in north India, Bollywood's predilection for feel-good urban India stratified the entertainment industry.[3]

And yet paradoxically, Bhojpuri films are also attracted to Bollywood in equal measure; perhaps, a fascination with the stronger, bigger and more domineering culture. In these times of globalization, every society is part aspirational, even while it tries to retain old values and norms. So, while new-generation Bhojpuri films have partly emerged out of a reaction to Bollywood's indifference, they are also consumed by its attraction and allure.

This has led to the genre creating its own version of Bollywood even as it resists the influence. There is a willingness and openness to go beyond village-level family dramas. This phenomenon, however, has blurred the distinct identity of the regional film.

In the opening shot of the film *Janam Janam Ke Saath* (2007), hero Manoj Tiwari is shown strumming a guitar and wearing a smart cap with the peak turned backwards. It may appear ludicrous as a fashion statement in a regional film, but it affirms a social aspiration. Satellite television and the internet have affected every aspect of entertainment and it would be unrealistic to hope that Bhojpuri cinema would remain an island.

* * *

The popularity of Bhojpuri cinema is a complex question also because the audience of Bhojpuri films has changed significantly. Back in the 1960s and 1970s, the audience was largely confined to people from eastern Uttar Pradesh and central and western Bihar. Now, the movies are seen across Bihar: Rohtas, Aurangabad, Bhabhua, Buxar, Bhojpur, Saran, Siwan, Gopalganj, West Champaran, East Champaran, Patna, Muzaffarnagar, Samastipur, Darbhanga, Supaul, Begusarai, and other districts.

That is the reason why Hindi films—that once ruled the cinema halls of western and central Bihar and eastern Uttar Pradesh—now have to fight for space with Bhojpuri films, and often end up getting out-muscled. *Bunty Aur Babli* (2005) a big hit in cosmopolitan Delhi, did not evoke the same response in Bihar from an audience that preferred *Panditji Bataeen Na Biyah Kab Hoee*, a breathlessly-paced masala movie.

With Bhojpuri films being released every week, distributors prefer exhibiting these films because they do not cost them much. Distributors say that Bollywood A-list star and producer Aamir Khan's *Taare Zameen Par* (2007), a film on a child's learning disability, did not interest theatre owners in Bihar. According to a newspaper report, 'Distributor Sanjay

Sharma says not only Aamir, even the big films of other so-called saleable Mumbai stars are not a patch on Bhojpuri cinema these days. The exhibitors prefer to screen the films of Bhojpuri stars Manoj Tiwari and Ravi Kishan because they ensure better returns at the box-office.'[4]

Further, the report says, 'The John Abraham-Bipasha Basu starrer *Goal* failed to get a release in Patna because most theatres were running either a Tiwari or a Kishan film. And when it finally hit the screens, it failed to woo the audience, who preferred *Sajanwa Tohre Khatir*, a Ravi Kishan movie.'[5] Obviously, what the audience wants is to see something else.

That's not all. Ticket clerks and gatekeepers point out that the rise of Bhojpuri cinema has even caused the demise of C-grade skin flicks and bikini-budgeted dacoit films made by the likes of Kanti Shah and Kishen Shah, which were extremely popular in the late 1990s and early 2000s.[6]

The genre has also expanded to include other states. As discussed earlier, migrants from Bihar and Uttar Pradesh have created film territories in Maharashtra and Punjab, and to a lesser extent, in Bengal, Gujarat and Rajasthan. With the passage of time, this 'diaspora within the diaspora'[7] has become an important market. Distributors and exhibitors estimate that about thirty per cent of the Bhojpuri film market is located outside Bihar and Uttar Pradesh. This market is largely powered by migrant money.

At one level, for the migrant audience, Bhojpuri films are the aesthetic equivalent of homemade food. For them, these films are about memories, yearnings, companionship and togetherness. For a few hours, the auditorium becomes their home away from home. The proud hero, the plotting zamindar or bahubali, the egotistical father and the crooked sasurji—all reassure the viewer that their world has not changed. The films do not talk down to the viewer. They play along.[8]

But the migrant labourer is also exposed to the other world. He also wants a slice of this larger, richer world served in the movies he sees—not in the Bollywood style, which he finds totally alien, but something that is given to him on his own terms, in a milieu he enjoys, and in a language that he is most familiar with. In other words, his needs are a mix of the home and the world, and needless to say, getting this delicate blend right is not easy.

Kirit Desai, who manages Moti cinema in Delhi's Chandni Chowk, was extremely impressed with *Slumdog Millionaire* and booked the Hindi version for his cinema hall. 'But my audience did not like it. They prefer to watch Bhojpuri films or dubbed Hindi versions of Telugu films these days,' he says.[9]

In its gender as well as class composition, the Bhojpuri audience of the new millennium is different from the older audience on which the foundation of the industry was built in the 1960s and sustained in the 1980s. Going to the cinema was one of the few recreational avenues for rural women then. Well-made family socials like *Ganga Maiya Tohe Piyari Chadhaibo* (1962), *Ganga Kinare Mora Gaon* (1983) and *Naihar Ki Chunri* (1985) brought them in droves to the qasbah theatres.

Top Bhojpuri star Ravi Kishan is perceptive about the audience's changing needs, and articulate enough to illustrate them. He says, '*Dehat dehat nahi raha* [The village is no longer like the old village]. The farmers still own the fields. But they have mobile phones, electric converters and DVDs too. More people are reading newspapers and watching satellite TV. Awareness levels are much higher. Earlier popular music used to reach the small towns and villages after a long time. Today's village boys dance to the same music as a Mumbai teenager.'[10]

The new target audience is the underclass youth, and he adds, 'The core ticket-buying audience ranges from age ten to thirty-five or forty. They want to see the fields, a village, Gangaji, *ma ka sindoor* [mother's vermilion, a marker of her married, un-widowed status] and the hero touching his father's feet. But they also want a lot of entertainment. Today the hero can wear jeans. But to provide the flavour of Bhojpuri, I also wear kurtas and keep a *gamcha* [an all-purpose cloth generally kept on the shoulder]. I wear a *tilak*. Even when I am driving a bike or a tractor, this is my dress.'[11]

For this core audience, the issue is not about good or bad cinema. The new audience, especially the migrant section, now wants movies that not only suit its aesthetics and idea of entertainment but also reaffirm its regional identity. 'The masses want *tamasha* [entertainment] in their own language and now they are getting it,' says Rajesh Kumar Singh, who distributes Bhojpuri films in Mumbai.[12] Most Bhojpuri films have at least eight to ten songs, with plenty of hip-swinging dances, something that its core audience enjoys. For instance, *Panditji Bataeen Na Biyah Kab Hoee* had fourteen songs, *Daroga Babu I Love You* had thirteen, and *Nirahua Rickshawala* had ten.

To sum up, at a time when regional political parties continue to assert their identity, the rise of Bhojpuri films is only part of the remodelling of Indian cinema. The availability of cheap technology has allowed dozens of 'little cinemas' to flourish in dialects such as Chhattisgarhi, Kumaoni, Garhwali and Khariboli.[13] Even Ladakhis have begun making films in their local dialect.[14]

* * *

The growth of Bhojpuri cinema also reflects how the region has evolved. For instance, most top Bhojpuri film heroes—from Ravi Kishan to Manoj Tiwari—are upper-caste Hindus. But at a time when Laloo Prasad Yadav and Mulayam Singh Yadav are two important leaders of Bihar and Uttar Pradesh, can the caste effect be far away? An obvious case, of course, is the rise of Dinesh Lal Yadav 'Nirahua', an OBC, as the premium star of Bhojpuri films after 2007. Slowly but surely, Other Backward Classes (OBCs) as well as Dalits are also making their presence felt. Birendra Paswan, who wrote the dialogues of *Ego Chumma De Da Rajaji* (Give me a kiss my darling, 2008) is one such person.

Over the decades, even the content and presentation have changed dramatically. In several early Bhojpuri films, the city was presented as a dangerous place where the ideals, morals and values that the village embodies are lost. The village continues to be idealized even now, but the hero is no longer overawed by the big, bad urban world. Rather, he seems keen to conquer it.

With time, the genre's villains have changed. The zamindar and the money-lenders are no longer the favourite bad guys—the local MLA or a bahubali with political patronage takes pride of place.

Superhits of recent years—*Sasura Bada Paisewala, Panditji Bataeen Na Biyah Kab Hoee* and *Nirahua Rickshawala*—are vastly different from the early blockbusters. *Sasura Bada Paisewala* blends comedy with family drama. The movie talks of family values while ensuring that the westernized heroine is tamed by the English-speaking hero whose soul is Bhojpuri. *Panditji Bataeen Na Biyah Kab Hoee* has elements of *Sholay* and a graphic rape scene. In *Nirahua Rickshawala*, the hero kisses the girl he loves, which is rather revolutionary for a Bhojpuri film.

Bhojpuri film songs too have changed dramatically. The 1960s were about melody, but by the 1980s, rhythm had made its presence felt. After the mega success of *Sasura Bada Paisawala* (2004), rhythm has completely overshadowed melody and every film has at least four or five dance tracks. Producers and directors are continuously experimenting to attract a wider audience. For instance, director Javed Sayyed says that in *Ego Chumma De Da Rajaji*, they included a non-Bhojpuri song titled *Jhaaruwali bai tujhe heroine bana doonga* ('Hey sweeper maid, I will make you a heroine').[15]

And there is an epidemic of explicit songs where imaginative lyricists often compare the shapes of fruits with parts of the female anatomy. The actresses are dressed scantily and blouses worn by item girls are often smaller than handkerchiefs.

Undeniably, dance tracks with suggestive movements and risqué lyrics have adversely affected the image of Bhojpuri films, though, interestingly, Bhojpuri films have very little sex. Love-making scenes are almost absent because it appears that the audience feels uneasy about watching 'visual' sex. They are much more accepting of explicit audio tracks since 'risque' folk songs are traditionally sung in these parts during festivals like Holi and during weddings.

The heroines of Bhojpuri films have become far more urban in the new age. Often, they are portrayed as city-bred girls who dress in western clothes. The heroines of hits such as *Sasura Bada Paisewala, Daroga Babu I Love You* and *Nirahua Rickshawala* represent this stereotype. In *Daroga Babu*, heroine Rinku Ghosh appears in the opening shot in a tight T-shirt and tighter trousers. One can only imagine the reaction of the audience when she thrusts her breasts against the hero and makes him fall down—a scene that was unimaginable even for a vamp of the 1960s and 1970s.

The heroine is not restricted to the courtyard and sugarcane fields either—in *Pandit*, heroine Nagma plays a journalist! As the title suggests, *Saas Rani Bahu Naukrani* (2007), is about courtyard politics involving a mother-in-law and daughter-in-law, but unlike the past, the heroine refuses to be ill-treated. The demure heroine of the 1960s is now clearly an exception rather than the rule.

But that's one side of the coin. Back in the 1960s, heroines like Kumkum were the main box-office draw. Stories were written around her character. Even in the 1980s, heroines like Padma Khanna and Gouri Khurana were stars in their own right. But with the passage of time, stardom acquired a gender angle in Bhojpuri films. Now it is the male stars—Nirahua, Kishan, Tiwari—who command centre-stage both in terms of the script as well as the price. Screenplays are written to suit their personalities.

* * *

In this scenario of cultural give-and-take, traditionalists lament that the genre has lost its soul and mourn the fact that the regional flavour is dying. Arti Bhattacharya, who became the first woman director of Bhojpuri films with *Dagabaaz Balma* (1988), says that producers ask for two or three suggestive item numbers in their films. She says, 'People say, "*Jab Hindi film dekhne jaate hain to lagta hai ki angrezi film dekh rahe hain. Jab Bhojpuri film dekhne jaate hain to lagta hai ki Hindi film dekh rahe hain. Hamari film kahan hai?*" [When we watch a Hindi film, it feels like a Hollywood film. When we go for a Bhojpuri film, it is like watching a Hindi film. Where's our film?].'[16]

Bhattacharya adds, 'During a visit to eastern Uttar Pradesh, young village boys told us that in family weddings they only show old Bhojpuri films on DVD because they are the only films that can be watched by the entire family.'[17]

There is a grain of truth in that argument. Family superhits of the 1980s still do good business during re-runs. '*Naihar Ki Chunri* was released again in November 2002. I remember entering the cinema hall during one of the afternoon shows on the fifth day. The entire hall was filled with women,' recalls Alok Dubey of Anand Mandir, Benares that now only shows Bhojpuri films.[18]

Critics too lament the absence of '*Bhojpuriyat*' in many new films. Reviewing *Sab Golmaal Ha* (2007), made by well-known Bollywood producers Inder Kumar and Ashok Thakeria, film critic Dr Shankar Prasad wrote in *Hindustan*, 'There is not a whiff of Bhojpuri earth [in these films]. There were crowds, whistles and fights but there was nothing Bhojpuri anywhere.'

There is also a strongly-held view that the Bhojpuri-speaking 'gentry' do not watch Bhojpuri films. Back in 1965, actor-writer-director-producer Nazir Hussain believed, 'The five crore Bhojpuri-speaking people should love their mother tongue like Bengalis and Marathis do. They should watch Bhojpuri films without any hesitation.'[19]

A 1965 *Rambha* article says, 'We do not love our mother tongue in the same way as a Bengali or a Marathi. We feel that watching Bhojpuri films is a sign of backwardness. People should love their mother tongue the way Bengalis and Marathis do. Only then will Bhojpuri films be made, released and become famous.'[20]

Hero Kunal Singh said in an interview published in *Hindustan* on 25 November 1993, 'The biggest tragedy of Bhojpuri films is that elite and modern families converse in Bhojpuri in their homes but believe it is below their dignity to go to a theatre and watch a film in the language.'

The truth is a little more complicated. In the 1960s, and even in the 1980s, the social elite watched Bhojpuri cinema to a greater degree.[21] A major part of that family audience—doctors, engineers, police officers, corporate executives, teachers, government clerks and others—now shun these movies. Why? To begin with, the movies are not in tune with their upwardly-mobile cinematic sensibilities. Besides television and VCDs are a cheaper and more comfortable alternative for women.[22]

It doesn't help either that most single-screen theatres in mofussil small towns are poorly maintained and many qasbah theatres resemble storehouses. The projection systems are old, though the ticket prices are low. And while one wonders if setting up costly multiplexes is the answer to the problem, something needs to be done to improve the quality of cinema halls to ensure that the middle and upper classes, and the women, who have largely abandoned the genre, are wooed back to theatres.[23] However, improving the infrastructure needs to go hand in hand with improving the quality of cinema.

There is also a view that producers who know nothing about 'Bhojpuri culture' have jumped into the fray, which has resulted in too many shoddily-made films flooding the market.[24] But the argument cuts both ways. Numerous producers, actors and technicians from different regions have contributed enormously to converting the genre from a cottage industry to a full-fledged one, but not many are willing to look inwards and ask the tougher question: are films being made by Bhojpuri-speaking producers any better?

Back in 1965, in a brochure brought out by an organization called Nav Sanskriti Sangh from New Delhi during the release of Nazir Hussain's *Hamaar Sansar*, a gentleman named Dr Bholanath Tiwary wrote how Bhojpuri films can be made on popular regional folk tales such as Loriki, Vijay Mal,

Shobhanayak Banjara, Sorthi Bihula, Raja Bharthari and Gopichand. Even the life of Babu Kunwar Singh, the zamindar from Jagdishpur who fought against the British during the revolt of 1857, he wrote, would make an interesting subject for a Bhojpuri movie. He also pointed out how different kinds of folk songs such as *sohar, khelavna, barahmasa, chaiti,* kajri, *phagua* and those sung during marriages can be used in films.

The 1970s actor Rakesh Pandey said in an interview that Bihar and Uttar Pradesh are treasuries of literature. He asked, 'Poets and writers like Phanishwar Nath 'Renu', Bhikari Thakur and Nagarjun have produced great literature. Why can't we adapt their works and make better Bhojpuri films? For that matter, why can't we make a Bhojpuri film based on a Tagore short story?'[25] How about a neo-realist film that captures the twenty-first century migrant experience? Or the Naxal problem that afflicts several Bhojpuri-speaking districts in Bihar? Or, even a murder mystery on the lines of *Manorama Six Feet Under?*

It's a catch-22 situation. Producers and financiers want masala movies because that is what the core audience of the single-screen theatres want. To create a different cinema to attract a wider audience, one first needs better infrastructure. This, along with a more family-friendly cinema, can radically change the content of the genre. That does not seem to be happening at the moment, but there is always hope.

Eight Bhojpuri movies you must see and why

Ganga Maiya Tohe Piyari Chadhaibo: One of the best for the first-rate acting and unforgettable songs.

Bidesiya: It has some incomparable folk numbers and memorable dialogues like '*Bhookha na jaane baasi bhat, neend na jaane tooti khat, preet na jaane jaat kujaat.*'

Ganga Maiya Tohe Piyari Chadhaibo (1962),
the first Bhojpuri feature film.

Sujit Kumar, the hero of *Bidesiya* (1963),
passed away on 5 February 2010.

Laagi Nahi Chhute Ram (1963) had melodious music by Chitragupta.

Hamaar Sansar (1965), a moving portrait of rural India,
was widely appreciated.

Dangal (1977), the first Bhojpuri film in colour.

Catchy songs made *Balam Pardesia* (1979) a superhit.

Dharti Maiya (1981) is the Bhojpuri film industry's *Mother India*.

Ganga Kinare Mora Gaon (1983)
celebrated its diamond jubilee in Benares.

Bihari Babu (1985) marked Shatrughan Sinha's entry
in the regional genre.

Kunal Singh and Meera Madhuri were the lead pair of
Ram Jaisan Bhaiya Hamaar (1986).

Starring Padma Khanna in the central role,
Mai (1989) was a hit.

Hamaar Betwa (1990).

Blockbuster *Sasura Bada Paisewala* (2004)
helped revive the Bhojpuri film industry.

Daroga Babu I Love You (2005)
was another Manoj Tiwari-box-office hit.

Directed by Anand D. Ghatraj, *Kab Hoi Gawna Hamaar* (2005)
won a national award.

Panditji Bataeen Na Biyah Kab Hoee (2005)
was a racy superhit starring Ravi Kishan and Nagma.

Hamaar Sansar: Because it authentically recreates rural India and shows how India Invisible used to think in the mid-1960s.

Balam Pardesia: Superhit of the late 1970s, with *Gorki patarki re* ('O lean and fair one'), one of the most playfully romantic songs of Bhojpuri cinema.

Dharti Maiya: Well-made social drama on the lines of *Mother India*. Padma Khanna's performance is excellent.

Ganga Kinare Mora Gaon: One of the biggest hits of all and because you need to carry at least three handkerchiefs to wipe away your tears.

Sasura Bada Paisewala: This film revived the genre in the new millennium and offers coarse comedy, risqué songs and roaring melodrama.

Nirahua Rickshawala: A perfect package of impressive action, emotion, drama, songs, and a kiss that was endlessly discussed by viewers.

PART II
PEOPLE
AND
PLACES

8

Twinkle Twinkle
Little Superstars

The early heroes

The stars of Bhojpuri cinema may not have been famous nationwide like Raj Kapoor or Rajesh Khanna, but in the Bihar and Uttar Pradesh hinterland, their appearance often led to immense crowd frenzy. Ashim Kumar, Sujit Kumar, Rakesh Pandey and Kunal Singh dominated the first three decades of Bhojpuri cinema. Together, they gave the nascent industry its most memorable hits.

* * *

Ashim Kumar acted in only four Bhojpuri films, but it was enough to earn him the title 'Dilip Kumar of Bhojpuri films'. An excellent actor who came from a prosperous Bengali family of Benares, Ashim was immortalized as the first hero of Bhojpuri films when he played the Devdas-like lover of *Ganga Maiya Tohe Piyari Chadhaibo*.

There was a gentleman's dignity to Ashim's personality, which made him quite suitable for the roles of the prosperous young men he essayed in *Ganga Maiya Tohe Piyari Chadhaibo* and *Laagi Nahin Chhute Ram*, two of his more successful films. On the other hand, Ashim's performance in *Hamaar Sansar* as an aggressive but lovable brother of a farmer was both confident and competent. He also played the leading role in *Balma Bada Nadaan*. His son Rana says, 'He was paid between Rs 11,000 and Rs 15,000 for these films.'[1]

Born in Benares in 1930, Ashim Kumar began his acting career at the age of five in a Bengali play, *Prafulla*, directed by his father, Moni Bhattacharya. 'I received my early education in Theosophical Society near Kamachha,' he once wrote.[2] As he grew older, he became part of the Benares theatre scene. Later, he joined Bimal Roy as an assistant. Ashim also played small roles in the master director's best films such as *Sujata* and *Devdas*. He played the stepson of Paro, the female protagonist of *Devdas*. He knew Nazir Hussain, who played the role of the family retainer in *Devdas*, and like him, also came from eastern Uttar Pradesh.

Ashim, who spoke fluent Bhojpuri, was extremely proud and fond of the city he grew up in: 'I love Kashi [Benares]. Even today the town is more precious to me than my life. If anyone can take the credit for my career in the movies, it is Kashi.'[3]

The success of *Ganga Maiya Tohe Piyari Chadhaibo* and *Laagi Nahin Chhute Ram* made Ashim a much sought-after hero. His son Rana recalls him saying that even producers from south India were keen to make Bhojpuri films with him.[4]

Unfortunately, none of these projects took off. The cast and credits of some of his incomplete films, however, are fascinating. One such film is *Shyam Se Neha Lagaye*: it was to be directed by the redoubtable Bengali film-maker Ritwik Ghatak, while the name of its composer is listed as Pandit Ravi Shankar, the world-famous sitarist. The film's dialogue was to be written by Nazir Hussain and the heroine was

Indrani Mukherjee, who later became as famous as a screen mother in the mid-1970s. It is not known whether the project was abandoned at the conceptualization stage or if it even entered the pre-production phase.[5]

Ashim Kumar's other incomplete Bhojpuri films were *Angna Mein Baaje Shehnai* (The shehnai plays in my courtyard; producer-director: Asghar; heroine: Kumkum; music: Bismillah Khan and Iqbal Qureshi), *Sajanva Se Karde Milanva* (Take me to my love; producer: Thadani; heroine: Kamini Kadam), *Sajna Bharihein Maang Hamaar* (My love will marry me; producer: Shankar Movies; music: S.N. Tripathi; story: Ashim Kumar; heroine: Saeeda Khan), *Lallu Ustaad* (director: Baburam; producer: Amir Khan; story: Ashim Kumar; music: S.N. Tripathi), *Goriya Chali Naiharwa* (The fair woman goes to her parent's home; director: Shakti Chatterjee; heroine: Lily Chakraborty; music: Hiren Ghosh), and *Maang Ka Sindoor* (The vermilion on the forehead; producer: Kalpana Movies; director: B. Dasgupta; heroine: Kumkum; music: Chitragupta).[6]

Later, Ashim Kumar produced the Hindi film, *Safed Jhooth* (1977), a pleasant comedy directed by Basu Chatterjee that crashed at the box-office.

* * *

The average Hindi film buff would remember Sujit Kumar as a character actor in Bollywood films. Some discerning fans might even remember him as the hero of small-time Bollywood flicks such as *Lal Bangla* (1966) and *Ek Saal Pehle* (1965). But in the world of Bhojpuri films, Sujit Kumar was king. He is undoubtedly among the most enduring and successful stars the genre has produced.

Sujit Kumar's real name is Shamsher Singh. Originally from Benares district, he established himself as a competent actor with an attractive screen presence in *Bidesiya*. Proficient both in action and emotional scenes, he played a major role in promoting the regional film industry through the 1960s to the 1990s. He got Rs 5,000 as the signing amount for *Bidesiya*, his first Bhojpuri film, and after its success, signed as many as eight films in three months.[7] Later in his career, he branched out as a character actor and director (*Paan Khaye Saiyan Hamaar, Balma Bada Nadaan*), until he had to stop working because of ill health.

During the first phase of Bhojpuri films (1962–69), he was the leading hero of the genre along with Ashim Kumar. Some of his well-known films from this period are *Bidesiya, Bhauji, Ganga, Ayeel Basant Bahar, Saiyan Se Bhaile Milanwa*.

In the second phase (1977–2001), his better-known films are *Dangal, Mai K Lal, Ganga Ghat, Sajai Da Maang Hamaar, Bhaiya Dooj, Ganga Kahe Pukaar Ke, Ganga Jaisan Bhauji Hamaar, Ganga Hamaar Mai, Saiyan Magan Pahelwani Mein, Paijaniya, Tulsi Sohe Hamaar Angna, Sajanwa Bairi Bhaile Hamaar, Patoh Bitiya, Piya Toote Na Piritiya Ke Dor* and more. He formed popular pairs with the heroines Kumkum, Prema Narayan and Padma Khanna.

Being a regular in Bollywood, Sujit Kumar also brought a certain star quality to his roles. His natural style of acting, especially in *Bidesiya*, is memorable and it came as no surprise when he got the best actor award for his performance. 'He is a very mature and professional actor,' says character actor Brijesh Tripathi.[8]

In 1984, Sujit Kumar turned director with, *Paan Khaye Saiyan Hamaar* (My lover chews paan), in which Amitabh Bachchan made a 'friendly appearance' with Rekha who performed a mujra. 'The movie didn't do as well as expected.

Amitabhji played the role of a do-gooder *lathait* [stick-wielding fighter] who helps the hero, played by Sujit Kumar himself,' says the movie's heroine, Bandini Mishra.[9]

Dipankar Bose, son of renowned Bhojpuri film director Dilip Bose and a director himself, recalls how crowds went wild wherever Sujit Kumar went: 'But he never threw any starry tantrums. While shooting for *Ghar Grihasti* in a village near Arrah, there was no decent hotel nearby. So he stayed in a house . . . no fuss.'[10]

Sujit Kumar maintained close links with his friends back home. Benares-based veteran film journalist Munnu Prasad Pandey recalls his visit to the actor's house in Mumbai. 'We had gone there to invite him for an all-India Bhojpuri meet. He agreed to come immediately. And he bought his own tickets to Benares and stayed in Hotel Clarke, again, paying his own money. He also served us *mattha* [a drink made from yoghurt]. He told us that when Amitabh Bachchan had come to his house, he had given him the same drink.'[11]

In 2004, Sujit Kumar directed *Balma Bada Nadaan*, a flop starring Samarth Chaturvedi and Divya Desai. He died of cancer at the age of seventy-five on 5 February 2010.

* * *

Rakesh Pandey was born in the hill town of Nahan in Himachal Pradesh. His father was the *rajguru* (royal priest) of the estate of the raja of Sirmaur. Pandey joined the prestigious Film and Television Institute of India in Pune.[12] He got his break as a hero in the Hindi film *Sara Akash* (1969), directed by Basu Chatterjee. Written by the famous Hindi writer Rajendra Yadav, this off-beat love story was a surprise hit. But after that, success eluded him in Bollywood.

Balam Pardesia (1979), his first Bhojpuri film, turned Pandey into a regional film superstar. 'I normally charged Rs 1.5 lakhs for a leading role in a Hindi film in those days, but for *Balam Pardesia*, I was paid Rs 25,000. After the film became a superhit, I started getting Rs 1 lakh per Bhojpuri film,' he remembers.[13]

After *Balam Pardesia*, Rakesh Pandey acted in many Bhojpuri films. Of these, *Dharti Maiya* (1981), in which he made a special appearance, became a superhit. 'I acted in about two dozen films as a hero and in twenty-odd films in character roles,' he says.[14]

He recalls being pampered during the shootings of these films in typical feudal style in the villages of Bihar and Uttar Pradesh: 'I used to be massaged with mustard oil before my bath at the village tubewell. People showered me with so much love and affection that I felt I was one of them.' A few years back, the actor discovered his enduring popularity in this region. He says, 'When I went to Hajipur for a film's shooting in 2006, I found that they still remembered me.'[15]

Pandey acted with many heroines, but formed a hit pair with Padma Khanna. The Pandey-Khanna pair was known as the Dharmendra-Hema pair of Bhojpuri films in the 1980s. Apart from *Balam Pardesia*, some of his other films were *Bhaiya Dooj*, *Saiyan Magan Pahelwani Mein*, *Roos Gayeele Saiyan Hamaar*, *Chanwa Ke Taake Chakor* and *Dharti Maiya*.

Actor Rakesh Pandey also directed two films: *Bansuriya Baaje Ganga Teer* (The flute plays on the banks of the Ganga, 1984) and *Tulsi Sohe Angna Hamaar* (The tulsi plant adorns my courtyard, 1986). *Bansuriya Baaje Ganga Teer* has six songs, two of which were written by veteran lyricist Anjaan. 'Anjaan told me I should give an opportunity to his promising young son and I did. Sameer wrote four songs and he wrote them quite well,' the actor reminisces.[16]

Pandey wanted Kishore Kumar to sing the film's Holi song. 'When I requested Kishore da, he sang over the phone, "*Tera gana hai to zaroor gaoonga, main zaroor gaoonga*" [Since it's your song, I will definitely sing it]. He was really a funny man and a genius.' The number turned out to be very popular.[17]

But the film only did average business. The actor's next directorial venture *Tulsi Sohe Hamaar Angna* died a quick box-office death. 'Later, when I went to eastern Uttar Pradesh and Bihar and spoke to those who had watched the film, I realized where I might have gone wrong,' says Pandey. 'In the film, I played Padma Khanna's *devar* [younger brother-in-law]. This was a casting blunder. Padma and I formed a popular pair in Bhojpuri films and people were used to watching us as lovers. They could not see us as a devar-bhabi [husband's younger brother and sister-in-law] pair,' he says.[18] The analysis seems to have some merit for fact and fiction often have a way of criss-crossing in hinterland India.

When the comatose Bhojpuri film industry burst back into new life in 2004, Pandey too got several offers to act in movies. Pandey says about those days: 'I refused the offers initially. But eventually, I ended up accepting a few of them. I did a film called *Dulha Babu* on the phenomenon of shotgun weddings in Bihar.'[19] He adds, 'The story was true to life. But the director failed to create the desired impact on screen.'[20] Some of his recent films are *Lal Chunariya Wali* (2007) and *Maiya Rakhiha Senurwa Aabaad* (2006).

Pandey was conferred the lifetime achievement award at the fourth Bhojpuri Film Awards in 2008.

* * *

In the 1980s, Kunal Singh emerged as the genre's most bankable star by delivering a clutch of hits—*Dharti Maiya*, *Ganga Kinare*

Mora Gaon, *Dagabaaz Balma* and *Ram Jaisan Bhaiya Hamaar*. The actor bears a remarkable resemblance to Hindi film star Jeetendra from certain angles. 'But my style is different,' he maintains. Today, he continues to play supporting character roles with élan.

As a child, Singh was once asked to read out from the script of a play titled *Jantantra Zindabad*. The young boy was extremely nervous and his hands started shaking at the audition. The impatient director snatched the script away and told him rudely, 'Acting isn't your cup of tea.' The incident apparently instilled a determination in the young Singh's mind to become an actor.[21]

Born in 1955, Kunal was the son of senior Congress leader Buddhadev Singh. His debut movie *Kal Hamara Hai* was directed by Girish Ranjan, a former assistant of Mrinal Sen. Released in 1980, the film had many artistes from Bihar and did excellent business in the state.[22] During the film's shooting, Kunal, who played the role of a garrulous tonga driver, fell in love with the heroine Arti Bhattacharya. The two soon got married.

Kunal Singh's first major success in Bhojpuri films came with *Dharti Maiya* (1981), in which he played an aggressive and slightly wayward youth on the lines of Sunil Dutt's character Birju in *Mother India*. But his biggest hit was *Ganga Kinare Mora Gaon* (1983).

Through his career spanning about a hundred films, Kunal spent many weeks shooting in different parts of Bihar and Uttar Pradesh. In a meeting, the ageing actor recounted some stories of fan worship.

In 1986, when he was shooting for *Beti Udhar Ke* in Tilauthu, about thirty-five kilometres from Dehri-on-Sone town, the producer had assembled a bunch of inexperienced local actors for a *lathi* (long stick) fight scene. One of them hit him on his left hand and caused a fracture. The shooting was stopped and when he reached the hotel, he found about a thousand people waiting for him outside! They were all worried about his health. As Singh says, 'I am no Amitabh Bachchan, but I was lucky enough to experience that moment when a star realizes what real fan worship is all about. Few actors get such adulation and with God's grace, I have.'[23]

On another occasion, during the shooting of *Ganga Jwala* in the same region, the actor saw an old woman shout out to him, 'Kunal *babua*, Kunal babua.' On meeting him, she began touching his hands and feet as if trying to find out if they were all right. Then she asked him, 'They are okay, aren't they?' It was later revealed that the old woman had seen *Ram Jaisan Bhaiya Hamaar* where Kunal played a handicapped person. His performance had been so convincing that she had walked all the way from home to the shoot just to find out if he was indeed physically challenged. 'What more can an actor ask for? I believe this is the finest compliment I have received as an actor,' he says.[24]

Singh's *Ram Jaisan Bhaiya Hamaar*, with Meera Madhuri as the heroine, was a successful film and ran for a record fifty days in Kishanganj, Bihar. It broke the record held by the Hindi film *Ram Teri Ganga Maili* (1985), which ran for four weeks.[25] Singh's five favourite films are *Ganga Kinare Mora Gaon, Dagabaaz Balma, Ram Jaisan Bhaiya Hamaar, Dulha Milal Dildaar* (2005) [a Bhojpuri take on Amitabh Bachchan's *Sooryavansham* (1999)], and *Maati* (2007), in which he plays a negative character.[26] *Dagabaaz Balma* (1988) was his home production and was directed by his wife Arti, who had also written the film's story, screenplay and dialogue.

In his long Bhojpuri cinema career, Singh acted with a host of heroines, including Gouri Khurana (*Dharti Maiya*, 1981), Rajni Sharma (*Sohag Bindiya*, 1986) and Jayshree T. (*Hamaar Bhauji*, 1983), although Meera Madhuri was his most regular leading lady. After acting as a hero for over a decade and half, Singh now divides his time playing character roles in Bhojpuri films and producing TV serials.

* * *

Lalitesh was a popular hero in Bhojpuri films during the 1980s and 90s. Born in Bhagalpur, Bihar, this psychology graduate got into movies by chance. A mutual friend introduced him to Javed Rehman, director of the film *Baaje Shehnaai Hamaar Anganaa* (1980). The film, incidentally, had plenty of shehnai music from old tapes of Ustad Bismillah Khan. Lalitesh ended up playing one of the two leads in the film, which turned out to be a flop. 'People used to look down on Bhojpuri films those days. A Bollywood film director once asked me, "Okay, you are a Bhojpuri film actor. But can you speak Hindi?" That was the level of ignorance about Bhojpuri films,' he says.[27]

The biggest hit of his career was *Naihar Ki Chunri* (1985). 'The film established me as a hero,' he says. Over the next decade, he starred in a number of Bhojpuri films such as *Aangan Ke Lakshmi* (1986), *Ganga Jwala* (1987), *Lagal Chunri Mein Daag* (1988), *Hey Tulsi Maiya* (1992), *Saat Phere* (1996), and *Dulhin Bani More Bahiniya* (2000). He has also acted in Maithili superhits such as *Sasta Zinagi Mahag Sinoor* (Life is cheap, vermilion is costly).

Lalitesh continues to work as a character actor, but he laments that there is no art, no discipline and no emotions involved in film-making these days. 'It is just about making money,' he says.[28]

* * *

Two other well-known heroes of the 1980s were Jai Tilak, who acted in *Piya Nirmohiya* (1983), *Ghar Grihasti* (1986) and *Ganga aur Gouri* (1988); and Manoj Verma, star of *Ganga Maiya Tohar Kiriya* (1985), *Dharti Ki Awaaz* (1986), *Ganga Hamaar Mai* (1986) and *Gawna* (1992).

9

New Heroes: The Three Aces in the Pack

Just as the Khan troika—Shah Rukh, Salman and Aamir—have lorded over Bollywood for over a decade, the new millennium Bhojpuri film industry is ruled by three major stars—Manoj Tiwari, Ravi Kishan and Dinesh Lal Yadav 'Nirahua'. These three stars have delivered the three biggest box-office successes of this era: Tiwari's *Sasura Bada Paisewala* (2004), Kishan's *Panditji Bataeen Na Biyah Kab Hoee* (2005) and Yadav's *Nirahua Rickshawala* (2007). Each of them has several other hits under their belt and they all charge hefty fees of Rs 40 lakh and more according to industry sources.[1]

Between 2004 and 2008, several new heroes emerged in Bhojpuri films—Sikander Kharbanda (who co-starred with Ravi Kishan in *Panditji Bataeen Na Biyah Kab Hoee*), Krishna Abhishek, Vinay Anand, Samarth Chaturvedi, Pankaj Kesri, Amar Upadhyay, Dev Joshan, Vikrant Singh, Sudip Pandey and Pawan Singh, among others. In a situation where demand outstripped supply, everybody had work.

In turning the third wave of Bhojpuri films into a tsunami of sorts, both Manoj Tiwari and Ravi Kishan played crucial

116

roles. They were the face of a genre that soon became a full-fledged regional film industry. Their stints in the reality shows *Bigg Boss*, *Bathroom Singer* and *Raaz Pichhle Janam Ka* (Kishan), and *Chak de Bachche* (Tiwari), helped them become well-known faces nationally.

Both actors are also political creatures. Tiwari contested the 2009 Lok Sabha elections on a Samajwadi Party ticket from Gorakhpur and came third. Kishan is a well-known Congress campaigner and has expressed his desire to contest elections in the future.[2]

Dinesh Lal Yadav 'Nirahua' is the premier star of Bhojpuri films at the moment, delivering box-office superhits such as *Nirahua Rickshawala* and *Nirahua Chalal Sasural*. In fact, his hit ratio outnumbers that of other actors in the genre.

* * *

Every Bhojpuri cinema fan knows Manoj Tiwari 'Mridul', the singer and actor. But not many are aware that he was passionate about cricket in college. A medium-pacer known for his in-swingers, Tiwari claims to have captained the Benares Hindu University team. 'When travelling in trains with fellow cricketers, we used to sing folk songs, keeping beat on suitcases,' he recalls.[3] Tiwari competed in the prestigious Vizzy Trophy tournament, and graduated in 1992. He confesses, 'I even played a season of professional cricket for Rajasthan Club in Calcutta. I took the game seriously and wanted to play for India. I used to feel very disheartened when I couldn't see myself breaking through. I was a poor fielder.'[4] Cricket's loss turned out to be Bhojwood's gain.

Tiwari, the fifth among four brothers and two sisters, was born in a government hospital in Benares's Kabir Chauraha in 1971. His native village is in Bihar's Bhabhua district and his earliest childhood memories are of village plays. 'I used to play Laxman in Ramlilas. Sometimes, I even played female roles like Kaikeyi. I often performed the singing parts. As I grew older, I also directed several plays such as *Aravali Ka Sher*, *Chandragupta*, *Vidrohi Shakti Singh* and *Bhagat Singh*.'[5]

Tiwari's rise as a film hero was preceded by his success as a singer. As a child he was fond of writing poems. 'I remember writing my first song in Bhojpuri after Indira Gandhi's assassination,' he says.[6]

The singer-actor comes from a family of rich farmers and his father was also a classical singer. 'But he never encouraged me to sing,' says Tiwari. The person who encouraged him to perform professionally was his elder brother. Tiwari says, 'Whatever I am today is because of his hard work. He was the first person to believe in my abilities.'[7]

'My brother helped me produce three audio cassettes of my songs. One was a collection of Ram bhajans and the other had Bhojpuri folk songs. Both failed. While recording the third cassette, I told my brother, "Let me do this my way." The cassette was titled *Kehla Pe Teet Lagela* [Feels bitter when you say it] and it became popular in my home district Bhabhua in west Bihar. Suddenly I found people being nice to me. And I started earning more than what I was making from club cricket, where I was barely earning Rs 4,000 to 5,000 for the entire season.'[8]

Manoj Tiwari hit bull's eye in 1996. 'After recording my fourth album, we still had a few hours of studio time left. I recorded some new songs during those two hours. I pursued T-series executives for months to release those songs. They were not too keen and I was told that young, modern boys would not like them. But I knew those songs would become popular.

'*Maata Ki Mahima* was released in March 1996. I had spent Rs 7,000 from my pocket to make that album. Later, the company paid me that amount. This was followed by another album a month later called *Hatath Naikhe Bhasura* [My husband's elder brother doesn't move away]. Both were hits. Amidst all this, I went on a trip to Vaishno Devi [a popular Hindu pilgrimage site]. When I went to the T-series office again after I returned, the miracle had happened!'[9]

Tiwari vividly remembers the day he discovered that his songs were a roaring success: 'A friend came running to me and told me in Bhojpuri, "Manoj, they are playing your songs all day at Gadauliya Chowk".'[10]

'I couldn't believe my ears,' Tiwari says. 'I went to six shops and couldn't find the cassette. Then I went to a shop called Cassette Sansar at Nai Sadak. The shopkeeper recognized me and decided to tease me. He said, "What's special about that cassette? I don't think it is available." Then he came over to the other side of the counter, hugged me and said, "Manoj bhai, you have sung some great numbers." I was still not convinced. I wondered whether he was the only person who had liked the songs. But his effusiveness convinced me that the cassette was a success. *Mujhe lag gaya ki main ab star hoon* [I felt I had become a star]. I was filled with joy. To be honest, I have never experienced the same intensity of happiness ever again."[11]

A compelling raconteur, Tiwari also narrates how his nom de plume 'Mridul' was created. In Tiwari's words, 'When I first met Gulshan Kumar of T-series, I told him my name was Manoj Kumar Tiwari. "It is a long name," he said, "why don't you shorten it?" Then he said, "*Tum bahut meethe bolte ho, tumhara naam Mridul hona chahiye*" [You speak so sweetly, your name should be Mridul]. It was a joke, but I changed my name to Manoj Mridul. Later, I realized there was no point in hiding my caste, so I added my surname. I became Manoj Tiwari "Mridul".'[12] Over the years, 'Mridul' has gradually disappeared from Tiwari's film credits.

After the success of his musical albums and brief appearances in Bhojpuri films such as *Humke Maafi Daee Da* (2004), Manoj Tiwari made his debut as a full-fledged hero in the box-office smash, *Sasura Bada Paisewala* (2004). The film was followed by two other hits, *Daroga Babu I Love You* (2005) and *Bandhan Toote Na* (2005).

'I was supposed to act in another film, but I finally only sang five of its songs,' he recalls. The film is *Panditji Bataeen Na Biyah Kab Hoee*, which stars Ravi Kishan. And when asked what stopped him from doing the film, he answers, 'I had some *ann bann* [differences] with director Mohanji Prasad.' The film, as we know, turned out to be a superhit.

As a hero, Tiwari was the right man in the right place. Being a successful folk singer, he was already well-known in the Bhojpuri-speaking parts of Bihar and Uttar Pradesh. The characters in his early films were also the right fit for the audiences' changing mindscape. As in other parts of India, satellite TV had opened up the qasbahs and small towns to big-city culture and Bhojpuri cinema's core audience was ready for a new kind of hero. In *Sasura Bada Paisewala*, Tiwari does not play an illiterate farmer, but a graduate who speaks fluent English. In *Daroga Babu I Love You*, he is the first daroga of his village. In other words, his characters typify the social aspirations of the underclass, the genre's core audience. With his moustache and well-fed, less than toned body, he exudes the aura of a homegrown hero.

Tiwari's acting is not characterized by stereotypical mannerisms. He is comfortable in action as well as dramatic scenes. In *Dhartiputra* (2005), a remake of Raj Khosla's *Mera*

Gaon Mera Desh (1971), he plays the role of the carefree outsider who rescues a village from dacoits with the same ease and élan as Dharmendra did in the Bollywood hit. Industry sources say that Tiwari is popular with the family audience as well as the migrant crowd. 'Emoting is his strong point. He managed to hold his own even against Ajay Devgan in *Dharti Kahe Pukaar Ke* (2006),' says producer Abhay Sinha.[13]

Besides, the singer's tenor suits high-pitched folksy tracks. Some of his numbers are extremely risqué, no doubt written and composed with an eye on the box-office. But the singer believes that this is only one part of the story. 'My non-filmi albums introduced variety to Bhojpuri music. Earlier, the genre was dominated by ribald songs. But we also sang songs on unemployment and female infanticide. I sang kajris and chaitas. We sang romantic songs which people with good taste could listen to. I sang about 2,000 songs before acting in films.'

Ajay Bhanot, who distributes Bhojpuri films in Punjab, says that Tiwari's voice is distinctive among Bhojpuri singers. 'He sings with feeling and heart,' he says.[14] Alok Dubey, who exhibits movies in Anand Mandir, Benares, has a similar view. According to Dubey, 'He has the great ability to control the audience from the stage.'[15]

Tiwari's fame has also travelled abroad—producer Abhay Sinha recalls that during the shooting of *Janam Janam Ke Saath* in Mauritius last year, Tiwari was mobbed by fans outside the radio station where he was interviewed.

Manoj Tiwari has also been involved in an unsavoury controversy. The actor had claimed that the Dutch government had issued a stamp in his honour. However, it turned out that the government had done no such thing—rather the stamp had been issued commercially by a company.[16]

Like fellow Bhojpuri star Ravi Kishan, Tiwari too has adapted impressively to various media. As a way of reaching out to a larger audience, he co-hosted the television programme *Chak De Bachche*. In 2009, he also compered *Sur Sangram,* a music show on Mahua.

Film journalist Munnu Prasad Pandey says that people in Benares were pleasantly surprised by Tiwari's incredible success. 'It was beyond their wildest dreams,' he says.[17]

The actor-singer has often spoken out on social and political matters involving the Bhojpuri-speaking community in Mumbai and elsewhere. Film distributor Ajay Bhanot says that when Tiwari visited the migrants of Uttar Pradesh and Bihar who were injured in a bomb blast in Ludhiana's Shingar cinema in 2007, there was almost a stampede. 'That's the kind of following he commands,' says the Punjab distributor.[18]

In February 2008, the actor's Mumbai office was attacked by activists of the MNS after he had received threatening telephone calls. But in March 2008, Tiwari distributed flowers among Marathi passengers travelling to Mumbai on Shivaji's birthday. This was his style of Gandhigiri.

In 2009, he became Gorakhpur's Samajwadi Party candidate for the Lok Sabha elections. 'Following the attacks [on north Indians by MNS workers], I decided to rally for the cause of actors and technicians working in Bhojpuri films. I want to be the voice of the whole Bhojpuri world,' he says.[19] Again, in November 2009, his Versova office was vandalized by a group of anti-north Indian activists.

Despite his success, Tiwari remains a simple man. He explains, 'I believe in clarity of mind and this reflects in my choice of food as well. I should be able to identify what I eat—I am not like a mixed vegetable stir fry . . . I am like *aloo gobhi* [potato cauliflower stir fry, a typical dish].'[20]

* * *

Another famous face of Bhojpuri cinema is Ravi Kishan (also spelt as Ravi Kissen and Ravi Kishen), who is called the Shah Rukh Khan of Bhojpuri films. Like the Bollywood *badshah*, Kishan has unhesitatingly played negative roles in films such as *Tu Hamaar Haoo* (2007)—a copy of the Shah Rukh Khan-starrer *Darr* where Kishan plays the part of the obsessive lover—and *Gabbar Singh* (2008).

He was the first Bhojpuri star to participate in the reality show *Bigg Boss* and left a lasting impression with his bold performance. His catch line, '*Zindagi jhand ba, phir bhi ghamand ba*' ('My life's in the pits but I am still proud'), gained immense popularity. Many still remember his performance for its calculated carefreeness, wit and rustic style.

However, his follow-up act on *Bathroom Singer* did not work, though the national exposure helped him launch a second innings in Hindi films with Shyam Benegal's *Welcome to Sajjanpur* (2008). And when Columbia Pictures wanted to dub Toby Maguire's voice in Bhojpuri, who do you think they went to? Now, with more and more Hindi films such as *Luck* (2009) coming his way, Kishan's Bollywood career is certainly looking up.

These are well-earned rewards for Kishan, the son of a priest from eastern Uttar Pradesh's Jaunpur district, who struggled for years to find a toehold in Hindi films before becoming a star in Bhojpuri films.

By his own account, Kishan's childhood was idyllic—he played outside the temple as a kid, and bathed in the Ganga. 'My father was a priest. He used to beat me a lot and used to think I was a good-for-nothing. But I can understand that because he had many expectations of me. I owe a lot to him. He taught me *sanskar* [the right tradition] and *sanskriti* [culture].'[21]

As a child, Kishan recalls being hugely impressed by Amitabh Bachchan. About the effect Bachchan's acting had on him after he had watched a film, he says, 'For a few hours after the film was over, I would be in a trance. Then I used to dream about the movie and its characters. I used to walk in a strange fashion. At school, friends teased me saying that I behaved like a hero. Stars like Amitabh Bachchan, Mithun Chakraborty, Shatrughan Sinha and directors like Manmohan Desai have influenced my life profoundly.'[22]

A commerce graduate, Ravi Kishan came to Mumbai in 1989. 'I stayed in a chawl in Bandra. People used to call me a Mithun look-alike. Being the son of a poor Brahmin, I didn't have the money to learn acting in a school. I wasn't sure how my career would pan out,' he says.[23]

He bagged a small role in *Udhaar Ki Zindagi* (1994), a flop. This was followed by several small parts. He says, 'In 1994, I acted in *Army* with Shah Rukh Khan and Sridevi. I observed Shah Rukh at close quarters during the shooting of *Army*. I noticed his high energy levels and also observed that he was always looking ahead.'[24]

Kishan recalls, 'Then I did about four or five films with Mithun such as *Justice Chowdhary* [2000] and *Marshal* [2002]. I also played a pandit in Salman Khan's *Tere Naam* [2003]. To make ends meet, I started acting for television. I did a serial called *Hello Inspector*. The serial created a fan base for me in Bihar and Uttar Pradesh. They liked my style and my dialogue delivery.'[25]

Then, one day, he got a call from director Mohanji Prasad who offered him a Bhojpuri film. 'I wondered who was going to watch it,' says Kishan. But the director was reportedly candid and told Kishan, 'Nobody watches Bhojpuri films these days. I am making a Bengali film and have some money left. That will be enough for us to finish the movie.' Kishan adds, 'He took my dates for forty days and I got Rs 75,000 for the movie.'[26]

The film, *Saiyan Hamaar* (2002), was shot in Falta. About forty kilometres from Calcutta, it was once the site of a Dutch factory. 'I really enjoyed the shoot. The song, *Bagalwali jaan mareli* ['The attractive girl in the neighbourhood torments me'], was a big hit. I played a poor flute player married to a rich zamindar's daughter, who gets paralyzed. One night, during the shoot, I told the director, "Mohanji, I can sense the revival of Bhojpuri films." He laughed and asked, "What are you saying?" I told him, "No, the audience is there. We just have to give them what they want."'[27] The film did well. This was followed by *Kanyadaan* (2003), which again enjoyed a decent run.

In 2004, Manoj Tiwari's superhit *Sasura Bada Paisewala* was released. Next came Ravi Kishan's *Panditji Bataeen Na Biyah Kab Hoee* (2005). 'That blockbuster made me a superstar. After that we started getting good money,' he says.[28] Nagma was the heroine of *Panditji* . . . and Kishan explains, 'I wanted a well-known name for the film. I called her personally and pleaded with her to do the film. I told her that Bhojpuri was an emerging industry and that she had to work in the film.'[29]

Ravi Kishan has acted in dozens of Bhojpuri films—*Pandit, Kab Hoi Gawna Hamaar, Pandav, Purab aur Paschim, Dulha Milal Dildaar, Hum To Ho Gaini Tohar, Raja Bhojpuriya, Banke Bihari MLA, Janam Janam Ke Saath, Ab Ta Ban Ja Sajanwa Hamaar, Babul Pyaare, Ganga, Kanhaiya, Hamra Se Biyah Karba, Ravi Kishan, Ram Balram, Gabbar Singh* and *Bidai*.

Kishan's strength lies in his intensity, a quality seen in films like *Pandit*, where he plays an innocent Brahmin forced to fight a land-grabbing henchman and his cronies. Throughout the film, Kishan maintains a silent, dignified countenance and there is symmetry to his performance, rarely seen in potboilers. No surprise then that the film got him the best actor award at the 2006 Bhojpuri Film Awards for the second year running after *Panditji Bataeen Na Biyah Kab Hoee*. In *Pandav*, Kishan plays the role of a quiet servant who finally rebels. This earned him the best Bhojpuri actor award yet again in 2007. In 2008—the fourth year running—he received the best actor award for his performance in *Dharam Veer* (2008).

Kishan is willing to take chances as an actor. In *Tu Hamaar Haoo*, he played an obsessed, over-the-top autodriver who worships heroine Nagma in much the same way Shah Rukh Khan admires Juhi Chawla, the heroine in *Darr*. In *Gabbar Singh*, he essayed the role of a dacoit. 'The film was doing quite well in Mumbai till the MNS agitators tore down the film's posters. The producer ended up losing a lot of money. The whole experience was painful for me,' says Kishan.

Ironically, it wasn't his performance in Bhojpuri films, but his role in the reality television show *Bigg Boss* that made Kishan a nationally-recognized face. 'Earlier, people loved me only in Bihar and Uttar Pradesh. Now people across the country love and know me. I had not expected the show to become such a rage. In fact, my kids have been asking me to participate in one more reality show. They like whatever I do on TV,' says the top Bhojpuri actor, who has also appeared in the television show *Rakhi Ka Swayamvar* as Rakhi's brother.[30] Apart from acting, Kishan says he works out for one hour every day and is a devotee of Lord Shiva.

* * *

With a plethora of box-office hits since 2006, Dinesh Lal Yadav 'Nirahua' has emerged as the top star of Bhojpuri films. A singer-actor, Nirahua generally lets his films do the talking.

Two of his films—*Nirahua Rickshawala* (2007) and *Nirahua Chalal Sasural* (2008)—are blockbusters. His other hits include *Lagal Raha Ae Rajaji* (Carry on my love, 2008) and *Pratigya* (Pledge, 2008).

Nirahua was the name of a fictional character, a simpleton, in Dinesh Lal Yadav's music album called *Nirahua Satal Rahe* released in 2003. 'Some songs were woven around the character and the cassette became extremely popular. The name became my identity as people started calling me Nirahua,' he says.[31] The word Nirahua, the actor says, is derived from the Sanskrit word, *nirhu*, which means sindoor (vermilion).

Nirahua's father worked in a factory in Calcutta. After his first wife died leaving three daughters behind, he married a second time, after which Dinesh Lal was born in 1979. His younger brother Pravesh Lal, now a rising star in Bhojpuri films, made his debut as a hero with *Chalni ke Chalal Dulha* (Super-refined bridegroom, 2009).

As a child, Nirahua saw Vijay Lal Yadav, his uncle's son, emerge as a well-known singer of birhas. 'My father had one heartfelt desire: that I should be a famous singer. He felt proud when people introduced him as the uncle of Vijay Lal Yadav and he wanted his own son to be a great folk singer,' says Nirahua.[32]

The actor-singer admits being nervous when he first began performing on stage. 'But my father often induced me to perform by promising me a new watch or some other gift. Whenever Vijay bhaiya hosted a stage show in Calcutta, my father used to take me there to sing a few songs. The compliments made me believe that I could be a singer too. Soon I dumped my ambition of being a chartered accountant. I formed my own group for stage shows in 1997. We would earn about Rs 400 to 500 per show. I would distribute the amount among the troupe members because I wanted to create a group of good musicians. My father used to tell me, "Don't think about money, just keep working hard and you will be successful one day,"' says Dinesh Lal Yadav.[33]

During the early phase of his career as a performer, he hosted shows in various towns of Uttar Pradesh and Bihar. This was followed by performances in Punjab and Mumbai. He says, 'Actually, I performed in almost every place with a decent population of Bhojpuri-speaking people. By 2001, I had done about 500 shows.'

Being Vijay Lal Yadav's cousin obviously helped. 'People who couldn't get him for a show if his calendar was full would sign me up. The audience listened to me attentively in those early shows because the buzz was that I was Vijay Lal's brother. After watching me perform and listening to my songs, people were impressed. I kept getting one show after another,' says the actor.[34]

His first cassette of songs was a big failure. 'But the ones that followed did much better. They were folk songs and *devi ke geet* [religious songs]. One of them was called *Malai khaye gurwa* [Jaggery eats the cream]. After that I got an opportunity to sing for T-series in 2003,' says Nirahua. 'I started getting film offers following the popularity of *Nirahua Satal Rahe*. Unlike other popular Bhojpuri folk singers like Vijay Lal Yadav, Chhaila Bihari and Manoj Tiwari, I decided to act and dance in the videos of all my songs. If I was singing about a politician or an old man, I acted out the part accordingly.

'Director Sanjay Srivastava saw a video where I had played a politician. He was making *Hamka Aisa Waisa Na Samjha* [Don't think I am riff-raff, 2006] and had wanted to cast Rajpal Yadav. But after watching the video, he felt that I could also do the role. The movie is about a boy's fight to make Bhojpuri a state-recognized language. But

Chalat Musafir Moh Liyo Re [The traveller has been ensnared, 2006], where I played the role of a police inspector, was my first release.'[35]

Among the films that followed was *Ho Gayeel Ba Pyaar Odhaniya Wali Se* (I have fallen in love with a girl wearing a stole, 2007). Nirahua said in an interview, 'After this film, I got plenty of offers. But I was not in a rush to sign films. My flourishing career as a singer gave me the confidence to do that. For me, doing selective but good work is the best thing.'[36]

He adds, 'The script I finally accepted to work with was *Nirahua Rickshawala* (2007), which ultimately became a superhit. *Kahan Jaiba Raja Najariya Ladaike* (2007) was another big success. I am known as a jubilee star now.'[37]

He isn't exactly in Bollywood actor Emraan Hashmi's category where sizzling scenes are concerned, but Nirahua's kissing scene in *Nirahua Rickshawala* was a much-discussed one. 'I was almost trembling when I came to know that I had to do a kissing scene. But when the director explained the scene to me, I found it was totally technical. The audience thinks I am kissing the heroine, but actually I was not. The kissing scene was a turning point in the film. And it played a huge role in making the film successful,' admits Dinesh Lal Yadav.

The film's success made the actor's market price soar. 'My fees are a result of my success. It is what my producer wants to give me at a certain point of my career. My biggest hit of 2008 was Ramakant Prasad's *Lagal Raha Ae Rajaji*. When he signed me again, he gave me Rs 50 lakh, and after that my rate became Rs 50 lakh. Films become superhits only when the audience visits the hall a second time.'[38]

Industry insiders believe that Nirahua is worth the price he commands. 'Nirahua tries to justify his price. He works hard on every role,' says Rajesh Kumar Singh, who distributes Bhojpuri films in Mumbai.[39]

Gatekeepers and ushers are unanimous that Nirahua is the hottest property in Bhojpuri films these days. 'He is way ahead of everyone right now. He is lean and dances well. When he ties the gamcha and jumps on screen, he looks like a great action hero too. When he kissed the heroine in *Nirahua Rickshawala*, the audience clapped and whistled. Even a flop Nirahua film runs for over three weeks. In comparison, a regular flop like *Baklol Dulha* ran for three days,' says Jaidev Karmakar, gatekeeper of Kanhaiya Talkies in Mughalsarai.[40]

Kamal Kumar Shukla, a small-time exhibitor, explains the extent of the singer-actor's popularity: 'When a Nirahua film comes to town, the audience seems to emerge from nowhere. Shopkeepers around the cinema hall often ask me in wonder, "Where has the crowd suddenly come from?"'[41]

Twelve-year-old Vicky Chauhan and fourteen-year-old Sukku Chauhan work in a tea stall near Kanhaiya Talkies and they say that Nirahua is their favourite hero because he dances and fights well. 'He is also slim, unlike Manoj Tiwari,' says Vicky.[42]

Like Tiwari, Nirahua's acting style is natural. 'During my student days in Calcutta, I had learnt karate. I had no idea the martial art would turn out to be such a handy tool,' says Nirahua, who loves watching Dharmendra movies.[43]

Now the singer-actor has started his own production house called Nirahua Entertainment. 'We want to make clean films which people can watch with their families. I have already produced a social film, *Chalni Ke Chalal Dulha* with my younger brother Pravesh Lal Yadav as the lead. Pakhi Hedge [a popular actress in Bhojpuri cinema] has also co-produced one of our films *Prem Ke Rog Bhayeel*,' he says.[44]

In addition, Nirahua has performed successful stage shows in Fiji, Australia and New Zealand. 'In 2007, I performed eleven shows to packed houses. Those who couldn't get tickets would sit on the ground and listen. In Fiji, the stadiums were as jampacked as those at a cricket match in India,' he says.[45]

'I was pleasantly surprised to discover that local singers had created their own songs based on my tracks. People used to come with their kids and tell me, "My boy doesn't drink milk without listening to your songs on a CD."'[46] He adds, "Many of those who came for the show were third-generation migrants from India. They also told me that they watched my music CDs and had come to see me perform in person. Even the waiter in the hotel I was staying in used to hum my tunes.'

10

The Directors

Now close to completing five decades of its existence, Bhojpuri cinema has produced some first-rate directors who helped the genre fashion a distinct identity. The best of them always managed to get decent box-office results without compromising on aesthetics. Here's a look at some of them.

* * *

Many still regard the first Bhojpuri feature film, *Ganga Maiya Tohe Piyari Chadhaibo* (1962), as the finest ever in the genre, not for nostalgia alone. Even today, the movie does not seem outdated, which is a tribute to director Kundan Kumar's cinematic vision.

Kumar was from Benares and had already directed Hindi films like *Neel Mani* (1957), *Teesri Gali* (1958), *Raj Sinhasan* (1958) and *Bade Ghar Ki Bahu* (1960). Known to be extremely soft-spoken and well-mannered, he proved his mettle in the regional genre with *Ganga Maiya Tohe Piyari Chadhaibo*.

Kumar went on to direct *Laagi Nahin Chhute Ram*, *Ganga*, *Loha Singh* and *Bhauji*, which he also produced. Of them, *Laagi Nahin Chhute Ram* and *Bhauji* fared well at the box-office. The 1965 promos of *Bhauji* show how the 'silver jubilee director' Kundan Kumar was a big success—his name is more prominently displayed than the names of the film's stars, Kumkum and Sujit Kumar. Barring *Loha Singh*, all these films featured music composed by Chitragupta.

In 1965, when several Bhojpuri films flopped, producers of this nascent genre panicked. Kumar, however, remained optimistic about the industry's future. 'Bhojpuri films will always have a market. But they must have a regional flavour. If some films have flopped, it is only because some producers have forgotten the importance of geography in their movies,' he said.[1]

During the years when Bhojpuri films went through a slump, Kumar established himself as a successful Bollywood director with *Aulad* (1968) starring Jeetendra and Babita. Later, he also produced and directed films like *Anokhi Ada* (1973) with Jeetendra, Rekha and Vinod Khanna, and *Aaj Ka Mahatma* (1976) with Randhir Kapoor and Rekha. His untimely death in 1979 was a big loss to the Bhojpuri film industry.

* * *

Sri Nath Tripathi, also from Benares, was one of the greatest all-rounders of Bhojpuri cinema: producer, director, actor, singer, story and screenplay writer, and music director. Born in 1913, Tripathi was trained in Hindustani classical music. He joined Bombay Talkies as a violinist in 1935 and got his break as a music director in *Chandan* (1939).[2] Slowly, he carved a niche for himself in Hindi mythologicals and historicals. Some of his hit songs were heard in Hindi films like *Janam Janam Ke Phere* (1957), *Sangeet Samraat Tansen* (1962), *Rani Roopmati* (1957) and *Lal Qila* (1960).

His musical score for *Bidesiya* (1963) remains the benchmark for music in Bhojpuri films. That apart, he also directed the film and acted as a police inspector in it. The movie not only shows his understanding of the sociology of the region, but also his control over film-making.

Being a music director first, Tripathi filmed his songs beautifully. An example of Tripathi's talent appears in *Bidesiya*, when there is a long shot of a tree towards the end of the song *Dinwa ginat* ('Counting the days'). In showing a tree without leaves, with outspread branches studded with thorns, the emotional state of the film's female protagonist bemoaning her absent lover is figuratively represented. No dialogue could have illustrated the feeling of lost love better than that broken-hearted-looking tree.

After *Bidesiya*, Tripathi made the first Bhojpuri mythological, *Sita Maiya* (1964), which he reportedly readied in five months.[3] Tripathi believed that it was the duty of regional film-makers to bring the true form of their language, culture and music to the audience. He also felt that regional films needed to retain a 'purity of language'.[4]

During the low period of Bhojpuri cinema in the late 1960s and early 1970s, Tripathi went back to directing and composing music for Hindi mythologicals.

In the second phase of Bhojpuri films, he made *Jaagal Bhag Hamaar* (My stars are rising, 1980) with Sujit Kumar, Prema Narayan and Heena Kauser. Eight years after this film was released, in 1988, he passed away.

* * *

Another director who left his mark on Bhojpuri cinema was Nazir Hussain. He was born and brought up in Lucknow, but his family was from Osia, a village near Dildarnagar in eastern Uttar Pradesh's Ghazipur district. 'Osia is my ancestral village. We were agriculturists,' says Mumtaz Hussain, his son.[5]

Nazir's father was a railway guard earning European grade salary and all his children, including Nazir, were educated in Lucknow.

Nazir himself worked as a fireman for a few months in the railways. He then joined the British Army during World War II and was posted in Malaysia and Singapore, where he became a prisoner of war. When he was freed, he joined national leader Subhash Chandra Bose's Indian National Army (INA).[6]

Nazir always had an artistic bent of mind and he found the platform to express it in the INA. Initially, 'After a hard day's work as a field propagandist, [he] used to return to his camp and waste time doing absolutely nothing.' But soon, he 'decided to spend the long, barren hours reading and writing. [He] formed a literary circle with some of [his] INA colleagues and started writing poems and plays in the light of a feeble candle.'[7]

Nazir Hussain also said that the most memorable recognition he ever received as an artiste and playwright was during his INA days.[8] In January 1945, the INA organized week-long festivities to celebrate its leader's birthday. It was for this occasion that Nazir Hussain wrote the play *Balidan*, which was staged by platoon members. Bose, who watched the performance, couldn't hold back his tears. It won Nazir the highest award, the gold medal of the Azad Hind Force.'[9]

After the cases against the INA were closed, the army's soldiers were released. Unable to find jobs, a few of them, including Nazir, got together and began performing plays. Among others, they enacted a play called *Sipahi Ka Sapna*, written by Nazir during his INA days.

B.N. Sircar of New Theatres happened to see a show, and impressed by Nazir's performance, called him to Calcutta to join New Theatres. In Calcutta, Nazir met director Bimal Roy and became his assistant. He also wrote the story and co-wrote the dialogues for the Hindi movie *Pehla Aadmi* (1950). Nazir continued acting in films and his role in *Devdas* as Dharamdas, the faithful servant of the protagonist, is remembered to this day. 'My father used to say it was one of the best roles of his career,' says Mumtaz.[10]

Nazir was part of the core team of *Ganga Maiya Tohe Piyari Chadhaibo*—he wrote the film's story, screenplay and dialogues, and even acted in it. But above all, he helped put the team together.

Nazir Hussain turned producer with *Hamaar Sansar*, a moving portrait of the lives of farmers and migrant labourers. Between *Hamaar Sansar* and *Balam Pardesia*, the first film that Nazir Hussain both produced and directed, there was a gap of fourteen years—coinciding with the period of slump in Bhojpuri cinema in the late 1960s. When *Balam Pardesia* was released in 1979, it ran for over twenty-five weeks and became a superhit.

Later, Hussain directed *Roos Gayeele Saiyan Hamaar*, which did reasonably well at the box-office. His other two movies were *Chanwa Ke Taake Chakor* and *Chutki Bhar Senur* (A Pinch of Sindoor, 1983), although *Chutki Bhar Senur* was released several years after his death.

As a director, Nazir Hussain displayed a keen sense of detail. He was a firm believer in the need to depict local cultural practices accurately on celluloid. 'It is easier to make Hindi films than Bhojpuri films. In Hindi films, you can show skirts, night clubs, dance clubs and gambling dens; but not so in Bhojpuri films. While watching a Bhojpuri film, our core audience wants to feel close to their village life and culture. They want solutions to their everyday problems, not just entertainment. For that they already have Hindi films.'[11]

Actor Kunal Singh, who worked in *Chutki Bhar Senur*, says that Nazir Hussain used to narrate a film's story like a villager. 'His expressions, his words, his style, all gave you that feeling. You knew what he wanted. He would take care of small things—the way a goatherd speaks, walks and dresses; the way a mother serves food; even the way food is prepared over the *chulha* [indigenous stove to cook food]. He believed in authenticity. He made me get a hair cut to suit the script. Right from *Ganga Maiya Tohe Piyari Chadhaibo* to *Balam Pardesia*, you can see how he works on the details. In *Balam Pardesia*, see how he makes Padma Khanna run in the fields with her sari hitched a little high like village women. No discussion on Bhojpuri films is complete without considering Nazir Hussain's films.'[12]

Rakesh Pandey, who worked in *Balam Pardesia*, says that since Nazir Hussain was an actor, he could also visualize a frame from an actor's point of view. 'That made things much easier for us. He was very passionate about his work. I dedicated *Bansuriya Baje Ganga Teer* to him. He was meticulous about sets and costumes. He was a director in the true sense of the term. Since he was from the Bhojpuri-speaking region, he knew everything about its culture: the *vrat*s [religious fasts] and the *tyohar*s [festivals]. He never used raunchy dialogues or songs. He was true to his origins.'[13]

* * *

For someone who could not speak Bhojpuri, Dilip Bose had an amazingly successful career in the genre. He directed ten Bhojpuri films, most of them emotional tear-jerkers. His films attracted rural women in droves. He was undisputably the most successful Bhojpuri film director in the 1980s. Some of his well-known films are *Ganga Kinare Mora Gaon*, *Ganga Maiya Bhar De Acharwa Hamaar*, *Sajanwa Bairi Bhaile Hamaar*, *Ghar Grihasti*, *Bihari Babu* and *Piya Ke Gaon*. 'Both

Bihari Babu and *Piya Ke Gaon* were released on the same day in Patna. On the first day, the crowd broke the gate of Elphinstone cinema where one of the films had been released. Both films turned out to be box-office hits,' recalls Dilip Bose's son, Dipankar, who assisted his father on these films.[14]

Bose was born in Khulna in present-day Bangladesh. After his graduation, he made his debut as a director with the Bangla film *Dui Bechara* (Two pitiful fellows, 1960). But his Hindi debut film, *Chandi Ki Deewar* (1961), which had the hit Talat Mehmood song *Ashkon ne jo paya hai, woh geeton ne diya hai* ('What the tears have got is due to the songs'), was a dud.[15] His first Bhojpuri film, *Ganga Maiya Bhar De Acharwa Hamaar* (1982) was a moderate success—but the second one, *Ganga Kinare Mora Gaon* (1983), became one of the biggest money-spinners of all time.

Bose was a master of emotions and managed to capture the flavour of the region though he did not speak the language. Lalji Gupta, who produced the first Bhojpuri film directed by Dilip Bose, *Ganga Maiya Bhar De Acharwa Hamaar*, recounts an incident that shows Bose's sharp powers of observation. During a visit to Allahabad, the two witnessed a fight between rickshaw-pullers. 'Later, when directing the movie, he drew on the mannerisms of the rickshaw-pullers during the on-screen fight. It became part of a comedy scene. He was a mature and sensitive director who understood the pulse of the public.'[16]

In time, Bose's understanding of the language improved. In fact, he also wrote the dialogues of some Bhojpuri films such as *Piya Ke Gaon*, a first-rate melodrama.

Actor Kunal Singh says it is unfortunate that Bose never made it as a top Hindi film director. 'He had a tremendous understanding of script and had the uncanny ability to get good work out of a bad actor. He was the *shahenshah* [monarch] of emotional scenes. He used to say that while performing a poignant scene, an actor must go through three steps. First, his heart must feel heavy. Then, his voice must choke. And, in the end, there should be tears in his eyes. Dilip Bose taught me all this.'[17]

Well-known character actor Vijay Khare affirms, 'He was a master of emotions. And he could make good films at a low cost. These were his two specialties.'[18]

Bose died on 7 July 2002. His sons continue to ply the same trade and in the past five years, Dipankar Bose and his brother, Diwakar, have together directed four low-budget Bhojpuri films: *Nadi Ke Lahariya Bole* (2003), *Humke Maafi Dei De* (2004), *Hamaar Bahiniya* (2006) and *Raghupati Raghav Raja Ram* (2007).

* * *

An interesting director in the second phase of Bhojpuri films is Radhakant. Originally from Mathura, he began his career in the Hindi film industry assisting Nanabhai Bhatt and Homi Wadia, legends of low-budget fantasy films in Hindi. He began as a director of C-grade Bollywood action flicks in the 1960s such as *Tarzan Aur Jaadugar* (1963) and *Toofan* (1969).

Radhakant was making a Gujarati film for producer Sohanlal Kanwar when he got an offer to direct a film in Bhojpuri titled *Saiyan Tohre Karan* (For you my love, 1981). The film was about a love triangle and did reasonably well, but Radhakant feels that the movie might have done better if the story had not been so similar to Rajshri's *Tarana* (1979), which had been released a couple of years earlier. 'Since this was my first Bhojpuri film, I travelled to Benares,

Gorakhpur and other places to gauge the public's reaction. I found out that the surfeit of similar stories had worked to our disadvantage,' he says.[19]

His second Bhojpuri film, *Bitiya Bhayeel Sayaan* (My daughter has grown up, 1982), was made for Rs 4 lakhs, one lakh less than his previous film. 'The producer had made a prior commitment to the financier that he would finish the film in that amount,' the director recalls.[20]

Having completed several small-budget films by then, Radhakant was well-versed in cost-cutting techniques. He shot the film on 16mm and blew it up to 35 mm later. The director recalls, 'But you had to avoid too many long shots or the grains would show. That's how I saved Rs 1 lakh on raw stock and other things.'[21]

The film's heroine was Jayshree T., famous for her cabaret tracks, which always evoked wolf-whistles. According to Radhakant, 'We had worked together before and she readily agreed to do the role of a bride who becomes a *nautanki* dancer after she is abandoned by her husband. Jayshree T. [who is a Maharashtrian] was a professional and had no problems speaking Bhojpuri.'[22]

After this, Radhakant directed two more Bhojpuri films: *Saiyan Magan Pahelwani Mein* (1984) and *Birhin Janam Janam Ke* (1992), but neither of them were successful at the box-office.

* * *

Successful in equal measure as producer and director is Mohanji Prasad. He was born in Ribilganj in Bihar's Chhapra district, but from the age of eight, began living with the family of his mother's brother, Bishwanath Prasad Shahabadi, in Giridih.[23] Shahabadi, who later produced *Ganga Maiya Tohe*

Piyari Chadhaibo, brought Prasad into the film business. 'He opened a distribution centre in Benares and I used to look after it,' he recalls.[24] The two split up following some differences. Then Prasad wrote the story of *Gangadham* (1980), which was a box-office success, and this was followed by the flop, *Geet Ganga Ke*.

Prasad's Bhojpuri film career took of with the silver jubilee hit, *Hamaar Bhauji* (1983), which he produced. 'The film was based on the famous south Indian production house AVM's *Bhabhi* (1957) and it did well. There were no Bhojpuri-speaking actors in the film, but the language was not a problem because Bhojpuri is just like Hindi,' says Prasad.[25]

Over the next couple of decades, he wrote, produced and directed several good, bad and indifferent Hindi films. His first Bhojpuri film as a director, *Saiyan Hamaar* (2002) was a modest success. The film was also Ravi Kishan's first film as a Bhojpuri hero. Prasad says about Ravi Kishan, 'Character actor Brijesh Tripathi introduced him to me. I liked him immediately.'[26]

As has been mentioned earlier, *Panditji Bataeen Na Biyah Kab Hoee* (2005), written and directed by Prasad turned out to be a blockbuster. Though evasive about why Manoj Tiwari and he parted ways,[27] Mohanji is more forthcoming when explaining the film's success: 'It was like a commercial south Indian film. It had plenty of fast action and didn't allow the audience to think.' [28]

The director feels that Bhojpuri cinema is too influenced by Hindi movies at the moment and laments the genre's increasing vulgarity. He believes that only the audience has the power to rein in such tendencies. 'They are the ring masters,' he says.[29]

* * *

Another director whose name is assured in the history of Bhojpuri films is Ajay Sinha. He will always be credited as the director—and co-producer—of *Sasura Bada Paisewala,* the superhit that turned the fortunes of an ailing Bhojpuri film industry.

The son of a small businessman in Patna, Sinha is a science graduate from Magadh University who always wanted to be an actor. Sinha's early career in Mumbai included small roles in serials and movies such as *Arjun Pandit* and *Bichchoo.* 'I had a decent role in *Hum Panchchi Ek Daal Ke* (2000), alongside Sunil Shetty, but the movie flopped,' he says.[30]

This was followed by a phase during which he made telefilms for Zee TV. His first foray into Bhojpuri films as a producer ended disappointingly when *Sajna ke Angna* (2002), made for Rs 13 lakhs, failed to make profits.

Sinha's life changed with the stupendous success of *Sasura Bada Paisewala.* His subsequent films, *Dulhaniya Naach Nachaye* (2005) and *Kasam Dharti Maiya Ki* (2007) failed to create the same magic. However, his latest film, *Chalni ke Chalal Dulha* (2009), starring Pravesh Lal Yadav, Nirahua's younger brother, has fared better.

* * *

Aslam Sheikh is an A-list director in Bhojpuri cinema's current phase. His films include *Bandhan Toote Na* (2005), *Balma 420* (2006), *Dharti Kahe Pukaar Ke* (2006, in which he directed Bollywood star Ajay Devgan), *Pyaar Ke Bandhan* (2006), *Janam Janam Ke Saath* (2007), *Pappu Ke Pyaar Ho Gayeel* (2007), *Dharam Veer* (2008) and *Bidai* (2008). For the last film, he also got the 2008 Bhojpuri Film Award for best director and best story.

Born in 1961, Sheikh grew up in Mumbai's Ghatkopar area where his father ran a dry cleaning business. 'But my family roots go back to Azamgarh district in eastern Uttar Pradesh. My *sasural* [wife's natal family] and my relatives live there,' he says.[31]

Sheikh had first joined an automobile engineering course, but was more interested in the engineering institute's dramatic society, of which he was the secretary. An abiding love for theatre also fuelled Sheikh's interest in the movies. He joined director Prem Singh, known for *Bairi Saawan* (1984), as an assistant. His break as a full-fledged director came at the young age of twenty-four when he was asked by producers R.B. Sharma and Mohammed Aslam to direct *Paijaniya* (1986)—that was the time of low-budget social dramas. Aslam says, 'The film was completed in about Rs 8 or 9 lakhs. I got just Rs 21,000 for my work, but even top Bhojpuri heroes like Sujit Kumar weren't paid much then.'[32]

In the 1990s, Sheikh worked hard to establish himself in the film industry. He made two more Bhojpuri films, *Patoh Bitiya* (1989) and *Hamaar Sajna* (1994). With the films being shown only in morning shows in Mumbai and shot on 16mm, money was in short supply.[33]

Eventually, Sheikh hit bull's eye in the post-*Sasura* boom, delivering hits such as *Bandhan Toote Na* (2005) and *Bidai* (2008). Now, sometimes, the budgets for his films go as high as Rs 1.5 crore. He also directed the multi-starrer *Janam Janam Ke Saath*, shot partly in Mauritius.

The buzz is that Sheikh charges anything between Rs 7 and 10 lakhs for directing a film these days. 'But,' as Aslam says, 'there is always room for a concession for friends or for people I know.'[34] He is smart enough to recognize that the Bhojpuri film industry flourished after a majority of Hindi film producers began targeting the overseas market and making multiplex films. 'The Bhojpuri film industry might go through ups and downs but as long as single-screen theatres remain, these films will live,' he says.[35]

* * *

Anand D. Ghatraj, a commerce graduate from Calcutta, is director of *Kab Hoi Gawna Hamaar* (2005), *Kab Kahbu Tu I Love You* (2007), *Ee Rishta Anmol Ba* (2008) and *Tu Babua Hamaar* (2008).

Kab Hoi Gawna Hamaar received the national award for best Bhojpuri film in 2005. 'I didn't know the language, but during my college days, I had plenty of friends from Bhojpur, Balia, Chhapra and Siwan. Before doing my first film, I started researching *gawna pratha*. That's when I began learning the language,' he says. [36]

The film's shooting took him to Mauritius. Ghatraj recalls, 'We met plenty of Bhojpuri-speaking people there. We saw a ghat called Ganga *talab* [lake], a beautiful Shiv *mandir* [temple] and an auditorium named after Indira Gandhi there. I felt I was in India!'[37]

* * *

One of the most talented personalities in Bhojpuri films these days is choreographer, actor and director Bali. Swarthy and stylish, the actor is a very good dancer too. Anybody who has seen him gyrate to the tracks *Gamchha bichhai ke* (in *Sasura Bada Paisewala*) and *Chhodi ke aankh mein ajab nasha ba* (*Dhartiputra*) would agree with this. His roles in *Sasura Bada Paisewala*, *Dehati Babu*, *Chacha Bhatija* and *Daroga Babu I Love You* have also been appreciated. Many fans fondly refer to him as Chhedi, one of his popular on-screen characters. But Bali has really made his name as director through films like *Daroga Babu I Love You*, *Dehati Babu*, *Dhartiputra*, *Chacha Bhatija* and *Kahan Jaiba Raja Najariya Ladaike*.

In June 2009, Bali was seriously injured in an accident in Surat, where he had gone to celebrate the release of *Munnibai Nautankiwali*, his first film as a lead actor. He slipped when jumping from a diving board and was seriously injured on his head and neck. [38]

* * *

Director Braj Bhooshan specializes in making family audience friendly, low-budget Bhojpuri social dramas. In Bhooshan's words, 'A film should be aesthetically appealing. I don't believe in filling up a film with double-entendre dialogues. It is my social responsibility to make decent films. I have concentrated on making films which the Bhojpuri-speaking audience can identify with.'[39]

Known for giving breaks to newcomers, Braj Bhooshan does not believe in the star system and has introduced actors such as Pratibha Pandey and Gunjan Kapoor. Urvashi Dholakia, who is famous as the vamp in a Hindi television serial was awarded for her performance in *Saas Rani Bahu Naukrani* (2007).

After having earned a diploma in film editing from Chennai in 1977, Braj Bhooshan assisted well-known editor Waman Guru in films like *Ghar* (1978) and *Kitaab* (1977). Then he assisted Gulzar on *Angoor* (1982). His first Hindi movie as a director was *Insaaf Ki Manzil* (1988) with Shekhar Suman in the lead and Chitragupta as the music director. Before he came into his own in Bhojpuri films, Braj Bhooshan had also made several notable documentaries such as *Mehnat Aur*

Manzil and television serials such as *Nanha Jasoos* and *Bostaan Ki Kahaniyan*.[40]

His first Bhojpuri film was *Piya Ke Ghar Pyaara Lage* (2003), a family drama centred around two brothers. Made on a frugal budget of Rs 22 lakh, the film was shot in Bihar's Maharajganj area and filming was completed in three months. 'It managed to gain business amounting to triple the investment,' he says.[41]

Ganga Ke Paar Saiyan Hamaar, based on the tried and trusted lost-and-found theme, ran for sixteen weeks, while *Ganga Mile Saagar Se*, an award-winning film made for Rs 45 lakh, was on the inevitabilty of fate.

His other films are *Hamra Se Biyah Karba* (2006), *Phoolva Se Mahke Angna Hamaar* (2007), *Saas Rani Bahu Naukrani (2007)*, *Saajan Sang Laagi Laganiya Re* (2008) and *Saiyan Anadi Ba Hamaar* (2008).

The director recalls an interesting incident that occurred during the filming of *Hamra Se Biyah Karba*, whose producer Sridhar Shetty was from Karnataka. "We were shooting in a village in Uttar Pradesh's Balia district. The village was dominated by two castes: Bhumihar and Rajput. One of them was against the shooting, the other was determined that the film be shot at any cost. Handling the two contrary standpoints was a sensitive and delicate task that I had to carry out," he recalls.[42]

Braj Bhooshan believes that a director also has a certain economic responsibility: 'The tickets in the single-screen theatres in the interior areas are priced at Rs 12, 15 and 18; so how can one make big-budget films? That's why I don't want my films to be too expensive. I don't charge more than Rs 4 lakhs, though I know top directors ask for double that amount.'[43]

* * *

K.D. (Dinkar Kapoor), the director of blockbuster *Nirahua Rickshawala*, was born in a small qasbah in western Uttar Pradesh called Muradnagar. He grew up in Mumbai where his father produced and directed several low-budget Bollywood films that flopped—*Jhoom Utha Akash* (1973), *Teen Chehre* (1979) and *Gumnaam Hai Koi* (1983).

As a child, Dinkar grew up watching his father in action on the sets. He began his career assisting director duo Abbas-Mustaan in films like *Khiladi* (1992), *Baazigar* (1993) and *Daraar* (1996) before he directed the Hindi film, *Yeh Kaisi Mohabbat* (2002).

Nirahua Rickshawala, the blockbuster of 2007, was his first Bhojpuri film. 'I am a quality-conscious person. I know that in these times of thousands of Hindi television serials, you must make a decent regional film to attract the audience. But I had no idea it would become such a roaring success,' says Kapoor, who understands the language, but cannot speak Bhojpuri.[44] Since then, he has made *Shreeman Driver Babu* (2007), *Munna Bajrangi* (2008), *Dulha Albela* (2008) and *Hum Hai Khalnayak* (2009).[45]

* * *

Given the sheer number of Bhojpuri films being made in the past three decades, several other directors deserve an honourable mention.

Rajpati (*Mai K Lal, Ganga Ghat, Sampoorna Teerth Yatra, Ganga Ke Teere Teere, Palkan Ke Mehman*), Tejesh Akhauri (*Aangan Ki Lakshmi, Bahuriya* and *Gawna*), Lalji Yadav (*Sonwa Ke Pinjra, Saiyan Bina Ghar Soona, Birha Ke Raat, Guru Dakhshina, Saiyan Bedardi, Hamaar Goriya*), Prem Singh (*Piya Nirmohiya, Bairi Saawan, Piya Ke Pyaari, Ganga Maiya Kar Da Milanwa Hamaar, Bhaile Piya Guleri Ke Phool,*

Mai Tohre Khatir, Des Mein Lautal Pardesi), Jagdish Singh
(*Piya Nirmohiya, Ganga Aur Gouri, Ganga Maiya Bhar Da
Godiya Hamaar, Neha Lagauni Saiyan Se*), Nihal Singh (*Bairi
Kangna, Saat Phere, Suhagin, Senura Ke Laaj, Toote Na
Sanehiya Hamaar*), K. Vinod (*Piya Rakhiha Senurva Ke Laaj,
Piya Bin Nahi Chain*), Dipankar and Diwakar Bose (*Humke
Maafi Dei Da, Jaane Tohara Hirday Hamre Jiyara Ke Haal,
Raghupati Raghav Raja Ra*).

In the ongoing third phase, some well-known directors
are Jagdish Sharma (*Uthaile Ghoongta Chand Dekh Le,
Devaa*), Harry Fernandes (*Bhojpuriya Bhaiya*), Jai Prakash
(*Pandav, Tu Hamaar Haoo*), Rajkumar Pandey (*UP Bihar
Bambai Express, Kangna Khanke Piya Ke Angna*), Abhishek
Chadha (*Ganga*) and Babloo Soni (*Banke Bihari MLA*).

An emotional drama, *Bandhan Toote Na* (2005)
was a superhit.

Amitabh Bachchan played an important role in
Ganga (2006).

Shreeman Driver Babu (2007).

Ravi Kishan won a best actor award for
Pandit (2006).

Parts of *Balma 420* (2006)
were shot in London.

Well-known Bollywood heroine Bhagyashree acted in
Uthaile Ghungta Chand Dekh Le (2006).

संयोगिता फिल्म्स
प्रस्तुत

आलोक कुमार कृत

होगईल बा प्यार ओढ़निया वाली से

Dinesh Lal Yadav 'Nirahua' and Sunil Chhaila 'Bihari' starred in
Ho Gayeel Ba Pyaar Odhaniya Wali Se (2006).

अंक मीडिया आर्टस प्रा. लि. कृत

"निरहुआ"
रिक्शावाला
NIRAHUA RIKSHAWALA

निर्माता : अशोक के. कोटवानी, निर्देशक : के. डी.
संगीत : राजेश-रजनीश, गीत : श्याम देहाती
कलाकार : दिनेश लाल यादव 'निरहुआ', पाखी,
विजयलाल यादव 'बिरहा सम्राट' व अन्य

Nirahua Rickshawala was the biggest box-office success of 2007.

Nautanki (2007)
had plenty of songs and dances.

Pandav (2007) is a take-off on the Bollywood hit, *Hum Paanch*.

Tu Hamaar Haoo (2007)
is based on the Bollywood hit, *Darr*.

Naag Nagin (2008)
was a rare Bhojpuri film on a supernatural theme.

Nirahua Chalal Sasural (2008)
is another superhit film in the Nirahua series.

Anand Mandir in Benares showing
Nirahua Chalal Sasural.

Dalit Bhojpuri film writer, Birendra Paswan.

Veteran Bhojpuri film journalist, Munnu Prasad Pandey.

Mohanji Prasad

Bhojpuri film heroine Rani Chatterjee.

II

The Heroines

Contemporary Bhojpuri films are quite male star-centric, but in the 1960s, it was a different story. There was a marked preference for social dramas and several films revolved around female protagonists. To some extent, the trend continued even in the 1980s. Two heroines who ruled the first phase of Bhojpuri films were Kumkum and Naaz. Scripts were often written around their characters and to their credit, they often proved equal to the task.

* * *

Kumkum added great value to the movies she acted in. In *Laagi Nahin Chhute Ram*, she got higher billing than the hero Ashim Kumar, which is an indication of her star power. Kumkum's real name is Zeba Khan, and in her words, 'I was born in Hussainabad in Bihar. I began learning kathak from the late *kathak samrat*, Shree Shambhu Maharajji when I was only nine years old. After learning kathak, I wanted to pursue my career in the film industry for which I went to Mumbai.'[1]

It was not easy to break into Hindi films, but Kumkum, who spent a part of her early life in Benares, finally got her chance as a dancer in *Sheesha* (1952). This was followed by several other films. Says Kumkum, 'One day, to my surprise, I had a visitor at my house. He was a close associate of Guru Dutt sahib and had come with an offer for me to do a song sequence for *Aar Paar* [1954].' The song was *Kabhi aar kabhi paar, laga teer-e-nazar*. She adds, 'The song became so popular that I was flooded with offers from different producers and directors. My career took off from there.'[2]

But the success of *Ganga Maiya Tohe Piyari Chadhaibo* (1962) opened another door for her—regional cinema. The character she played in the film had three different aspects: a village girl who becomes a wife, a widow, and a nautch girl who faces many obstacles in her efforts to win her self-respect back.[3] Kumkum's performance was one of the film's highlights and contributed in no small measure to its success.

Over the next few years, Kumkum acted in a string of Bhojpuri films in author-backed roles—*Laagi Nahin Chhute Ram, Balma Bada Nadaan, Naihar Chhutal Jaiye, Ganga* and *Bhauji*.

In her home production *Ganga*, she played the role of a simple village girl who is strong and brave enough to face the world to support her family. She said in an interview, 'In *Bhauji*, I played the role of a mother who gives away her only child to her sister-in-law who has just lost her own child. *Ganga Maiya Tohe Piyari Chadhaibo, Ganga* and *Bhauji* were all shot in different locations in Bihar. Shooting for these films would bring back many childhood memories.'[4]

Kumkum, whose career includes well-known Hindi movies such as *Son of India, Ganga Ki Lehren* and *Geet*, gave up films after marriage. She justifies her move and says, 'I have been offered several roles in Bhojpuri and Hindi movies. But I am not taking them up because I am happily married.'[5]

* * *

Once famous as Baby Naaz in Hindi films, actress Naaz even got a special mention in Cannes for her performance as a child actor in *Boot Polish* (1955). Naaz, whose real name was Salma Baig, became a sought-after Bhojpuri star after her stellar performance in *Bidesiya* (1963). In the 1960s, she also played the leading lady in many Bhojpuri films such as *Saiyan Se Neha Lagaiba*, *Ayeel Basant Bahar* and *Solaho Singaar Kare Dulhaniya*.

Later, she switched to character roles. In 1980, she acted in the flop, *Baaje Shehnai Hamaar Anganaa*. Then, in 1983, she reintroduced herself to a new generation of viewers in the diamond jubilee hit, *Ganga Kinare Mora Gaon*. Playing a woman who ages from a young woman to a grey-haired mother, Naaz effortlessly tapped the emotions of her audience.

While shooting for the film in the rural outskirts of Benares, she said that by doing the role of a mother of two sons, she wanted to erase the image of Baby Naaz from the audience's mind. She had once famously said, 'I enjoy working more in Bhojpuri films because there is no star system in regional films.'[6]

Having acted in Bhojpuri films for a long time, she always empathized with the regional film industry: 'If financiers do not hesitate in investing in Bhojpuri films and if the government makes regional films tax free, then the future of Bhojpuri films would be bright. The Bhojpuri language can be kept alive through films. Every film is a living document of Bhojpuri literature.'[7]

Naaz worked with leading directors in outstanding Hindi films. These included K.A. Abbas' *Munna* (1954), Hrishikesh Mukherjee's *Musafir* (1957) and the Nargis-Balraj Sahni starrer, *Lajwanti* (1958). She died of cancer at the age of fifty-three in 1995.[8]

* * *

Younger film lovers will remember Lily Chakraborty (also spelt as Lily Chakrawarty) for her picture-perfect portrayal of the widowed aunt in Rituparno Ghosh's *Chokher Bali* (2002). But four decades back, this well-known theatre and film actress from Calcutta played the leading lady in *Hamaar Sansar* (1965). Lily performed admirably in the role of Sugiya, a poor widow's only daughter.

Lily was born in Dhaka, but grew up in Madhya Pradesh's Chhindwara district. 'I spoke Hindi quite well. But when Nazir Hussain came to my home in Calcutta with an offer to act in a Bhojpuri film, I was a little unsure because I had not spoken the language before. But I took it up as a challenge. I also wanted to do films in different languages,' she says.[9]

She says about the shoot of the film: 'We shot part of the film in Mumbai's Mohan Studio. There was some outdoor shooting too. Hussain was a very encouraging producer. He would speak out the dialogue and I would repeat it.'[10]

Hamaar Sansar turned out to be the only Bhojpuri film she acted in since her other film in the regional language, *Gori Chali Naiharwa* with Ashim Kumar, was never completed. She says, 'The film's director was Shakti Chatterjee. We had shot several reels in Begusarai and Sasaram. I remember shooting a scene at a railway station. In fact, the producer had spent a lot of money.'[11]

* * *

They too served

The other leading ladies of the first phase of Bhojpuri cinema were Preetibala (*Naag Panchami*), Saeeda Khan (*Saiyan Se Bhaile Milanwa*), Anita Guha (*Solaho Singaar Kare Dulhiniya*), Vijaya Chowdhury (*Loha Singh*) and Amita (*Mitwa*), the stunning heroine of Bollywood hits such as *Tum Sa Nahi*

Dekha (1957) and *Goonj Uthi Shehnai* (1959). Mumtaz too acted in a Bhojpuri film: *Vidhana Naach Nachawe*.

* * *

No heroine was as successful as Padma Khanna in the second phase of Bhojpuri films—she not only excelled as a heroine, but also became the second woman director of the genre with *Hey Tulsi Maiya* (1992) after Arti Bhattacharya's *Dagabaaz Balma* (1988).

She made her Bhojpuri debut as 'Kumari Padma' (according to the film's credits) in *Ganga Maiya Tohe Piyari Chadhaibo* (1962) in a supporting role. In *Bidesiya* (1963), she again played a character role, but showed remarkable maturity as an actress. As an ornament-laden, straight-talking and domineering wife of an aging lascivious villain, Padma made subtle shades of grey in her character come alive. Her negative act as the younger daughter-in-law in *Hamaar Sansar* was again spot on.

During the low years of Bhojpuri films, Padma became popular playing dancers and vamps in Hindi films. But she also excelled in character roles in *Saudagar* (1973) and *Us Paar* (1974), probably the finest flop directed by Basu Chatterjee.

Bhojpuri films gave her the opportunity to become a major actress and Padma came into her own after *Balam Pardesia*'s super success in 1979. Interestingly, Mumtaz Hussain recalls his father giving heroine Padma long blouses to wear. At a time when the Hindi film industry was eager to see her perform cabaret dances or play the vamp in hotpants, the veteran actor-producer's vision helped her develop a more conservative image and emerge as a top actress in the regional genre.

Her pairing with Sujit Kumar and Rakesh Pandey always drew the crowds. But Padma also had films written around the characters she played. *Dharti Maiya* gave her the most expansive role of her acting career. She also had roles in *Mai* and *Thakuraeen*, which were specially written for her. In *Champa Chameli* (1987), she played a double role. In fact, in several films, Padma stole the show from the hero. In *Sajai Da Maang Hamaar* (1983), she glows throughout the film even as hero Sujit Kumar looks over the hill.

In a sense, Padma Khanna successfully built a career across Hindi and Bhojpuri films. She says, 'Both Hindi and Bhojpuri films are important to me in different ways. I remain grounded in both cases.'[12] After marrying producer Jagdish Sadanah, Padma Khanna shifted to the USA where she runs a dance academy.

* * *

Prema Narayan, the beauty queen, acted in several Hindi films as a heroine, including in Mahesh Bhatt's debut film, *Manzilein Aur Bhi Hain* (1974), but she made a name for herself as a supporting actress in *Amanush* (1975), *Ghar* (1978), *Umrao Jaan* (1981) and *Mangalsutra* (1981). She became a familiar face for Bhojpuri film lovers after playing a spunky village girl who never shies away from a verbal duel in the box-office smash *Dangal* (1977).

Prema Narayan, who was a convent school teacher before winning a beauty contest, played the heroine in several other Bhojpuri films such as *Mai K Lal* and S.N. Tripathi's *Jaagal Bhag Hamaar*, where she enacted the role of a knife-throwing *madaran* (street performer). Her other films include *Ganga Ghat*, *Sonva Ke Pinjra* and *Bansuriya Baaje Ganga Teer*.

* * *

Gouri Khurana started her career as a Bollywood child artiste, but went on to have a fairly decent run in Bhojpuri films. In 1970, every kid was singing the popular *Hai na, bolo bolo* from the Shammi Kapoor-Hema Malini hit *Andaaz* (1971) in which Khurana had acted. As a teenager, Gouri also acted in several Hindi films—as Rajesh Khanna's younger sister in *Thodi Se Bewafaai* (1980) and with Jeetendra in *Judaai* (1980).

In danger of getting typecast as a sister in Bollywood, she found herself playing more substantial parts in Bhojpuri films where she soon became a major star. Khurana made her mark in effervescent, chirpy parts. In *Dharti Maiya*, she excelled as a garrulous *banjaran* (gypsy girl) who wanders from one village to another with her cow. In *Ganga Kinare Mora Gaon*, she again played the role of a gregarious girl who falls for the shy hero. This pleasantly plump heroine formed a highly successful pair with Kunal Singh in movies like *Ganga Kinare Mora Gaon* and *Dulha Ganga Paar Ke*.

* * *

Fair-skinned, slim and gifted with a winsome smile, Meera Madhuri was the queen of tear-jerkers. Known as the Meena Kumari of Bhojpuri films, this girl from Darjeeling acted in some successful social dramas like *Naihar Ki Chunri, Piya Ke Gaon, Ram Jaisan Bhaiya Hamaar* and many more. In *Piya Ke Gaon*, she convincingly played a simple girl whose life changes dramatically when her soldier husband is given up for dead. However, she faded from the scene after her marriage.

* * *

Another heroine who was popular during the 1980s was Bandini Mishra. Born in 1962 in Uttar Pradesh's Sultanpur district, Bandini Mishra grew up in suburban Mumbai. An army man's daughter, she learnt kathak at an early age. After doing bit roles in Hindi films such as *Noorie* (1979) and *Payal Ki Jhankar* (1980), she gained a heroine's part in the Bhojpuri *Paan Khaye Saiyan Hamaar* (1984).

Shooting in the hinterland of Bihar was always exciting, says Mishra. She recalls an incident while filming *Ghar Grihasti* (1986), near Arrah: 'It was early in the morning and I was getting ready for the shoot of the song, *Jeth mahinwa ke bhari dopahariya* [In the afternoon of the Jeth month]. I saw a man outside my tent with a gun slung across his shoulder. He told me that he was carrying it to shoot birds. Later, while we were filming the number near a canal in the afternoon, we heard gunshots. I learnt later that there was a gunfight between two thakurs and that the man outside my tent was one of those shooting! We immediately packed up and the rest of the song was shot in another village.'[13]

Mishra also refers to a similar incident during the shoot of the famous song *Saikilia pe hoke sawar* ('Riding on the bicycle') for *Ganga Maiya Tohar Kiriya*: 'We were shooting in a field near Patna when a couple of guys asked us to stop shooting. We tried to reason with them, but they would not listen to us. We had no option but to leave. The song was shot later in Kolhapur.'[14] Mishra now plays character roles in Bhojpuri films.

* * *

Seema Vaz, who played the leading lady in films such as *Paijaniya* (1986), *Lagal Chunri Mein Daag* (1988) and *Patoh Bitiya* (1989) is a Goan Christian. Born and brought up in Mumbai, Vaz readily accepted the role of a village girl who ends up being a *kothewali* (brothel-keeper) in *Paijaniya*. 'I had no problems speaking Bhojpuri,' she says.[15] Vaz, who later acted in a number of Bollywood horror films such as *Khooni Panja* (1991) and *Aakhri Cheekh* (1991), says heroines were paid very little in those days. According to Vaz, 'I got around Rs 40,000. The films used to be completed in one schedule.'[16]

* * *

Abha Dhulia, the actress who performed in Hindi off-beat films like *Paheli* (1977) and *Chameli Memsaab* (1981), also acted in a Bhojpuri film: *Baaje Shehnaai Hamaar Anganaa*. Dhulia, whose family is from Uttarakhand's Garhwal region, grew up in eastern Uttar Pradesh's Gorakhpur town. She recalls the reactions of locals to actresses those days: 'During the shoot, we stayed in a village near Patna. A woman radio journalist accompanied me for safety reasons. The village women never came out. They would stare at us from the *jharokha*s [balconies]. No village woman interacted with us during the shooting. For them, we were *nati*s [female performers]. Our presence was a culture shock for them.'[17]

* * *

A Bollywood dancer and character actress, Jaishree T. showed her mettle as a heroine in several Bhojpuri films. Some of her films are *Bitiya Bhayeel Sayaan* (1982), *Hamaar Bhauji* (1983) and *Saiyan Magan Pahelwani Mein* (1984). In the 1980s, most distributors wanted a Jaishree T. dance number in the film and sometimes, a song would even be added on special demand from them! In some posters, the photographs of the hero and the heroine were smaller than those of Jaishree T. 'Producers and dance directors liked me because I picked up the moves very fast. There were hardly any retakes. They used to call me *bijli* [lightning],' she says.[18]

At times, the very presence of Jaishree T. could excite crowds during the shooting. According to her, 'On several occasions, crowd control was a problem. Once in Chhapra, there was a knife fight and we had to call the police.'[19] Even now her association with Bhojpuri films continues as a senior character actress in films such as *Hamaar Izzat* (2007).

* * *

Several heroines who failed to make it big in Hindi films also tried their luck in Bhojpuri films. For instance, Rajni Sharma of *Balika Badhu* (1976) fame was the leading lady in *Bairi Saawan* and *Sohag Bindiya* (1986).

Kumud Chhugani, who acted in Hindi films such as *Poonam Ki Raat* (1965) and *Vaasna* (1968), was the heroine in *Saiyan Tohre Karan* (1981).

Well-known item girl of the 1980s, Kalpana Iyer, also acted in a Bhojpuri film titled *Senurwa Bhayeel Mohal* (1986). Even Hindi film star Rekha put in a guest appearance in *Paan Khaye Saiyan Hamaar* (1984).

Some other Bollywood actresses also made special appearances in Bhojpuri cinema. Anita Raj performed an item number in *Bihari Babu* produced by Shatrughan Sinha to a song that starts with the line, *Kalkatta se Bambai tak hum lootli kitna baar, ab ta lootle aayeel bani UP aur Bihar* ('I have robbed Calcutta and Mumbai many times, now I have come to loot Bihar and UP'); Tina Munim did a painful mujra (*Ik ta chadhal jawaniya*) in the same film; and Kimi Katkar danced to a song in *Sajanwa Bairi Bhaile Hamaar* (1987).

* * *

The third wave of Bhojpuri films saw the emergence of a new set of heroines: Rani Chatterjee, Nagma, Rambha, Rinku Ghosh, Pakhi Hegde, Divya Desai, Monalisa, Chandni Chopra, Shweta Tiwari, Gunjan Kapoor, Maansi, Sweety Chhabra, Sadhika Randhawa, Pratibha Pandey, Arti Patel, Divya Dwivedi, Mona Thiba and many more.

Bollywood heroines such as Hrishita Bhatt, Suman Ranganathan, Priya Gill, Bhagyashree, Bhumika Chawla and Hema Malini have also acted in Bhojpuri films.

The former Jammu beauty queen, Anara Gupta, who was falsely accused in a porn racket, did well for herself with *Vidhaata* (2008) and *Rang De Basanti Chola* (2008). 'I want to play a long innings in Bhojpuri films,' she says.[20]

* * *

Among those who have played a fairly long innings in Bhojpuri cinema is Rani Chatterjee. Born in Thane, Maharashtra, as Sabiha Sheikh, Rani made her debut in the superhit *Sasura Bada Paisewala* (2004). She got the name Rani Chatterjee by accident: 'We were shooting a scene in a temple and the crowd asked the producer my name. He felt that there could be a problem with my original name, so he said, "Rani", the name of my character in the film.'[21] In fact, the film's credit only shows her name as Rani, but since there was already a Rani Mukherjee, she became Rani Chatterjee.

'None of us had even dreamt we would become stars. I just wanted to finish the film and go back to my studies. But I could never do that because after the film became a roaring hit, offers started pouring in one after another,' she says.[22]

Rani has acted in over twenty-five Bhojpuri films so far, including another big box-office success, *Bandhan Toote Na*.

As she basks in the glory, she says, 'People recognize me even in Mumbai and ask for my autographs.'[23]

Tall and certainly not size zero, Rani's innocent face is among her greatest assets. She easily fits into the roles of village women as well as city-bred girls, and performs dance numbers with a certain degree of abandon as can be seen in her *paisa vasool* dance track, *Chale thain thain more jobna pe rifle re* ('The rifle goes bang bang over my chest') in *Baklol Dulha* (2007).

* * *

Then there is Nagma, whose first film in Bhojpuri was *Panditji Bataaen Na Biyah Kab Hoee* (2005). She enjoyed the advantage of being one of the first Bollywood actresses to take the risk of acting in Bhojpuri films. When *Panditji* became a superhit, Nagma became a big star in the regional genre.

Having started out in Hindi films, Nagma had enjoyed success in Telugu and Tamil films. Forthright when asked why she started acting in Bhojpuri films, she says, 'I could not have worked in B-grade films. With the passage of time, the next best option for me was to switch over to Bhojpuri cinema, which has tremendous potential and viewership, not only in the Hindi heartland, but also abroad in places like Mauritius.'[24]

Her other well-known roles are in *Pandit* (where she plays a television journalist), *Dulha Milal Dildaar*, *Ganga*, *Raja Thakur*, *Tu Hamaar Haoo* (a Bhojpuri version of *Darr*), *Hanuman Bhakt Havaldar* and *Thela No 501* (2008). For her performance in *Dulha Milal Dildaar* (2005) and *Ganga* (2006), she also won the film best actress awards in 2006 and 2007 at the Bhojpuri Film Awards.

Nagma also increases the glamour quotient of a film. Those

who have seen *Pandit* will remember her in *Bahiyan mein bahiyan dala, akhiyan mein akhiyan dala* ('Put your hands in mine and look into my eyes'). Filmed in the style of *Kaate nahin katthte hain yeh din* from *Mr India* (1987) Nagma's performance is as sizzling as that of the 1980s Bollywood star Sridevi. Again, in *Tu Hamaar Haoo* (2007), she is credible in the role of a woman stalked by an obsessed lover.

She once said, 'I feel Hindi movies are overrated; may be because they give national and international fame. But regional cinema emphasizes tradition and culture. My Bhojpuri films always have a social message.'[25]

A well-known Congress party supporter and campaigner, Nagma was seen doing the rounds of the Congress headquarters at Delhi before the fifteenth Lok Sabha elections. She wanted a ticket from Mumbai's north-west constituency. 'I am young. I am a Mumbaikar. I have been a dedicated Congress worker for six to seven years. Mumbai's north-west is also the hub of Bhojpuri-speaking people,' she says.[26] Clearly, she is keen to enjoy the fringe benefits of acting in Bhojpuri films.

* * *

Like Nagma, Rambha has also had a successful career in Telugu and Tamil films. Which regional producer would not like to cast a heroine who has also acted opposite stars like Salman Khan and Govinda in superhit Bollywood movies? Her bathing scene in *Banke Bihari MLA* prompted plenty of wolf whistles in mofussil theatres. *Janam Janam Ke Saath, Ram Balram* and *Rasik Balma* are some of her other movies. Rambha can be both sweet and sexy at the same time and that makes her a saleable heroine in Bhojpuri films.

* * *

Svelte and spunky, the Mumbai girl Rinku Ghosh already has over a dozen films in the regional genre under her belt with *Daroga Babu I Love You* and *Bidai* being her notable successes. For *Bidai*, she also received the best actress award at the 2008 Bhojpuri Film Awards.

A naval officer's daughter, Rinku started modelling during her teenage years. But after being spotted on the sets of a Hindi film, *Tumse Milke Wrong Number* (2003), she got an offer to act in the Bhojpuri film *Sohagan Bana Da Sajna Hamaar* (2004), starring Ravi Kishan and Avinash Wadhawan.[27]

It turned out to be the most eventful decision of her career. She explains, 'It was a women-oriented subject. And I got the role of a middle-class woman who has to take care of her entire family. On the third day when I was given two pages of dialogues for a single-shot scene, I was a little nervous. But I went with the flow of my emotions and completed the scene in my first take. When I finished, there was pin-drop silence on the set. Everybody clapped. Doing that scene successfully became my biggest motivation and inspiration.'[28]

Her next film, *Daroga Babu I Love You* (2005), was a big hit. 'During the promotional tours, people started calling me *darogain* [the daroga's wife]. I am always asked to recite dialogues from the film,' she says.[29]

Since then, she has acted in a host of other Bhojpuri films such as *Hamaar Gharwali, Suhaag, Saugandh, Ankiya Ladiye Gayeel, De Da Piritiya Udhar, Lal Chunariya Wali, Pinjrewali Muniya, Sajanwa Tohre Khatir, Uga Ho Suraj Deo Arag Ke Bhail Ber, Kishan Arjun, Hum Bahubali* and *Bidai*.

Successful stints in television serials such as *Durgesh Nandini* and *Mohe Rang De* have further helped her become a well-known face. But being a sought-after heroine in the regional genre has enabled her to taste adulation.

She has had some fearful experiences too. During the shooting of *Hamaar Gharwali* in Buxar, a boy barely seventeen-years-old met her with a letter written in his blood. But rather than shooing him away, Rinku counselled him. 'I told him we were normal, regular people like him so why was he wasting his energy? He came to the shooting every day but was normal after that,' she says.[30]

Rinku also recalls visiting small qasbahs for the promotion of *Sohagan Bana Da Sajna Hamaar*. She says, 'We used to sit in the manager's cabin before being introduced to the audience. I remember an old women walking up to me, touching my hands, and telling me, '*Savitri* [the name of Rinku's character in the film], *tum kitni acchhi ho* [You are so good].'[31] Clearly, she is enjoying her fame and adds, 'Every actor dreams of being successful. Through Bhojpuri films, I got my first box-office hit. I owe my success to the industry.'[32]

* * *

Divya Desai, a Gujarati, also made her debut in the same film as Rinku. As a child, Divya wanted to be an air hostess because she was fond of travelling. But this daughter of a mechanical engineer was destined to become an actress. 'I was just a teenager and I was pretty scared giving the first shot. But everyone, especially Ravi Kishan, was very encouraging,' she recalls.[33]

Gifted with an extremely innocent face, Divya is a sensuous dancer. Anybody who has seen her dance in the track *Thoda* ('A little') in *Bambai Ke Laila Chhapra Ke Chhaila* (2006) would agree with that. Having learnt dance from Kanu Mukherjee, well-known dance director of Bhojpuri films, her confidence shows in many foot-tapping numbers. Some of her other films are *Kab Hoi Gawna Hamaar*, *Tohse Pyar Ba*, and *Pappu Ke Pyaar Ho Gayeel*. Of late, Divya has recast herself as Rashmi Desai and is doing television serials.

* * *

A Calcutta-girl, Monalisa (Antara Biswas), is another 'happening' heroine in Bhojpuri films. A graduate in Sanskrit, Monalisa started out working in the hospitality business. Following a string of jobs, including as a guest relations executive in Calcutta's Oberoi Grand, she entered films. After doing small parts in Bengali movies such as *Shatrur Mokabila* (2002) and in low-brow Bollywood flicks like *Tauba Tauba* (2004), Monalisa was called for an audition by well-known producer Sunil Boobna, who had earlier given breaks to Rinku Ghosh and Divya Desai.

Monalisa was soon chosen for *Kahan Jaiba Raja Najariya Ladaike* (2007) with Dinesh Lal Yadav 'Nirahua' playing the hero. She says that during the shooting, she actually cut her veins by accident and needed stitches to seal the wound.[34] The film did reasonably well and offers started coming in. Since then, she has acted in several Bhojpuri films including *Shreeman Driver Babu*, *Tu Babua Hamaar*, *Dulha Albela*, and more. 'I am very happy doing Bhojpuri films,' she says, 'and I hope my good run continues.'[35]

* * *

With Dinesh Lal Yadav 'Nirahua', Pakhi Hegde has formed the strongest box-office Bhojpuri pair in recent years. The two have delivered many box-office hits—*Nirahua Rickshawala*, *Kahan Jaiba Raja Najariya Ladaike*, *Nirahua Chalal Sasural* and more.

Pakhi was born and brought up in Mumbai where her family, originally from Karnataka's Udipi district, was involved in the hotel business. She lost her father at the age of ten. 'Women were homemakers in our family. But I always wanted to do something on my own,' she says.[36]

A commerce graduate, she first wanted to be a chartered accountant. But life obviously had different plans for her. Pakhi got her break in the entertainment business with the serial *Main Banoongi Miss India* (2004). 'It was about a village girl who aspires to become a beauty queen. The serial was very successful and I became a familiar face in the hinterland,' says Pakhi, who speaks Hindi, English, Bhojpuri, Marathi, Kannada and Gujarati.[37]

Her first break in Bhojpuri films was in Gyan Sahay's *Bairi Piya*. 'The story was similar to the 1960s Hindi film, *Saraswatichandra*, and my role was similar to Nutan's. It was a good film which could not get a proper release because of the untimely death of its producer,' she says.[38]

But her impressive performance attracted other producers. She did *Saiyan Se Solah Singaar* (2006), a Bhojpuri take on the Hindi film *Judaai* (1997), the Anil Kapoor-Sridevi-Urmila Matondkar hit. 'I did Urmila's role. And even a senior artiste like Nagma appreciated my performance,' she says.[39]

Then *Nirahua Rickshawala* came her way. She says, 'Many heroines had rejected the role. Even I had said no at first. But the movie went on to become a golden jubilee hit! It came at a time when Bhojpuri films had been flopping one after another, and its success stemmed the downslide.'[40]

The film's climax centres on a long dialogue by her. 'The scene is about four minutes long and I did it in one shot,' she says.[41] Indeed, her melodramatic performance in a red sari— along with the much-talked-about kissing scene—clinched the film's fortunes.

She has also travelled with Nirahua for song and dance shows to Fiji, Australia and New Zealand. 'In Fiji, in the airport, shops, everywhere, people would recognize Nirahua. That's because his songs were very popular there. Our shows were a big success. When I went there, I was just another artiste—but I came back a star,' she says.[42]

Pakhi has turned a co-producer with Nirahua in *Chalni Ke Chalal Dulha* (2009) and she says, 'We want to make clean films.'[43]

Bengali Sweets

Many Bengali actresses have acted in Bhojpuri films: Lily Chakraborty, Sabita Chatterjee, Indrani Mukherjee, Bela Bose, Rinku Ghosh, Monalisa Biswas, Indrani Banerjee, Saraswati Chatterjee, Arpita Pal (now Tollywood superstar Prosenjit's wife), Rupali Ganguly, Priyanka Moitra, Ritika Dey, Bidisha Banerjee, Madhumita Sarkar, Mahima Mukherjee, and many others. Rani Chatterjee is not a Bengali. Her real name is Sabiha Sheikh.

12

People and Places

Giving shape to the genre

Over the years, Bhojpuri cinema has produced its own stars. In places where the regional genre has influence, they are idolized and feted. There are others who have made invaluable contributions to Bhojpuri cinema, but are not known to the larger public. These people are driven by their passion for the genre and have spent a lifetime supporting and promoting it.

For sheer commitment, few individuals come close to Munnu Prasad Pandey, who has been publishing *Rambha*, a weekly Hindi film newspaper from Benares since 1964. Probably the first newspaper of its kind, the first issue of *Rambha* appeared on 15 August 1964, two years after the first Bhojpuri film was released. It sold about a thousand copies for 15 paise each. The newspaper not only published weekly gossip, but also interviews of film stars.

News on the Bhojpuri film industry always occupied prominent space in the newspaper. When going through editions from the 1960s, one finds numerous interviews of Bhojpuri film stars, synopses of films, debates on the content of Bhojpuri films—everything printed out in detail. Few publications have done more to promote the cause of Bhojpuri films than *Rambha*.

Now nearing eighty years of age, Munnu Pandey is a little hard of hearing. But with his son acting as a prompter, he starts reeling off anecdotes from the past: '*Hamaar Sansar* was first released in Bihar and didn't do well at the box-office. The film's producer Nazir Hussain came to my office and said, "*Hamaar picture ke naiyya par kara da*," roughly meaning, "Please help my film at the box-office." I organized a press conference at the Benares Lodge located on Nai Sadak. *Hamaar Sansar* was a good movie anyway, but we ensured proper publicity for the film and created a buzz around it.'[1] The film ran for twenty-five weeks at Kanhaiya Talkies in Benares—a single-screen theatre that is now a multiplex.

Pleased by the success, Nazir Hussain offered to make Munnu Pandey his public relations officer, but like any self-respecting journalist, Pandey refused. 'I told him that I had helped him only because he had made a Bhojpuri film.'[2]

Pandey also talks about Laxman Shahabadi, a well-known Bhojpuri lyricist who worked in the Bihar government's irrigation department. Shahabadi made *Dulha Ganga Paar Ke* in spite of major financial problems. 'But the film turned out to be a major box-office hit. After the success of the film, there was a long queue of financiers outside his door. Unfortunately, he did not live to enjoy the film's success. He was making *Ganga Jhoot Na Bolawe* when he passed away suddenly,' says Pandey.[3]

Undeniably, Pandey remains a treasure trove of information on Bhojpuri films. Incredibly, *Rambha* continues to be published even today, though it has lost much of its charm and clout.

* * *

In eastern Uttar Pradesh and Bihar, older people would immediately recognize Vijay Khare—one of the most successful character actors in Bhojpuri films. Known for his negative roles, Khare was born in 1947 in Bihar's Muzaffarpur district. He made his Bhojpuri film debut as a villain in *Ganga Kinare Mora Gaon* (1983) and continues to be popular. A post-graduate in psychology, he came to Mumbai in the 1970s and performed bit roles in a few Hindi films such as *Raeeszada* (1976), *Toote Khilone* (1978), *Sarkari Mehmaan* (1979) and several others. 'But I could not carve out my own identity,' says Khare.[4]

His role in *Ganga Kinare Mora Gaon* gave him the much needed recognition he was looking for. The actor says, 'Many people, including the director, did not want me to do the villain's role. But producer Ashokchand Jain backed me. Thankfully, everybody liked my performance. The film turned out to be a diamond jubilee hit.'[5]

Khare recalls an interesting anecdote from the movie: 'After filming a fight scene, I overslept the next day. Unit members kept banging on my door, but I just wouldn't wake up. Finally, they had to bring down the door.'[6] After this film, Kunal Singh, Gouri Khurana and Khare became a sound box-office package and were cast together in several films.

In a career spanning over two and half decades in Bhojpuri films, Khare singles out his roles in *Dulha Ganga Paar Ke* and *Mai* as two of the best in his career. 'I earned plenty of appreciation for the role of a simpleton in *Dulha Ganga Paar Ke*. In *Mai*, I played a crooked zamindar called Hazuri Singh. After watching the film, many people told me that the film should have been named Hazuri Singh,' the actor reminsces.[7]

Khare still features regularly in Bhojpuri movies. He has recently produced a film called *Saiyan Anari Ba Hamaar* (2008) with his son as the hero. He also plans to do a film on female infanticide called *Betwa Se Badhkar Bitiya*. The actor says that he enjoyed doing movies in the 1980s—'Those movies had the feeling and flavour of the land. These days we only mouth the dialogues in Bhojpuri.'[8]

* * *

Another well-known character actor for over two and half decades now is Dev Malhotra, whose career passed through four stages: business, sports, theatre and films. Born in 1941 to a family of Benarasi sari dealers, Malhotra is a postgraduate in sociology. 'I was also a well-known weightlifter,' he says.[9] Anybody who has seen him in real life or on screen would find no reason to contend that.

Like Khare, Malhotra made his Bhojpuri film debut with *Ganga Kinare Mora Gaon* in 1983 and quickly established himself as a top character actor. Since then, he has done over forty films. Of these, he says, 'I enjoyed my role of a Muslim in *Dulhin* and the father's role in *Naihar Ki Chunri*.'[10] He has also played negative characters in films like *Piya Ke Gaon*.

In a film career spanning over twenty-five years, Malhotra has several anecdotes to relate. One of these is, 'During the promotion of *Ganga Kinare Mora Gaon*, the crowd went wild in Balia. We were surrounded by hundreds of people. I recall carrying heroine Gouri Khurana on my shoulders and running to escape the crowd.'[11] Malhotra has also acted in dozens of Hindi films such as *Saudagar*, *Refugee* and *Ghulam-e-Mustafa*. He continues to act in Bhojpuri films.

* * *

Arti Bhattacharya became the first woman director of Bhojpuri films with *Dagabaaz Balma* (1988). She also directed *Ghar Angna* (1998) and *Kanhaiya* (2006). Arti is also the writer of *Hamaar Dulha, Bairi Kangna* and *Ram Jaisan Bhaiya Hamaar*.

Arti came to films by chance. Born in Jamshedpur, as a young girl, she performed the role of well-known Bengali film actress Sabitri Chatterjee's daughter in a Calcutta theatre production.[12] Impressed by her performance, a well-wisher recommended her to eminent director Mrinal Sen for his Hindi film, *Ek Adhuri Kahani* (1972), which was shot in Bihta, near Patna. She also acted in Satyajit Ray's Bengali film *Jana Aranya* (The Middleman, 1976) and starred with actor Uttam Kumar in the Bengali box-office hits *Stree* and *Aami Shey O Shakha*.

Arti was the heroine of the Hindi film, *Kal Hamara Hai*, in which Kunal, whom she would later marry, played the hero. She also wrote and directed the Bollywood flick *Mashooka* (1987) starring Kunal Kapoor, Zarina Wahab, Arun Govil, Moon Moon Sen and Amjad Khan. 'Due to the vagaries of the star system, making the movie was a bitter experience for me,' says Arti.[13] The harrowing experience forced her to look towards Bhojpuri films where Kunal had become a top star. That is when she directed *Dagabaaz Balma*, which turned out to be a success.

During the film's shoot in Kunal's native village Maner, Arti often wore a pair of jeans. A bahu (daughter-in-law) in jeans was a rare sight in an area where patriarchy still reigned and where the best place for a married woman was supposed to be in the courtyard. 'But I never faced any problem because my in-laws and Kunal backed me,' she says.[14]

There was once a minor incident though. During the film's shooting, she had shouted at a group of people who were intruding into the frame. One of them, an elderly relative, complained to Kunal's grandfather. 'Why did you scold him?'

she was asked, but she replied boldly, 'It is part of my job to control the crowd.' The matter ended there.[15]

* * *

The family of Alok Dubey of Benares's Anand Mandir cinema hall, which screens only Bhojpuri films, has been involved in the business for three generations. Alok's grandfather Ganesh Dutt Dubey was a manager for a touring cinema company in Lahore that showed movies in tents to the qasbah crowds. His father Shankar Dutt Dubey was a man of many parts—he distributed Satyajit Ray's films as well as Nazir Hussain's *Hamaar Sansar* in north India, and also wrote on Bhojpuri films.

Alok now manages Anand Mandir. He says, 'We have been showing only Bhojpuri films since 2004.'[16] Well-versed in the business, he feels that many producers have no idea what the public wants. He recounts an anecdote to illustrate his point: 'The producer of *Ganga Tohre Des Mein* told me that action is his film's USP. It was being released on the same day as the Bollywood action film *Race* that went on to be a hit. So I asked him if his film had better action scenes than *Race*. He had no answer to that.'[17]

Dubey adds, 'People making Bhojpuri films must understand that there is no point in imitating and competing with Hindi films. Bhojpuri films should have their own identity. A good Bhojpuri film must have two essential aspects: emotions and music. But the tragedy is that the financier is deciding the content of Bhojpuri films today.'[18]

* * *

Art director Anjani Tiwari has also made a mark in Bhojpuri cinema. Born in the mid-1940s in Bihar's Vaishali district, he always wanted to be in the arts. His father, a doctor, wanted him to get a decent government job, but Tiwari decided to follow his own path. After earning a diploma in fine arts from Patna College, he opened a photography studio. But in 1975, he gave it all up for a career in films in Mumbai.[19]

Tiwari started out by assisting well-known art directors Mansoor and Shanti Das, before working independently on the suspense film *Sannata* (1981) directed by the Ramsay Brothers, directors known for horror movies. He started out in Bhojpuri films with a low-budget flick *Nautanki* in the early 1980s. 'I don't remember much about the movie except that the name of its director was Debashish,' he says.[20]

Since then, he has done over seventy-five Bhojpuri movies as art director—from *Dulha Ganga Paar Ke* and *Dagabaaz Balma* in the 1980s, to the more recent *Bandhan Toote Na* and *Kab Hoi Gawna Hamaar*. Interestingly, his son Shammi made his debut as a hero in a home production titled *Shammi Bhaiya* (2006). The film, made for about Rs 40 lakhs, had good music, but failed to excite the box-office. Tiwari reasons, 'The release co-incided with the massive Bihar floods of 2007.'[21]

Tiwari says that Bhojpuri films have witnessed major technical improvements over the years. 'Earlier, much of the shooting was indoors. Now it has shifted outdoors. The budgets have gone up for art direction, so the quality of work has improved. Earlier, a producer would spend a maximum of Rs 50,000 on art direction, but now the amount is between Rs 2 to 3 lakhs. Sometimes, it goes up to Rs 5 lakhs. It helps you do better work.'[22]

* * *

Character actress Pushpa Verma is a well-known 'mother' in Bhojpuri films. 'People say I am Bhojpuri cinema's Nirupa Roy, Lalita Pawar and Leela Mishra rolled into one,' she says rather immodestly.[23] These three character actresses were the ubiquitous mothers, mothers-in-law and grandmothers in many a Hindi film between the 1960s and 80s.

Verma came into prominence after playing Meghnad's wife in the television serial *Ramayan*. Also the songwriter for *Dharamsankat* (1991) and *Najayaz* (1995), she has acted in several Hindi films such as *Maharaja* (1998) and *Kohram* (2000).

Her first Bhojpuri film was *Damadji* (2005). Since then, Pushpa has acted in at least twenty Bhojpuri films such as *Raja Thakur, Janam Janam Ke Saath* and *Uthai Le Ghoongta Chand Dekh Le*.

Her negative role as a scheming mother-in-law in *Uthai Le Ghoongta Chand Dekh Le* became her speciality. 'During a shoot in Bihar's Sitamarhi town, I heard kids shouting, "*Hare Krishna, Hare Krishna aa gayee*" [Hare Krishna has come]. I later realized they were shouting my dialogue from the film,' she recalls.[24]

A post-graduate in Hindi literature, Verma has also written lyrics for Bhojpuri films such as *Sasurari Zindabad* (2006). But she now refrains from writing songs. 'Producers come and say, "*Thoda non-veg gana chahiye, madam*" [We want sexually explicit songs, madam], but I am unable to write such lyrics,' she explains.[25]

* * *

Delhi girl Sambhavna Seth is known as the Helen of Bhojpuri films nowadays. Known for her seductive gyrations, Seth has done over twenty item numbers. The daughter of a Delhi-based property dealer, she never completed her graduation because she always wanted to be in the movies. In 2001, she acted in the Bollywood flop *Paagalpan*.

Success and adulation came her way through dance numbers in Bhojpuri films. Two of her most popular numbers are *Misir ji* from the superhit *Nirahua Rickshawala* and *Tanika lahe lahe ho* ('A little slowly, man') from *Pyaar Ke Bandhan.* 'I have also got plenty of lead role offers but I rejected them,' says Seth.[26]

Bhojpuri films have helped further her career. After working in Bhojpuri films, she appeared in *Bigg Boss 2,* a reality show that earned her national recognition. Some other films she has danced in are *Dharti Kahe Pukaar Ke, Hanuman Bhakt Havaldar* and *Kab Kahbu Tu I Love You.* Seth says, 'I don't understand the regional language. But it is close to my heart. These films have given me recognition among the common people.'[27]

* * *

Birendra Paswan, a Dalit writer of Bhojpuri films, has many bitter memories of his struggle in Mumbai. But there is one incident that he remembers clearly. A film producer asked him to wait outside his office, so Paswan, then a novice actor-writer who had just come to Mumbai, kept waiting—for more than three hours. He recalls, 'I could hear him chatting loudly and laughing. Even today his laughter echoes in my ears. He clearly had no intention of granting me an audience. After waiting for that long, I left.'[28]

Paswan was livid with rage—but he opted to harness that anger. 'I use that incident to motivate myself, to strengthen my resolve to succeed in the Mumbai film world,' he says.[29]

The thirty-five-year-old Dalit is from Bihar's Aurangabad district and is slowly finding his feet and establishing his identity. He wrote the dialogues of *Ego Chumma De Da Raja Ji* starring Manoj Tiwari and Ravi Kishan. He has also been involved with several other Bhojpuri films such as *Nautanki* (2006) as writer, and *Najariya Kahe ke Ladavla* (2003) as writer-director. The last film is loosely based on the life of an infamous henchman-politician from eastern Uttar Pradesh.

Paswan is just one in a bunch of young Dalits who are mapping out a brave new world for themselves in Bollywood and Bhojpuri films. With no connections, so essential to Bollywood, they have all struggled hard. Some of them come from places where abysmal conditions exist—where, for example it is common to wade through knee-deep water to reach home during the monsoon. But the hurdles notwithstanding, many young Dalits are determined to find a place in Hindi and Bhojpuri films.

One of them is Gopal Paswan, who started out doing small roles in films like *Shararat* (2002), the flop Abhishek Bachchan starrer, and then became the casting director for the gripping television serial, *Bahubali* (2008–09), shown on the Bhojpuri channel Mahua TV.

* * *

Rajpipla, a former princely state in southern Gujarat, is the most popular outdoor venue for Bhojpuri films. Over the years, about a hundred Bhojpuri films have been shot here. What matters for producers is that Rajpipla is relatively close to Mumbai (360 kilometres) and it offers a couple of budget hotels that are part of a palace owned by Raghubir Singh Gohil.

The hotel and palace usage rates vary according to different needs, but roughly, a unit can book eight air conditioned and twelve non-air conditioned rooms for a total payment of about

Rs 15,000 to Rs 20,000 a day. There are small outhouses too for lesser mortals like lightboys, dressers, and so on. Additionally, units are allowed to shoot on the palace premises free of charge. Ask any regional producer, that's a steal.

Spread over eight acres, the palace also has it own lawns and swimming pool. 'Units are free to set up their temporary sets. The surrounding villages offer a variety of places to shoot in: temples, hills, lakes and waterfalls,' says Gohil.[30]

He adds, 'In all, about 500 films and television serials in different languages—Hindi, Gujarati, Bengali—have been shot here. There are three waterfalls in the area—Jerwani, Junaghata, Ninai—and two rivers, Narmada and Karjan, besides two wildlife sanctuaries. The Narmada Dam is just thirty-five kilometres away and there are several beautiful temples along the banks of the two rivers. Rajpipla also boasts of two palaces for shooting.'[31]

'For a producer, Rajpipla is a charming and affordable locale,' says Sunil Prasad, who has directed four Bhojpuri films in Rajpipla.[32]

The first Hindi film to be shot here was *Rakshabandhan* (1972), a Sachin-Sarika starrer. The first Bhojpuri films were shot here in the 1980s. Director Radhakant recalls shooting in Rajpipla for *Bitiya Bhayeel Sayaan* (1982). 'Believe it or not, they allowed the entire crew to stay in the palace as well as shoot there for Rs 500 per day,' he remembers.[33]

Purists believe that Rajpipla does not duplicate the villages of eastern Uttar Pradesh or Bihar. Even the horns of the cattle have a different shape in these parts, they say. Others differ. According to director Radhakant, the rustic surroundings of Rajpipla have the same feel as eastern Uttar Pradesh and Bihar. 'The prints of the saris that women wear in that area are similar to those worn in Uttar Pradesh. Even the fields of mustard and sugarcane are similar. Besides, Gujarat is close to Mumbai. Which means we save more money,' says the veteran director.[34]

Over the past few years, Rajpipla has become a major venue for all kinds of shoots. Gohil says, 'There are times when three film or television units shoot at the same time. Sometimes we are full up. In 2009, between January and June, ten movies were filmed here.'[35]

Some of the Bhojpuri films shot in Rajpipla are *Ganga Jaisan Mai Hamaar*, *Bhojpuriya Daroga*, *Phoolva Se Mehke Angna Hamaar*, *Ab Ta Ban Ja Sajanwa Hamaar*, *Pyaar Ke Bandhan*, *Dulha Milal Dildaar*, *Bandhan Toote Na* and many more.

The shooting of these films has revitalized the local economy. 'Every film ensures employment to at least twenty-five locals. They also get catering orders,' says Srikant Jai Mahato, who has been working at the Rajvant Palace Hotel since 1994.[36] Adds Gohil, 'About hundred taxis now operate in the area.'[37]

The rush for Rajpipla has surprised everybody, including Gohil, who says, 'I didn't think the boom would last so long. But now it looks like it will continue for at least a couple of years.'[38]

* * *

The villages of Wai taluk in Maharashtra's Satara district are also preferred as locations for Bhojpuri films. About 300 kilometres south-east of Mumbai and situated on the banks of the Krishna river, the area appears in over forty Bhojpuri films. However, according to a newspaper article, 'Now villagers allege that local MNS activists try to create trouble every time a Bhojpuri film is being shot, they demand money, order the use of local actors or threaten to disrupt shooting.'[39]

PART III

THE EVOLUTION OF BHOJPURI FILM MUSIC

13

Melody to Rhythm

In most parts of rural north India, singing is a part of everyday life. Whether it is sowing, harvesting, marriages, festivals, seasons, or the birth of a child—there is a song for every occasion. Thousands of folk songs have been passed down over generations. The Bhojpuri-speaking belt has a rich repertoire of such songs, variations of which have found a place in Hindi films. Traditionally, songs have played a central role in Bhojpuri films and often have been the key to their success or failure. '*Gaana Bhojpuri filum ke jaan ba*,' says veteran Benares-based film journalist Munnu Prasad Pandey—Songs are the heart, the very life of a Bhojpuri films.[1]

The trend continues even today. However, the character of songs has altered dramatically. In the 1960s, the songs were primarily woven around melody, but now there is more rhythm and tempo. This is not to suggest that the 1960s Bhojpuri films did not have dance numbers. But those tracks were limited to the nautankis, while now, much like Hindi films, even duets are dance-driven.

From its very inception in 1962, Bhojpuri cinema attracted several talented songwriters and composers. Apart from Chitragupta and S.N. Tripathi who were regulars, several well-known Bollywood composers provided music for Bhojpuri films in those early years: Jaidev (*Naihar Chhutal Jaiye*), Hemant Kumar (*Ayeel Basant Bahar*), Ghulam Mohammed (*Saiyan Se Neha Lagaibe*), Shyam Sharma (*Hamaar Sansar*), C. Ramachandra (*Mitwa*), Iqbal Quereshi (*Kab Hoi Gawna Hamaar*) and Dattaram (*Vidhana Naach Nachaye*).

The compositions that earned both commercial success and critical acclaim were from *Ganga Maiya Tohe Piyari Chadhaibo, Laagi Nahi Chhute Ram* (both by Chitragupta) and *Bidesiya* (S.N. Tripathi). The music of these films has endured just as the songs of *Guide* or *Madhumati* are enjoyed by discerning Hindi film music lovers even today.

Not that the music from other films were insignificant. Shyam Sharma's compositions for *Hamaar Sansar* such as *Cham cham chamke ee mehnat ke moti* ('The pearls of hardwork shine brightly', singer: Manna Dey, lyrics: Shyam Sharma) and *Ka boli saiyan bataolo na jay* ('What should I say, my love', I can't even say it, singers: Talat Mehmood and Suman Kalyanpur) are excellent.

Other songs like *Jiyara kasak masak more rahe lagal, man me aake kehu chor rahe lagal* ('My heart is behaving strangely, for a thief has started living there') from *Naihar Chhutal Jaiye* and *Phulwa neeyar nar sukuwaar gagariya chhal chhal ke la* ('A woman delicate like a flower walks with a pitcher that shouldn't spill') from *Saiyan Se Neha Lagaibe*, have all the romantic naughtiness that Mohammed Rafi infused in those songs, where the hero woos the heroine by gently teasing her.

Few Bollywood composers could infuse the flavour of rural central India with as much elegance as Chitragupta, who was born in Bihar's Gopalganj district and was educated in economics and journalism. At one point of time, he used to be the highest-paid person in Bhojpuri films. Producers knew that a good score by him would improve the box-office chances of a movie far more than the presence of any director or actor. As veteran writer-director of Bhojpuri films Anirudh

Tiwari says, 'Chitragupta's music was a guarantee that the distributors would buy the film.'[2]

Every song composed by Chitragupta for *Ganga Maiya Tohe Piyari Chadhaibo* is a remarkable melody. The title track sung by sisters Lata and Usha Mangeshkar has a folksy devotional feel and is still sung by village women in festivals. Over the years, it has acquired the stature of a hymn.

Three other songs stand out in this musical feast. Two are Lata solos: *Kahe bansuriya bajaole* ('Why did you play the flute?') and *Luk chhip badra mein chamke* ('In the clouds, it plays hide and seek'). Till the 1980s, these numbers were often heard on the radio. The third is the hauntingly heart-breaking *Sonva ke pinjra mein band bhayeel hai ram chiraai ke jiyara udaas* ('Trapped in the golden cage, the bird is sorrowful'), which can easily find a place among the best songs sung by Mohammed Rafi.

Even the Suman Kalyanpur number, *Ab hum kaise chali dagariya logwa nazar lagavela* ('How can I walk on the streets people stare'), lip-synched by Helen onscreen, is a pleasing track. The lyrics by Shailendra tell the story of a child bride whose husband left home many years ago to earn a livelihood in Calcutta and never came back. Having grown up since, she pines for her husband: *Hum ta khelat rahni amma ji ki godiya, kar gayeel tabhin biyaah re bidesiya, chavre mahina kahike gayeele kalkatwa, beet gayeel barah baras re bidesiya* ('I was married off to a migrant when I was playing in my mother's lap, he went off to Calcutta saying he would be back in four months and it has been twelve years since'). Indeed, it reflects the lives of many labourers who left their homes to seek a better life elsewhere, as much a phenomenon then as it is now.

Every song written by Shailendra in *Ganga Maiya Tohe Piyari Chadhaibo* is worth exploring for its nuances. In *Kahe bansuriya bajaule*, Shailendra writes, '*Tohre bansuriya mein ginti ke chhedwa, manwa hamaar piya chalni* [sieve] *bhayeel ba'* ('Your flute has a few holes but my heart has been punctured like a *chalni'*). The metaphor is just right for the setting.

At an awards function held in April 1965 for all Bhojpuri and Magadhi films, Shailendra got the best lyricist award for *Ganga Maiya Tohe Piyari Chadhaibo*, though Pandit Rammurti Chaturvedi gave him close competition with his *Bidesiya* lyrics. The best male singer prize went to Mohammed Rafi for his rendition of *Sonva ke pinjra mein band bhayeel hai ram*.

The music and lyrics of *Laagi Nahin Chhute Ram* too endure. The score was again by Chitragupta and the lyrics were by Majrooh Sultanpuri, who knew the language as his father was a police officer who was posted in different parts of Uttar Pradesh.[3] The movie had two great duets by Talat Mehmood and Lata Mangeshkar: *Laal laal oonthwa se barse lalaiya ho ke ras choowela* ('Your red lips drip nectar') and the title track, *Ja ja re sugna ja re kahide sajanwa se* ('Hey parrot, go give my message to my lover').[4]

In the 1960s, Chitragupta also composed music for *Balma Bada Nadaan, Ganga* and *Bhauji*. A lullaby from *Bhauji, Chanda mama aare aawa, paare aawa, nadiya kinare aawa*, even topped the weekly charts of the radio countdown show, *Binaca Geet Mala*.[5]

Unfortunately, Chitragupta suffered a heart attack in 1968, which was followed by a paralytic stroke in 1974. 'One half of his body was paralysed. Though he recovered slowly, he had a problem with his memory,' says his son, Anand, who is one half of the famous composer duo Anand-Milind.[6]

Chitragupta had started his film career providing scores for C-grade stunt movies, but over the years graduated to top banners like AVM. His music in films like *Bhabhi, Main Chup Rahoongi, Kaali Topi Lal Rumaal, Oonche Log* and

Vaasna had already ensured his place in the Bollywood music pantheon.

But following health complications, a second period of struggle began for him. 'My father was fond of cars but he had to sell off his pink Plymouth. During this period we travelled by bus. He seriously thought of going back to Patna,' recalls Milind.[7]

In this situation, providing music for *Balam Pardesia* was a very emotional experience for Chitragupta and the music went on to become the key to the film's super success. 'We went to Patna after the film was released. On every street corner, the loudspeakers were blaring out songs from the movie. We saw the film in Patna's Elphinstone cinema and were amazed to see people throwing coins at the screen during the songs,' says Milind.[8] Then he adds, 'My father never looked back after that. Soon he was recording ten to fifteen songs a month.'[9]

The hero of *Balam Pardesia*, Rakesh Pandey, went for the recording of *Gorki patarki re* ('O fair, slim woman'). He recalls, 'When I first heard the tune, I thought it was a little *dheela* [loose]. But the song became a superhit and I congratulated Rafi sahib who had sung the track along with Asha Bhonsle. I told him, the film is not my hit, it's your hit.'[10]

Chitragupta's second innings was prolific: *Roos Gayeele Saiyan Hamaar, Chanwa Ke Taake Chakor, Dharti Maiya, Ganga Kinare Mora Gaon, Piya Ke Gaon, Bihari Babu, Sajanwa Bairi Bhaile Hamaar* and many more. Of them, *Dharti Maiya* and *Chanwa Ke Taake Chakor* had the most memorable music.

Actor Kunal Singh says, 'You could feel the *mitti ki khushboo* [fragrance of the earth] in Chitragupta's music. You can feel it in a song in *Dharti Maiya*—*Jaldi jaldi chala re kahara* ["Hurry up o palanquin bearer"]. Anybody could hum the tunes he composed. I was fortunate enough to sit with him in several music sessions of *Dharti Maiya*. When the director narrated a situation to him, he listened in rapt attention. He asked for details of the script and composed accordingly. With his music you never felt as if the film's narrative has been put on "pause" mode for a song.'[11]

Chitragupta was very particular about the tunes he gave for Bhojpuri films. 'He used a lot of flute and clarinet for nautanki songs and the *sarangi* for mujras. He also used the mandolin, sitar, tabla and *dholak*. My father had a strong sense of rhythm,' says son Milind.[12] Songs such as *Gaj bhar ke gujariya gazab kare ho* ('The yard-long stole is wrecking havoc') from *Chanwa Ke Taake Chakor* exemplify that.

Chitragupta was born in 1917. His elder brother, Brij Nandan Azad, was the editor of the Patna-based English newspaper, the *Indian Nation*. He also played the tabla and was an early teacher of the composer. When he was a child, Chitragupta sang patriotic songs during a rally at the Gandhi Maidan in Patna. 'He was also involved in the national movement and went to jail for a brief period. At a young age, he ran away from home to try his luck in Mumbai with Madan Sinha, who became a cameraman in Hindi films. He assisted composer S.N. Tripathi before venturing out on his own,' says Anand, his son.[13]

* * *

The only other music director who matched Chitragupta both in quantity as well as in quality, at least in the first phase of Bhojpuri films, was S.N. Tripathi. It was Tripathi, not Chitragupta, who got the best music director award for *Bidesiya* in the first Bhojpuri-Magadhi Film Awards. Contemporary journalists also praised the effective use of folk tunes in *Bidesiya*.[14]

Each of the eleven tracks in the film is a crafted with care. Manna Dey's voice—along with Mahendra Kapoor's—infuses life into *Hasi hasi panwa khiole beimanwa* ('The cheat made me chew paan casually'), one of the finest songs of his long career. The song has been beautifully picturized on an old man riding a camel and the voice seems to emerge from his weary, vagabond soul. Dey is equally good in the track *Na darbe na darbe, na darbe ram* ('Won't be afraid, O god'), which he sings along with Geeta Dutt and Koumudi Mazumdar. There is a scene in the film where hero Sujit Kumar just sings two lines—no instrument plays in the background and only Dey's uncomplicated voice can be heard. Those few seconds in the movie are touched by magic.

Bidesiya's songs include a kajri (*Ishq kare oo jiske jeb mein maal bare balmu* ['Only the well-heeled can afford to fall in love']) and a chaiti (*Bani jaihein*). The song *Dinwa ginat mori ghisli ungariya* ('My fingers have chafed counting days'), is another impressive track by Suman Kalyanpur. Only a poet like Pandit Rammurti Chaturvedi could have conjured the image of fingers getting chafed counting the days waiting for the lover. *Lei badarwa se kajarwa* ('Take the kajal from the cloud') is another beautiful track penned by Pandit Chaturvedi.

Indeed, in *Bidesiya*, the Tripathi-Chaturvedi combine raises the film's music to a level that perhaps will never be matched. In the other films that he provided scores for such as *Jekra Charanwa Mein Lagle Paranwa* (1964), *Sita Maiya* (1964, also directed by him), *Jogin* (1964), *Loha Singh* (1966) and *Jaagal Bhag Hamaar* (1980, also directed by him), he was competent without ever reaching that same sublime level.

* * *

As a lyricist and dialogue writer, Pandit Rammurti Chaturvedi is one of the finest artists Bhojpuri films has seen. He was born in Mathurapur village near Benares and was educated in Bhagalpur. His father was a lecturer and poet and even his grandfather was a poet. His talent for literature was evident at an early age—he was the editor for four years of a handwritten school magazine.[15]

Chaturvedi entered Hindi films in 1940 with *Station Master*. In all, he wrote the songs and dialogues of over a hundred films, but the Bhojpuri film that became his calling card was *Bidesiya*. Sample the lyrics: *Hasi hasi panwa khiyole beimanwa ki apna basere pardes, kori re chunariya mein dagiya lagai gayeele maari re karejwa mein thhes.*

His work for Shakti Samanta's Bhojpuri production, *Ayeel Basant Bahar*, also came in for praise. 'The film's music [by Hemant Kumar] is weak. But if the movie has become extremely popular, it is only because of its story, dialogue and lyrics. At every step you can taste the flavour of Bhojpuri and listen to its heartbeat.'[16] Chaturvedi also wrote the lyrics of *Amar Suhagin* (1978) and *Jaagal Bhag Hamaar* (1980).

* * *

Shailendra was the most prolific lyricist in the first phase of Bhojpuri films. He wrote lyrics for at least six films: *Ganga Maiya Tohe Piyari Chadhaibo, Mitwa, Naihar Chhutal Jaye, Ganga, Saiyan Se Neha Lagaibe* and *Vidhana Naach Nachave*. Even Majrooh Sultanpuri, an Urdu poet and lyricist, was the songwriter for at least three Bhojpuri films: *Laagi Nahi Chhute Ram, Bhauji* and *Hamaar Sansar*. One of his songs refer to child marriage, a common practice in the 1960s, in *Hamaar Sansar*: *Aath hi baraswa mein kaile biyahwa* ('I got married at the age of eight').

* * *

The second phase of Bhojpuri films began with *Dangal* in 1977. The compositions of Nadeem-Shravan, who were still some years away from becoming superstars of Hindi cinema music, was the film's highlight. In the following years, the duo also gave the music for *Mai K Lal* and *Ganga Ghat*. *Dangal*'s chartbuster—*Kashi hile, Patna hile, Kalkatta hile la*—sung by Manna Dey, is a take-off from a famous Bhojpuri folk song. The lyrics of a sensuous mujra number written by Kulwant Jaani and sung by Asha Bhonsle went like this: *More hotwa se nathaniya kulel kare lala, jaise nagin se sapera athkhel kare la* ('My nose ring teases my lips as the cobra plays with the snake charmer').

Then there is a funny track, again written by Kulwant Jaani—*Phoot gayeele kistmatwa*—sung on screen by comedienne Shobha Khote and well-known character actor Hari Shukla, with six children in tow. The song is reminiscent of *All line clear*, sung on screen by Johnny Walker in the Raj Kapoor-Nargis superhit *Chori Chori* (1956) where Walker parades about with his obese wife and platoon of kids.

Many successful songs of this period retain the regional flavour but a few are also bereft of identity. For instance, the popular Kishore Kumar number, *Hum ta ho gayeeni tohar ae saanwar goriya* ('I have become yours, o dark one') in *Dharti Maiya*, could easily have been a Hindi film number. But these were exceptions to the rule.

The lyrics of *Dharti Maiya* were written by Laxman Shahabadi whose songwriting revealed his knowledge of the region's traditions. In the superhit track, *Jaldi jaldi chala re kahara* ('Hurry up o palanquin bearer'), he writes, '*Chahe kahin dana mare paani piye soogwa, sanjhi ke beriya uu khojela apna khotwan, oeise hi dulhaniya ke lalke paranwa, oodi ke pahun jayee piya ke aganwa*' ('The parrot may drink water anywhere in daytime but at night comes back home. Similarly the bride [in the palanquin] wants to fly to her husband').

He wrote many other hits for films such as *Ganga Kinare Mora Gaon*. But he was also a creative composer and provided music for *Dulha Ganga Paar Ke, Ganga Jwala, Dagabaaz Balma* and *Ram Jaisan Bhaiya Hamaar* (he wrote lyrics for this film too).

Dulha Ganga Paar Ke was also produced by him. One of the tracks sung by Mahendra Kapoor and Usha Mangeshkar, *Bol bam ke naara ba, ee hey ek sahara ba,* became a hit. Shahabadi could have been a much more successful composer-lyricist but for his untimely death shortly after the film's release.

* * *

After *Qurbani*'s success with *Aap jaisa koi* ('Someone like you', 1980), it became almost mandatory to have a disco track in every Hindi film. The beat fever afflicted regional producers too, who wanted more rhythm-oriented music. Consequently, even a traditional film like *Ganga Kinare Mora Gaon* had a folk-disco track.

Actor Kunal Singh says that the disco track in *Ganga Kinare Mora Gaon* was an experiment of folk and western music. 'Chitragupta never abandoned the regional flavour of a song even when he was experimenting,' says Singh.[17]

Interestingly, *Preetam More Ganga Teere* (1985), which advertised itself as the most expensive Bhojpuri film ever made, incorporated traditional '*gaari*' (abuse) songs sung by women during weddings. One of them was, *Samdhi layein hain baaraat* ('The bridegroom's father has brought the baraat').

In the 1980s, there was a profusion of asinine and vulgar songs in Hindi films. The effect could be seen in Bhojpuri song-writing too. By the mid-1980s, Bhojpuri films were also flirting with 'double-meaning' lyrics. The low-budget hit, *Piya Ke Gaon* in 1985, was a clean family social drama but a couple of lyrics by Dr Ramnath Pathak 'Pranayi' bordered on the risqué. In one of the songs, a lovelorn woman asks for a remedy and the doctor advises her that an injection will cure her. Then she says: '*Naari tu dekhla, tu aala lagavla, upar se neeche le dekhla parakhla, tab hoon asli daradiya samajhla, suiya gada ke tu tu kitna dukhavla, hava na dactar, tu hava kasai*' ('You felt my pulse, you pressed the stethoscope, you felt my condition from top to bottom, yet you couldn't understand my pain when you inserted the injection, it hurt a lot, you are no doctor, only a butcher'). The song reminds one of the track *Saat saheliyan* in Subhash Ghai's *Vidhaata* (1982).

In the family drama *Ganga Se Nata Ba Hamaar* (1991), well-known music director Ravindra Jain not only provided the score, but also penned the lyrics for a couple of songs. In one of them he wrote, '*Kahin nimbua to kahin be anaar sajni, nimbua bechari kisi ginti mein na aaye, yeh zamana hai anaaron ka beemar sajni*' ('There is a lemon at one place and a pomegranate in other. Nobody spares a second thought for the poor lemon, this is the age where everybody is mad about pomegranates'). It is obvious the composer-lyricist is not talking about different sizes of fruit.

Such examples abound. But what was only hinted at in the 1980s has become overt nowadays. The level of bawdiness varies from one track to another. Some songs are downright lewd; others might just have a hint of coarseness. It is another matter that the song picturization often accentuates the vulgarity these days. There is little effort to present sexually-tinged numbers aesthetically.

Sasura Bada Paisewala's superhit number, *Chue lagal, chue lagal* ('It's dripping, it's dripping'), is sung by a *launda*, a man dressed as a woman. The setting is a natural one—the launda sings on a stage with a white spreadsheet acting as the backdrop, while villagers watch and dance to the tune. It is a scene anybody from the Bhojpuri-speaking belt in Bihar and Uttar Pradesh can easily identify with. But it is the catchy tune and the double-entendre lyrics that turned the song into a chartbuster. The lyrics say that palm toddy is dripping from the tree, but it is evident from the last shot of the song, when a man grips his own thigh and says, '*Ab ta chue lagal*' ('Now it is dripping'), what he really means.

Other naughty numbers in the same movie such as *Saiyan dilwa mange re, gamchcha bichhai ke* ('My lover asks for my heart by spreading out a small piece of cloth') and *Ego chumma na deba je sarkar to khetwa kaise kodhai* ('How can I plough the fields if you don't kiss me').

Sample another gem, a Holi song written by Vinay Bihari and sung by Manoj Tiwari and Anand Mohan, in *Daroga Babu I Love You*. At one level, it is about how a couple wants to celebrate the festival of colours. At another level, it is coarse sex talk. The song goes, '*Dalwaib na, dalwaib na, jab le na laibe Benares ke paan dalwaib na*' ('Won't let you put it in till you get me a paan from Benares'). At another point, the song goes, '*Aage se aai ki peechche se aai, sochi le tohra se kaise dalwain*' ('From the front or from the back, I am contemplating from where you will put it in').

Another film, *Dhartiputra*, has a brusque double-entendre track: *Kab daalin, kahwan daali, ihwan daali, uhwan daali, hum daalein ke baani taiyyar* ('When should I put it in, where, here or there, I am ready to put it in'). And then the male says, *Kab debu apan pyar* ('When will you give me your love').

Another track says '*Mamla garam ba, kahe ke saram ba, loha garam ba chala da na hathoda*' ('Everything is hot. Why are you shy? The iron is hot. Why don't you just bang the hammer?') from *Bambai Ke Laila Chhapra Ke Chhaila*.

In *Pyaar Ke Bandhan*, singer Rekha Rao croons to the lyrics by Vinay Bihari, '*Tani lahe lahe dheere dheere dala kamsin ba dukhala raja ji*' ('Put it in slowly, darling, I am very young, it hurts'), while on screen Sambhavna Seth dances to the tune and as she gyrates, a launda tries to slip bangles into her arms. That is double-entendre at its best.

Again in *Shreeman Driver Babu*, a dancer sings '*Kamaal kar gayeel ho kamaal kar gayeel, sipahiya ke danda kamaal kar gayeel*' ('It did wonders. It did wonders. The policeman's stick or baton did wonders'). As the lyrics proceed, nobody has any doubts about the identity of the joy stick that gets the girl dancing with pleasure.

Lyricist Vinay Bihari, who has written many songs with double-meanings, narrates an incident that illustrates why risqué songs have become so popular. 'I once asked a truck driver, why don't you listen to the bhajans that I have written? Why do you listen to singers such as Radheshyam Rasiya, famous for his bawdy numbers. He replied that naughty songs keep him awake or else he will fall asleep at the wheel,' recounts Bihari.[18]

Producers and directors justify such presentations as compulsions of market economics. It is a case of demand and supply, they say. Director Aslam Sheikh says, 'Nautankis are part our culture. And people must be entertained. But sometimes producers go overboard in stuffing their films with risqué numbers.'[19]

Take the song, '*Kehu aaye pardesi hamse pyaar karela*' ('An outsider comes and loves me,' in *Dhartiputra*), where the heroine is needlessly underdressed. One needs to watch this track on screen to understand how mismatched the melody and the heroine's frugal attire are.

Interestingly, few Bhojpuri films have sex scenes on the lines of Hindi films such as *Jism* (Body, 2001) and *Murder* (2004), known for their steamy sequences. In general, the Bhojpuri cinema audience enjoys listening to ribald songs, which is an integral part of the folk tradition, but being largely conservative, is wary of nudity or explicit scenes. The sexy bedroom track in *Ganga,* with Ravi Kishan and Nagma (looking incredibly hot in a pink night gown)—'*Man ke milan preet man ke badhaye, tan ke milan pyaas tan ke bujhave*'—is more an exception than the rule.

In recent years, some songs offer interesting sociological insights. The upwardly mobile aspirations of the region are evident in the songs on litti-chokha, a popular dish made of wheat and black gram powder in the Bhojpuri-speaking belt. In *Daroga Babu I Love You*, the hero sings about the virtues of litti. The song written by Vinay Bihari says that those who eat litti-chokha have proved their mettle all over the world, including Surinam and Mauritius. Similar sentiments are echoed in *Ganga*'s song, *Litti-chokha bada majedaar* ('Litti-chokha is very delicious'), where Europeans are shown eating the dish. In other words, the Bhojpuriya, just like the Punjabi, has also conquered the world.

Mobile phones (*Piya number mila da ishtyle mein, kabo kate na connection mobile mein* ['Darling please dial the number in style, so that the connection is never interrupted']), and girls in jeans (*Ego jeans pant waali se pyaar ho gayeel ba* ['I have fallen in love with a girl in jeans']) have also been the focus of attention of songwriters in several films.

As in Bollywood films, *antakshari* (a game where everyone has to sing a song beginning with the last letter of a number sung by the previous participant) is often used to raise a movie's potential box-office quotient. For instance, *Daroga*

Babu I Love You has an antakshari culled from famous Bhojpuri songs from *Dangal, Ganga Maiya Tohe Piyari Chadhaibo* and *Ganga Maiya Tohar Kiriya*.

Another song in *Banke Bihari MLA* uses former Bihar chief minister Laloo Prasad's name to create a connection with the people. In a pleasing track with heroine Rambha dancing, the lyrics go like this: '*Har dil mein aag lagai denge, sansad mein balwa karai denge, hum hain Laloo ke gaon ke, hum jab chahein, jab chahein, hum sarkar girai dembe*' ('I will put every heart on fire, I will create a ruckus in Parliament, I am from Laloo's village, whenever I want, I can make the government fall').

Simply put, the lyrics are in the simple conversational style and very aware of recent developments.

There is some experimental music too. In *Bandhan Toote Na*, the song *Kabhi dekha humke bhi dil mein basa ke* ('For once let me into your heart and see') has a rap interlude. *Bambai Ke Laila Chhapra Ke Chhaila* has an interesting quick tempo *qawwalli*-like track filmed on a bus, *Chalal chalal gaadi Bambai sahariya* ('The vehicle is going to Mumbai').

Bairi Piya has a pleasant semi-classical track, *Preet ki muratiya ba tohari suratiya* ('Your face is the statue of love'), and mujra too gets a rare semi-classical twist in the track, *Zila hilat badue* ('The district is shaking') in *Godhan*. *Saiyan Bedardi* has a superb unadulterated folk track with only traditional instruments, *Chala chaani kata goriya jawaniya mein*, and Manoj Tiwari sings an exquisite folk number in *Ganga*, *Sootal saiyan ke jagaave ho rama, koyaliya badi papi* ('The koel is a sinner, it wakes up my beloved').

In *Nirahua Chalal Sasural*, the folk song, *Dhaani rang chunariya*, is again quite outstanding for the singing. The sad number, *Mile khatir dil bekarar kahe hola, pyar mein logwa beemar kahe hola* ('Why does the heart pine to meet you, why do people fall ill in love?') in *Nirahua Rickshawala*, has evocative lyrics, great tune and earnest singing. It is one of the best Bhojpuri songs composed in recent years.

To sum up, Bhojpuri film music has evolved significantly since the 1960s. While it is near impossible to improve on the songs of *Ganga Maiya Tohe Piyari Chadhaibo* and *Bidesiya*, plenty of good music is being written, composed and sung in the new millennium too. However, many of these songs give the impression of being recorded in a hurry. Listening to them one gets the feeling that a few more hours of hard work would have further improved the quality of the final output.

Nevertheless, with cheap CDs being sold across north India, Bhojpuri film songs have become easily accessible and are being bought more than ever before. Songs continue to be the backbone of Bhojpuri movies, reflecting the ethos of the Bhojpuri people and enlivening the content of each film.

Seven tracks to treasure

- *Kahe Bansuriya bajaule* (Why did you play the flute), film: *Ganga Maiya Tohe Piyari Chadhaibo*, music: Chitragupta, lyrics: Shailendra, singer: Lata Mangeshkar
- *Sonva ke pinjra mein* (In the golden cage), film: *Ganga Maiya Tohe Piyari Chadhaibo*, music: Chitragupta, lyrics: Shailendra, singer: Mohammed Rafi
- *Luk chhip badra* (Hide and seek in the clouds), film: *Ganga Maiya Tohe Piyari Chadhaibo*, music: Chitragupta, lyrics: Shailendra, singer: Lata Mangeshkar
- *Hasi hasi panva kheeole beimanwa* (The cheat made me chew paan casually), film: *Bidesiya*, music: S.N. Tripathi,

lyrics: Rammurti Chaturvedi, singers: Manna Dey and Mahendra Kapoor
* *Dinwa ginat mori* (Counting the days), film: *Bidesiya*, music: S.N. Tripathi, lyrics: Rammurti Chaturvedi, singer: Suman Kalyanpur
* *Laagi nahin chhute ram* (Love cannot be stamped out), film: *Laagi Nahin Chhute Ram*, music: Chitragupta, lyrics: Majrooh, singer: Talat Mahmood and Lata Mangeshkar
* *Lal lal othwa se* (From the red, red lips), film: *Laagi Nahin Chhute Ram*, music: Chitragupta, lyrics: Majrooh, singer: Talat Mahmood and Lata Mangeshkar

14

The New Kings and Queens of Music

They may not be as famous as Chitragupta or S.N. Tripathi and nor are they as admired as Shailendra or Majrooh Sultanpuri. But the music directors and lyricists of Bhojpuri films in the new millennium have also carved out a niche for themselves.

Lal Sinha, the music director of *Sasura Bada Paisewala,* is one of them. As a child, Sinha grew up fiddling with the harmonium, the tabla and the sitar, instruments that he had bought to pursue his passion. 'Slowly I learnt to play them on my own,' says Sinha, the youngest of eight children of an assistant registrar in Bihar's Gaya town.[1]

The boy who aspired to become a musician graduated in English, but his mind was firmly focused on making melodies. Sinha spent his early youth singing and playing instruments for a local orchestra. In 1997, he left for Mumbai to make a career in music. He was only twenty-six years old. 'Bhajan was the big craze those days. I met Gulshan Kumar of T-series, the Tauranis and other music barons. Gulshan Kumar suggested that I do bhajans, so I returned to Bihar and composed some. But before I could go back to Mumbai, he had been killed,' he recalls.[2]

In the following years, Sinha brought out his first cassette, the devotional *Mata Rani Ka Jagrata*, which became a hit and ensured that he kept getting work. But his life-changing moment came in 2003 when he met Sudhakar Pandey. 'He ran a company called Hum Music and wanted to make a video cassette for that. From there, the concept evolved into a full-fledged feature film,' says the composer.[3] The film was *Sasura Bada Paisewala*.

Sinha knew this was his big chance and spared no effort to create a memorable score. He found a willing partner in lyricist Vinay Bihari. 'We worked on the songs for about six weeks and put in a phenomenal amount of effort,' he says.[4]

In the past, melody was king in Bhojpuri films. But Lal Sinha realized that over the years rhythm had gained primacy. 'I used eight dholaks and four tablas for the film—a really heavy rhythm section,' he says.[5]

In those days Bhojpuri films were scoffed at, which is why Sinha's job included cajoling Bolywood playback singers such as Shreya Ghoshal to lend their voices to his compositions. 'Shreya was initially reluctant when I approached her. Finally, she agreed. It was her first Bhojpuri film.'[6]

Popular folk singer Radheshyam Rasiya also sang for the movie. 'Earlier, Chhaila Bihari was supposed to sing the track *Chooe lagal*. But he didn't like the number so we decided to use Radheshyam Rasiya, who was in Mumbai. It turned out to be a superhit.'[7]

The music of *Daroga Babu I Love You* also turned out to be popular—the title track sung by Shreya Ghoshal and Tiwari's *Tohar solaho shingar kare jaan mar* ('Your ornamentation has bowled me over') were chartbusters.

Since then, Sinha has done more than twenty-five films. 'I believe in doing select work with a certain degree of involvement. Some music directors have given music in seventy-five films in five years. I can't,' he says.[8]

* * *

Vinay Bihari is the superstar songwriter of Bhojpuri films. Like his idol Anand Bakshi, he is extremely prolific. A graduate in sociology, the lyricist comes from Bihar's West Champaran district. 'As a child I used to write parodies of film songs and give them to my relatives who ran a *kirtan mandali* [a group of religious singers] in my *naunihal* [mother's natal home]. As a nine-year-old kid, I also parodied the hit, *Kehu lutera kehu chor ho jala* ["Some become looters, someone else a thief"] from *Dharti Maiya*. The parody was, *Master lutera chela chor ho jala* ["The teacher becomes a looter and his student a thief"],' recalls Bihari.[9]

A key moment in his life came as a Class VI student when he went to see *Dostana* (1980), the Amitabh Bachchan-Shatrughan Sinha starrer, with his elder brother. 'After watching the film, I told my brother even I could write such songs. He laughed. The sound of that laughter spurred me. I wanted to prove that I had the talent to write film songs,' he says.[10]

Bihari started writing professionally in 1989. By 1992, he started working for Gulshan's Kumar T-series. 'In 1995, he called me from Patna saying, "*Chalo beta, tujhko Sameer banaoonga*" [Come on, son, I'll make you famous like Sameer],' he recalls.[11] But Bihari's career received a setback when Kumar was murdered. 'I was broken from inside because sahib liked me a lot,' he says.[12]

In 2000, Darshan Kumar, Gulshan Kumar's younger brother asked him to join T-series. 'I got to write the dialogues and songs for *Saiyan Hamaar*,' he says.[13]

Since then he claims to have worked on over a hundred Bhojpuri films, including superhits such as *Sasura Bada Paisewala*, *Panditji Bataeen Na Biyah Kab Hoee* and *Nirahua Chalal Sasural*. 'I knew that *Sasura Bada Paisewala* was going to be such a hit. When we were recording the songs, I told co-producer Sudhakar Pandey that if the film does badly, it will be a silver jubilee. Otherwise it should be a golden jubilee. He told me, "If it is a silver jubilee, I will gift you a car." After the film became a superhit, he gave me Rs 2 lakh to buy a car,' he recalls.[14]

Sometimes, Bihari writes four to five songs in a day. 'I am often asked to produce songs at short notice. People even change songs in the studio. There have been times when a producer did not like a number after it was recorded. So I had to immediately write out another song,' he says.[15]

Bihari is also a master of double-meaning lyrics. He says there is a lot of pressure to write 'sexy' songs for producers. 'People dance to the tunes of double-meaning songs. But they also abuse the songwriter in the same breath,' he says.[16]

The lyricist claims to have written songs for an estimated 500 devotional albums, 'I have written shiv geet, ram bhajan, Muslim devotionals. But nobody talks to me about those songs,' he says.[17]

Vinay Bihari won the best lyricist award three times in a row for *Panditji Bataeen Na Biyah Kab Hoee* (2005), *Pyaar Ke Bandhan* (2006) and *Kahan Jaiba Raja Najariya Ladaike* (2007) in the Bhojpuri Film Awards.

* * *

Few artists have made such a remarkable contribution to Bhojpuri films in the past five years as Kalpana. Gifted with a rich, powerful and sensuous voice, the singer from Assam is almost considered mandatory for any film's score. 'She is a priceless gift to the industry,' says superstar actor Dinesh Lal Yadav 'Nirahua'.[18]

Music runs in her veins. Kalpana's father was a folk singer and a radio artiste. Born in Guwahati, she started singing at the age of four and trained in Hindustani classical music. 'But I wasn't singing folk music those days. I used to sing Mariah Carey, Whitney Houston and Shania Twain,' she recalls.[19] As a teenager, she tried her hand at almost everything, including crooning in a local rock band called Friends, and in 2001, she came to Mumbai to further her career.

'As a newcomer you have to sing all kinds of numbers. I sang remixes, devotionals, festival songs. I sang in Rajasthani, Telugu, Kannada, Punjabi. After singing the *Laxmi Puran* in Oriya, I developed confidence in my versatility,' she says.[20]

In 2002, she sang a devotional Bhojpuri album where the number, *Ae Ganesh ke Papa* ('O father of Ganesh'), became a superhit. When the Bhojpuri film industry took off after the super success of *Sasura Bada Paisewala*, she immediately became the favourite of all composers. Since then, Kalpana has sung over a thousand Bhojpuri songs. In terms of strength and in its ability to celebrate life with abandon, her voice is near-perfect.

Some of her superhit tracks are *Gamchha bichhai ke* ('The gamcha has been spread out' from *Sasura Bada Paisewala*), *Rasgulla* (from *Balma Bada Naadan*), *Ugal bade chanda mama* ('The moon has risen' from *Ho Gayeel Ba Pyaar Odhaniya Wali Se*), *Hamka utha le godiya mein* ('Pick me up in your lap' from *Bandhan Toote Na*), *Chale Thain Thain* ('Goes bang bang' from *Baklol Dulha*). In 2009, she was a judge in the music talent show *Sur Sangram* on Mahua TV.

* * *

One of the most successful music directors in contemporary Bhojpuri films, Dhananjay Mishra grew up in Ghazipur in eastern Uttar Pradesh. His agriculturist father loved singing bhajans and by the age of four, Mishra had started playing the banjo. He started doing shows by the time he was twelve years old. In 1996, he came to Delhi. 'I started doing music shows. I was also earning Rs 800 for a shift as a session musician in studio recordings,' he says.[21]

In 1997, he recorded his first album as music director. He claims to have recorded 350 cassettes and albums of Bhojpuri folk music by 2008. One of his biggest hits is *Bagalwali* (Neighbourhood girl), the album that introduced Indi-pop to popular Bhojpuri music. The title song was sung by Manoj Tiwari. Dhananjay went to Mumbai in 2003 and since then, has composed music for more than fifty Bhojpuri films.

In 2004, he got his break in the Bhojpuri film *Ganga Ke Paar Saiyan Hamaar* (My lover is on the other side of river Ganga), sharing the credits with veteran music director Surinder Kohli. By 2008, he was doing a film a month.

His hit films include *Balma Bada Nadaan, Raja Bhojpuriya, Bandhan Toote Na* and *Pyaar Ke Bandhan*. In 2006, he received the best music award for his score in *Pyaar Ke Bandhan* and again won it for *Hum Bahubali* in 2008.[22]

The composer is pleased that Bhojpuri films are thriving. But he believes that no one can produce the same quality of music as that of the 1960s and 1970s. 'That's because,' he says, 'both rhythm and melody change with time. Earlier songs were based on vocals; now they are rhythm-based.'[23]

Mishra believes that old folk songs can be interpreted and presented in a new style. He prefers employing variations even for item songs. 'In *Pandav*, I used *poorbi*, a style of folk music, for an item song,' he says.[24] He feels that that songs have a shorter shelf life now. 'First, there are too many songs in the market and second, the audience is overloaded with different forms of entertainment,' says Mishra.[25]

* * *

In recent years, many composers and lyricists have got opportunities to display their talent in Bhojpuri films. Some well-known composers of the ongoing phase in Bhojpuri films are: Rajesh Gupta, Rajesh-Rajinish, Aman-Shlok, Sujeet Chaubey, Satish Ajay, Rajendra Sahil, Ashok Ghayal, Ashok Kumar Deep, Anand-Milind, Sanjeev Rana, Nikhil-Vinay, Rajesh Prasad, Rajdhar Suresh, Baba Jagirdar, Pappu Srivastava, Surinder Kohli, Ajay Swami, Rakesh Trivedi, Madhukar Anand, Gunwant Sen-Raj Sen, Shams Jameel, Shashikant Sharma, Praveen Kunwar and Ajay Prasanna.

In 2006, Nikhil-Vinay received the best Bhojpuri film music award for their score in *Kab Hoi Gawna Hamaar* in 2005. In 2007, Rajesh Gupta got the best music director award for *Kab Kahbu Tu I Love You*. In 2008, Ashok Kumar Deep got the best lyricist prize for *Lagal Raha Ae Rajaji* (2008).

Some other Bhojpuri film lyricists in recent years are Phanindra Rao, Poonam Vishwakarma, Amol Donwar, Ashok Ghayal, Priyamvada Mishra, Shyam Dehati, Birendra Vatsa, Sahil Fatehpuri, Prem Bairagi, Ashok Kumar Deep, Shabbir Ahmed, Bipin Bahar, Rajesh Mishra, Rustam Ghayal, Vinay Panwari and Ashok Shivpuri.

Some other well-known singers in the genre are Vinod Rathod, Radheshyam Rasiya, Shreya Ghoshal, Kailash Kher, Udit Narayan, Kumar Sanu, Alka Yagnik, Sunidhi Chauhan, Sonu Kakkad, Priya Bhattacharya, Jyoti Jharkhandi, Indu Sonali, Manoj Mishra, Deepa Narayan, Sadhna Sargam, Pamela Jain, Shoma Banerjee, Suresh Wadkar, Mohammad Aziz, Rekha Rao, Anand Mohan, Aparna Bhagwat, Sunil

Chhaila Bihari, Poornima, Sapna Awasthi, Anuradha Paudwal, Anirudh Bhola, Anup Jalota, Chhotu Chhaliya, Hariharan, Babul Supriyo and Guddu Rangila.

Super seven tracks for dancing

- *Tanik lahe lahe ho* (Slowly, my love, slowly), film: *Pyaar Ke Bandhan*—Catchy melody, naughty lyrics. Sambhavna Seth—and the launda alongside her—form a delightful team on screen.
- *Chale thain thain* (Goes bang bang), film: *Baklol Dulha*—Rani Chatterjee's abandon is worth every wolf whistle in this paisa vasool track.
- *Misir ji*, film: *Nirahua Rickshawala*—A super track with Sambhavna Seth in top form. Macmohan (Sambha) delights as Misir ji.
- *Bagalwali* (Neighbourhood girl), film: *Saiyan Hamaar*—Pure delight.
- *Kamaal kar gayeel* (It did wonders), film: *Shreeman Driver Babu*—Great item track. Krishna Abhishek in a special appearance is stylish and amusing.
- *Hum hain Lalu ke gaon ke* (I am from Lalu's village), film: *Banke Bihari MLA*—Rambha makes all the right moves.

Super seven tracks for listening

- *Naina mein baselu tu* (You live in my eyes), film: *Saiyan Hamaar*—Not folksy but very melodious. On screen, Ravi Kishan and Arpita Pal gyrate energetically.
- *Kehu ayeel pardesi* (A stranger came), film: *Dhartiputra*—Dulcet track filmed on the underclad heroine.

- *Mile khatir dil bekarar* (The heart pines), film: *Nirahua Rickshawala*—Easy to hum. Impossible to forget.
- *Sun o anari tohe* (Listen o naïve one), film: *Banke Bihari MLA*—Melodious track by Sadhna Sargam.
- *Tor maathhe ke bindiya* (The bindiya on your forehead), film: *Tu Hamaar Haoo*—A fun-filled track with Nagma.
- *Jaisan tohri topi* (Like your cap), film: *Daroga Babu I Love You*—Not very folksy but this Shreya Ghoshal track is very peppy.
- *Tohse pyar ba* (I love you), film: *Tohse Pyar Ba*—A song that you can listen as well as dance to.

Epilogue

Much like Bollywood, the Bhojpuri film industry too remains in a state of furious flux. Most films flop, a few become hits. That's enough to keep the regional genre going.

As actor Aamir Khan pointed out in a recent interview, 'We have forgotten that we have an audience beyond [the A-town multiplexes]. You will be shocked by the number of people who have switched from watching Hindi movies to Bhojpuri movies.'

No surprise then that recent issues of trade magazines are full of reports about Bhojpuri films under production. The 23 January 2010 issue of *Film Information* carried reports of fifteen films under production. The overall number, of course, could be several times higher. One only hopes that quantity also translates into quality cinema.

There are some new positive developments on the business front. A report put out on several internet sites in January 2010 said that *Brijwa* is all set to become the first Bhojpuri movie to be released in Pakistan. The movie stars Vinay Anand, Sudip Pandey and Sadhika Randhawa, and deals with the Maoist insurgency in India.

There have been some setbacks too. The passing away of producer Sudhakar Pandey on 20 August 2009, and actor Sujit Kumar, on 5 February 2010, has left a huge void in the industry. Pandey's contribution to the revival of the Bhojpuri film industry is second to none. After all, he co-produced *Sasura Bada Paisewala*, a film that spurred the genre's recovery. Originally from Sultanpur district in Uttar Pradesh, he also produced *Daroga Babu I Love You*, *Chalat Musafir Moh Liya Re* and *Rang De Basanti Chola*. He was only thirty-seven when he died.

Sujit Kumar was one of the giants of the regional film industry. Describing his association with Kumar, Amitabh Bachchan wrote in his blog: 'A colleague of several films, a considerate neighbour, husband to a wife who remained an exceptional friend and fan till her tragic end some years ago. When life ends, it takes along so many moments of the past in quick succession. All those memories of time spent together, the films, the locations on outdoors, the camaraderie, all gone in one swift cruel move.'

May their souls rest in peace!

Endnotes

Introduction

1. The point was first raised by the author in the article 'The Mofussil's Revenge', *Times of India*, 1 November 2005.

2. Rajadhyaksha, Ashish and Paul Willemen, *Encyclopaedia of Indian Cinema* (New Delhi: Oxford University Press, 1999), p. 31.

3. This number is based on annual production statistics (till 1994) taken from the *Encyclopaedia of Indian Cinema* by Ashish Rajadhyaksha and Paul Willemen. Some figures are from the poorly maintained Indian Censor Board website.

4. There is a long-pending demand before the union government to include Bhojpuri in the Eighth Schedule of the Constitution. A report, 'Recognition to Bhojpuri, no final view till UPSC language policy is finalized,' in *Tribune* on 5 May 2008 said, 'The government has initiated action on the inclusion of Bhojpuri and Rajasthani in the Eighth Schedule of the Constitution, but a final decision on the matter would be taken only after the language policy for the Union Public Service Commission has been finalized.' Till 5 January 2010, nothing had changed.

5. *Bairi Kangna* was a silver jubilee hit, but *Piparwa Paar Ke Brahm* was a major flop.

6. Character actor Brijesh Tripathi, who acted in *Ho Jaye Da Naina Chaar*, says it was made for Rs 70 lakh, roughly double the amount spent on an average Bhojpuri film in those days. It was shot in Shalini Palace, Kolhapur. The film crashed at the box-office.

7. In an article 'Bhojwood dreams big' by Avijit Ghosh, *Times of India*, 27 May 2007, Vikramjit Roy, the then publicity head of Sony Pix India, was quoted as saying, 'We believe that entertainment must be localized. We want more of the Bhojpuri audience's mindspace.'

8. From reports carried in national newspapers. News channels also telecast the incidents.

9. For details, see Chapter 5.

10. Ghosh, Avijit, 'Cinema halls attack reveal envy, resentment,' *Times of India*, 5 February 2008.

1. Jai Ganga Maiya

1. Mumtaz Hussain, Nazir Hussain's son, recounted the story during an interview conducted by the author at his residence in March 2008. Mumtaz recalled that his father used to have long discussions with him on the making of *Ganga Maiya Tohe Piyari Chadhaibo*. The meeting between his father and the President most probably took place in 1958.

In a long article titled '*Bhojpuri cinema ke vikas yatra*' in *Bhojpuri Varta*, July–September 2000, Manoj Kumar Singh 'Bhavuk' mentions Hussain meeting Dr Rajendra Prasad and having a conversation on the same topic.

2. Ibid.

3. Moonis, in an e-mail response to a questionnaire by the author in March 2009. Contrary to popular perception, *Nadiya Ke Paar* is not a Bhojpuri movie.

4. From the article,'*Shooting dekhne gaye aur Bishwanath Prasad Shahabadi ban gaye amar producer,*' in *Rambha*, 25 January 1965.

5. Rajkumar Shahabadi narrated this in a telephone interview with the author on 1 February 2009.

6. Interestingly, no Hindi film by the name of *Paagal Premi* was released in the 1960s.

7. Shahabadi said this in an interview published in *Rambha* on 25 January 1965.

8. From the e-mail response to a questionnaire sent by the author.

9. Author's interview with Mumtaz Hussain.

10. Manoj Kumar Singh 'Bhawuk' gives this date in his article, '*Bhojpuri cinema ke vikas yatra*,' published in the July–September 2000 issue of *Bhojpuri Varta*.

11. Shahabadi's interview in *Rambha*, 25 January 1965. However, Ashim Kumar's son, Rana, recalls his father telling him that the film had cost Rs 2.38 lakh. Mumtaz Hussain recalls his father telling him that the film cost something between Rs 2 and 3 lakhs.

12. From an e-mail response by Kumkum to the author's questionaire. She was born in Hussainabad, Bihar.

13. From the author's Mumtaz Hussain interview.

14. Ibid.

15. The date is given in Manoj Kumar Singh 'Bhavuk's article.

16. From a telephone interview to the author on 13 March 2009.

17. See the article by Manoj Kumar Singh 'Bhavuk'.

18. Rajkumar Shahabadi narrated this in a telephone interview with the author on 1 February 2009.

19. Desai recounted the incident in an interview conducted by the author on 24 March 2009.

20. From Dubey, Shankar Dutt, '*Bhojpuri filmein tab aur ab*,' *Rambha*, 12 July 1965.

21. Ibid.

22. Rangoonwalla, Firoze, *A Pictorial History of Indian Cinema*, (London: Hamlyn, 1979), p. 92.

23. From an interview conducted by the author in Mumbai in March 2008.

2. High Noon

1. Director S.N. Tripathi at a press conference in Benares, *Rambha*, 5 September 1964.

2. From a brief telephone interview conducted by the author with Shakti Samanta on 2 June 2008.

3. '*Bhojpuri ki doob rahi kishti ko sahara mila Ayeel Basant Bahar ki apaar safalta se*,' *Rambha*, 29 March 1965.

4. Ibid.

5. The link continued till the 1980s. Alok Dubey, who manages Anand Mandir in Benares, recalls that the entire laboratory work of *Baaje Shehnai Hamaar Anganaa* (1980) was done in Calcutta. Dubey was interviewed by the author at his office in Benares in May 2008. In recent times, though, a few Bengal-based Bhojpuri films have been made. One of them starring Tollywood hero Jeet is *Pyaar Jab Kehu Se Ho Jala*.

6. Brief item titled, '*Angna Bhayeel Bides*,' *Rambha*, 30 November 1964.

7. Tripathi stated this at the premier of *Sita Maiya* in Benares, *Rambha*, 5 September 1964.

8. From the article, '*Bhojpuri sanskriti sangeet wa katha ki upeksha hi Bhojpuri chitron ke patan ka karan*,' *Rambha*, 7 September 1964.

9. From the article, '*Ayeel Basant Bahar ki apaar safalta se*,' *Rambha*, 29 March 1965.

10. From the article, '*Bhojpuri filmon ka nirman ateet aur vartman*,' *Rambha*, 1 March 1965.

11. Ibid.

12. Ibid.

13. Ibid.

14. Interview with Mumtaz Hussain.

15. This is how her surname is spelt in the credits.

16. These reviews were compiled in a *Hamaar Sansar* promotional brochure.

17. From Dubey, '*Bhojpuri filmein tab aur ab*'.

18. Several advertisements published in *Rambha* in 1965 highlight this point.

19. Ibid.

20. Pandey's statement in an interview to the author in May 2008. Anand Dubey, who manages Anand Mandir, Benares, also narrated a similar anecdote.

21. From a telephone interview of Rajkumar Shahabadi with the author on 1 February 2009. The film was directed by Romney Dey, who was the chief assistant director in the Hindi film, *Kali Topi Lal Roomal*.

22. For details of the awards, see '*Chitra Ganga Maiya va abhinetri Kumkum sarvashrestha ghoshit*,' *Rambha*, 10 May 1965.

23. Advertised in *Rambha*, 21 June 1965.

24. Moonis recounted this in a detailed e-mail response to a questionnaire sent by the author.

25. Ibid.

26. Ibid.

27. Ibid.

28. From Dubey, '*Bhojpuri filmein tab aur ab*'.

29. Ibid.

30. Ibid.

3. Life after Death

1. The censor board certificate spells it as *Dharati Maiya*.

2. From a telephone interview conducted by the author on 3 December 2007 and an interview at Pandey's Mumbai residence in March 2008.

3. Ibid.

4. Ibid.

5. Ibid.

6. Ibid.

7. From the interview conducted at Mumtaz Hussain's residence in March 2008.

8. From an interview conducted by the author at Rakesh Pandey's residence in Mumbai in March 2008.

9. Interview with Mumtaz Hussain by the author in March 2008.

10. Ibid.

11. Story narrated by Alok Kumar Dubey, who runs Anand Mandir, Benares, during an interview conducted by the author at his office in May 2008.

12. From an interview conducted by the author in May 2008.

13. From an interview by the author at Jain's Benares residence in May 2008.

14. Ibid.

15. Bachchan, Bholanath, '*Nirmata Ashokchand Jain: Bhojpuri filmon ke liye samarpit vyaktitwa,*' *Dewal Dainik*, Azamgarh, 4 October 1983.

16. Ibid.

17. Ibid.

18. Ibid.

19. From an interview conducted by the author in Mumbai in March 2008.

20. Ibid.

21. *Film Information*, 21 April 1984.

22. Ibid.

23. From an interview conducted by the author at Kunal Singh's Mumbai residence in March 2008.

24. Ibid.

25. From an interview conducted by the author in March 2008.

26. See *Rambha*, 14 January 1984, editorial.

27. From a telephone interview conducted by the author on 30 May 2008.

28. Ibid.

29. From a telephone interview conducted by the author in June 2008.

30. Ibid.

31. From a telephone interview conducted by the author in May 2008.

32. From a telephone interview conducted by the author in June 2008.

33. From a telephone interview conducted by the author in May 2008.

34. Ibid.

35. '*Naihar ki Chunri—Ek Lajawab Uttam Paarivarik Film,*' *Rambha*, 18 March 1985.

36. '*Aaj zaroorat hai aisi hi Bhojpuri filmon ki,*' *Rambha*, 25 March 1985.

37. '*Kashi mein nakli film nirmataon ki barh,*' *Rambha*, 10 June 1985.

38. From a telephone interview conducted by the author on 15 February 2009.

39. From a telephone interview conducted by the author in June 2008.

40. Ibid.

41. From the phone interview with Adarsh Jain conducted by the author in June 2008.

42. Ibid.

43. Ibid.

44. From a telephone interview conducted by the author on 2 June 2008.

45. Ibid.

46. Ibid.

47. Ibid.

48. Ibid.

49. From a telephone interview with the author conducted on 14 July 2009.

50. Ibid.

51. Ibid.

4. The Third Wave

1. A large section of this chapter was first published in an article, 'Father-in-law has pots of money' by Avijit Ghosh in *First Proof: The Penguin Book of New Writing from India* 3 (New Delhi: Penguin, 2007).

2. Interviewed on the phone by the author.

3. Interviewed in Benares at Dubey's office in May 2008.

4. From an interview conducted by the author at his Mumbai office in March 2008.

5. Ibid.

6. From an interview conducted on the phone by the author in 2006 and on 7 August 2009.

7. Ibid.

8. Quoted from interviews conducted on the phone by the author in 2006 and on 7 August 2009.

9. Ibid.

10. Ibid.

11. From a telephone interview conducted by the author in 2006. Pandey died on 20 August 2009.

12. Ibid.

13. Ibid.

14. From an interview conducted by the author in March 2008.

15. There is a similar scene in another Manoj Tiwari starrer, *Pyaar Ke Bandhan* (2006), where the cobbler-hero responds in English to the badly-behaved heroine.

16. Quoted from a conversation in Benares in May 2008.

17. Quoted from a telephone interview conducted by the author on 1 August 2009.

18. From an interview conducted by the author in March 2008.

19. Interviewed by the author at his Mumbai residence in March 2008.

20. Ibid.

21. From an interview conducted by the author in March 2008.

22. Quoted from, Ghosh, Avijit, 'Enter Bhollywood: Bhojpuri potboilers back with a bang,' *Times of India*, 1 July 2005.

23. Anuradha Raman in 'Bollywood's trying to read Bhojpuri,' *Indian Express*, 5 June 2005, says that around that time even top Bollywood producer-director Subhash Ghai was exploring what Bhojpuri films had to offer.

24. See Salam, Ziya Us, 'Feast from the East,' *Hindu*, 7 October 2005.

25. Quoted from Joshi, Namrata, '*Ab Hamaar Film Hit Hoi*,' *Outlook*, 3 October 2005.

26. From a telephone interview conducted by the author on 6 August 2009.

5. Widening Horizons

1. Quoted from Ghosh, Avijit, 'Bhojwood dreams big,' *Times of India*, 27 May 2007.

2. Trade magazine *Super Box Office* carried the advertisement of *Bairi Piya* on its front page in the 11 March 2006 issue. Actor Shatrughan Sinha launched a film trade magazine dedicated to the regional film industry called *Bhojpuri City*, according to a PTI report published in *Hindu*, 14 April 2008.

3. In 2007, the actor was involved in a major row with the Bihar-Jharkhand Film Distributor Association over the dubbing of one of his films, *Coolie* (2006), without his permission. The matter was resolved later.

4. Interviewed on the phone by the author on 1 August 2009.

5. *Super Box Office*, 3 December 2005.

6. Ibid., 26 November 2005.

7. Ibid., 14 January 2006.

8. Ibid., 25 March 2006.

9. Information taken from promotional catalogues of these films.

10. Shankar, A., 'The rise and rise of Bhojpuri cinema,' *Business Standard*, 21 February 2007.

11. *Film Information*, 16 September 2006.

12. Film review in *Complete Cinema*, 1 December 2007.

13. *Film Information*, 16 September 2006.

14. Ibid.

15. *Film Information*, 30 September 2006.

16. Ibid., 27 October 2007.

17. Ibid., 13 January 2007.

18. Distributor Joginder Mahajan said, 'The hype is huge. But the ground reality is different. The top stars are having a great time but a majority of producers are losing money' (Ghosh, 'Bhojwood dreams big').

19. Quoted from the interview conducted by the author at Dubey's office in May 2008.

20. Quoted from Shankar, 'The rise and rise of Bhojpuri cinema'.

21. Interviewed at his Naaz Building office in Mumbai by the author in March 2008.

22. Gujjar at the promotional press conference held for *Baklol Dulha* in New Delhi.

23. See Salam, 'Feast from the East'.

24. From an interview conducted by the author in March 2008.

25. Joshi, '*Ab Hamaar Film Hit Hoi*'.

26. Interview conducted by the author at his Palika Bazaar shop in New Delhi on 7 March 2009.

27. Ibid.

28. Ibid.

29. According to figures provided by the Ministry of Overseas Indian Affairs, the number of Indians in these countries is about 2.2 million. In an e-mail response, Pooja Vora of T-series says that these countries, even the United Arab Emirates, are good markets for Bhojpuri music.

30. Sheela Sahtoe also said, 'We have about 150,000 people of Indian origin who speak Sarnami. That is to say most of them speak Sarnami, as the language of the Indians is called. Sarnami is not pure Bhojpuri, as spoken in Bihar, but a language based on Bhojpuri, Avadhi and other languages like Braj and Maithali.'

31. In an e-mail response, Bhimull says, 'Only about two to three per cent of the Trinidad population understands Bhojpuri and an even smaller number can both speak and understand it.' But he believes that Bhojpuri films have a possible future in Trinidad. 'Once Trinidad Indians realize that there are films available in the dialect of their ancestors, it will catch on,' he says.

32. In a telephone interview conducted by the author in 24 March 2009, actor-singer Dinesh Lal Yadav 'Nirahua' spoke of his experience when he visited Fiji for his song and dance shows.

33. From an interview conducted by the author in March 2008.

34. Ibid.

35. Quoted from Ghosh, 'Bhojwood dreams big'.

36. Ibid.

37. From an interview conducted by the author in March 2008.

38. Ibid.

6. The Diaspora Within

1. From an interview conducted by the author in Mumbai in March 2008. Others in the Bhojpuri film business such as Alok Dubey of Benares say that the figures are accurate.

2. Kirit Desai was interviewed by the author at his office in the Moti cinema hall on 24 March 2009 and on 21 July 2009.

3. Ibid.

4. From Ghosh, Avijit, 'The Mofussil's Revenge', *Times of India*, 1 November 2005.

5. From an interview conducted in October 2005.

6. *Film Information*, 14 April 2007.

7. Ibid., 21 April 2007.

8. Ibid., 20 January 2007.

9. *Screen*, 23 September 2005.

10. *Film Information*, 11 August 2007.

11. Ibid., 15 July 2006.

12. Ibid., 29 March 2008.

13. Ibid., 25 August 2007.

14. Ibid., 10 June and 17 June 2006.

15. Joshi, '*Ab hamaar film hit hoi*'.

16. Quoted from article in *businessofcinema.com*, 'Bhojpuri reap rich returns in Bhiwandi,' accessed on 13 February 2007.

17. Ibid.

18. Joshi, '*Ab hamaar film hit hoi*'.

19. Quoted from Ghosh, Avijit, 'Bhojpuri flicks like oxygen for Ludhiana cinema halls,' *Times of India*, 16 October 2007.

20. Ibid.

21. Bharadwaj, Ajay, 'In Punjab, Bhojpuri films doing great business,' *DNA*, August 2007.

22. Ibid.

23. Ibid.

24. Ghosh, 'Bhojpuri flicks like oxygen for Ludhiana cinema halls'.

25. Ibid.

26. From reports carried in national newspapers. News channels also telecast the incidents.

27. Ibid.

28. Ibid.

29. Ibid.

30. Quoted from Mahapatra, Anirban Das, 'Cowbelt calls,' *Telegraph*, 16 November 2008. A Press Trust of India piece titled 'Anil Kapoor, Raveena to debut in Bhojpuri films', published in *DNA* on 9 November 2008 also spoke about the same incident.

31. *Super Box Office,* 30 April 2005.

32. Ghosh, Avijit, 'Cinema halls attacks reveal envy, resentment,' *Times of India*, 5 February 2008.

33. Ibid.

34. Borpujari, Utpal, 'Bhojpuri film with Marathi-speaking villains a big hit,' *Sakaal Times*, 24 September 2008.

35. Reports in *Rambha* mention such concerns in 1965 and 1985. A report, *'Kashi mein sheeghra hi studio wa lab sthapana ki sambhavna,'* quotes the then Uttar Pradesh industries secretary Mahesh Prasad as saying on 6 July 1985 that a state-of-the-art studio and laboratory would soon be set up in Benares.

36. From the article, *'Bhojpuri filmon ke censor ke saath hi uska manoranjan tax maaf ho,'* *Rambha*, 13 May 1985.

37. PTI, 'Bihar to have a studio for Bhojpuri films,' *Hindu*, 8 November 2008.

38. See Mane, Anuradha, 'Bhojpuri film wins Silver Bear at Berlin festival,' *Times of India*, 14 February 2008.

7. Deciphering Bhojpuri Cinema

1. See Chopra, Anupama, 'Bye-Bye Bharat,' *India Today*, 1 December 1997. Also Ghosh, Avijit, 'The Lost Village,' *Pioneer*, 4 January 1998.

2. The argument was made by the author in 'The Mofussil's Revenge'.

3. Ibid.

4. Jha, Giridhar, 'Bhojpuri films oust Bollywood from Bihar halls,' *Mail Today*, 23 December 2007.

5. Ibid.

6. Jaidev Karmakar and Shyam Kumar Singh who work in Kanhaiya Talkies, Mughalsarai (Bihar) said this during an interview with the author in May 2008. See also the article, Ghosh, Avijit, 'C for crisis: Seedy cinema runs out of steam,' *Times of India* 10 February 2008, in which film-maker Kanti Shah, who makes low-budget dacoit films, has admitted this.

7. Social scientist Shiv Viswanathan used this phrase in a conversation with the author.

8. From the author's 'The Mofussil's Revenge'. In Sahi, Ajit, 'The revenge of the Bhojpuria,' *Tehelka*, 15 March 2008, Sahi makes another interesting point. He points out that post-1991, 'The very core of Hindi cinema moved away from the Urdu-Hindi Hindustani of middle India to the Punjabi Hindi of Delhi and northwest India down to the themes, sensibilities, characters, idioms and lyrics.'

9. Interviewed at his office by the author on 24 March 2009.

10. Interview with Ravi Kishan conducted by the author at his residence in March 2008.

11. Ibid.

12. Quoted from an interview conducted by the author at Singh's office in Naaz building in Mumbai in March 2008.

13. Meerut is the centrepoint of western Uttar Pradesh's indigeneous cinema, a mix of Haryanvi and Hindi. These movies are not released in cinema halls but sold on VCDs. Generally shot on DSR 450 digital camcorders, they are made for anything between Rs 1.5 lakh and 8.5 lakh. The success of *Dhakad Chhora* (Cool Dude, 2005) started the trend. Suman Negi, the film's heroine, became the queen of this genre. See Ghosh, Avijit, 'Western UP carves its own Bollywood,' *Times of India*, 26 May 2006.

14. By 2009, the Ladakhi movie industry was twenty-six films old. These were filmed on DVCAMs with an average budget of Rs 5 lakh. See Gupta, Trisha, 'High Culture,' *Tehelka*, 1 August 2009.

15. From an interview conducted by the author in Mumbai in 2008.

16. Quoted from an interview conducted by the author in Mumbai in March 2008.

17. Ibid.

18. Quoted from an interview conducted by the author in Benares in May 2008.

19. '*Bhojpuri filmein tabhi safal ho sakti hai,*' *Rambha*, 12 July 1965.

20. '*Bhojpuri bhashi apni matribhasha ke prati mohabbat paida kare,*' *Rambha*, 19 July 1965.

21. The Vice-chancellor of Benares Hindu University went on record praising *Hamaar Sansar* (1965). Similarly, the *mahant* (priest) of Kashi's Sankatmochan temple lauded *Naihar Ki Chunri* (1985).

22. Gatekeeper Shyam Singh, who has been working in Mughalsarai's Kanhaiya Talkies for thirty years, maintains that there's no 'craze' for movies anymore. 'Now people don't stand in the queue for hours under the hot sun to buy a ticket,' he said in an interview to the author in May 2008.

23. A gentleman who works at Bhavani Chitra Mandir, Kachchwa, about thirty kilometres from Benares, told the author in May 2008 that the arrival of DTH, especially DD Direct, has affected the business of single-screen theatres in the qasbahs. 'Every village has five to ten dishes. Though the villages hardly get eight hours of electricity, they have batteries and invertors. Women, especially, prefer to watch the movies on VCDs and DVDs at home,' he said.

24. Producer-director Mohanji Prasad holds the same view. See Ghosh, 'Bhojwood dreams big'. In Bholanath Bachchan's *Nirmata Ashokchand Jain: Bhojpuri filmon ke liye samarpit vyaktitva*, Ashokchand Jain, who produced *Ganga Kinare Mora Gaon* and many other films, offered a similar reason. 'The reason why Bhojpuri films fail is because producers think commercially. In their attempt to stuff the film with masala, the producer forgets what the audience really wants. A majority of producers don't speak Bhojpuri. This is why they have no knowledge of the culture and language of the place.'

25. Quoted from an interview conducted at his residence by the author in March 2008.

8. Twinkle Twinkle Little Superstars

1. From a telephone interview conducted by the author with Rana in June 2008.

2. From '*Ashim Kumar swayam apni nazar mein,*' *Rambha*, 11 January 1965.

3. Ibid.

4. Ibid.

5. Ibid.

6. Ibid.

7. From Bhawuk, Manoj, '*Bhojpuri se hamaar uhe nata ba jawan bachchru ke gai se hola*,' online *Bhojpuri Sansar*.

8. From a telephone interview conducted by the author on 1 August 2009.

9. From an interview conducted on the phone by the author on 8 March 2009.

10. From an interview with the author in Mumbai in March 2008.

11. From an interview conducted by the author in Benares in May 2008.

12. Much of the information for this profile was provided by Pandey himself in an interview conducted by the author at his residence in March 2008.

13. Ibid.

14. Ibid.

15. Ibid.

16. Ibid.

17. Ibid.

18. Ibid.

19. Ibid.

20. Ibid.

21. The anecdote was narrated in a newspaper article by *Avdhesh Preet*. The name of the newspaper cannot be traced.

22. Quoted from Shukla, Shruti, 'Bihar's first hero,' *Youth Times*, 16–30 June 1980.

23. Ibid.

24. Ibid.

25. *Cine Advance*, 3 October 1986.

26. Kunal Singh listed these names in an interview with the author in March 2008.

27. From a telephonic interview with the author.

28. Ibid.

9. New Heroes: The Three Aces in the Pack

1. Producers, directors as well as trade experts quoted this figure in 2008.

2. Ravi Kishan, quoted in Sinha, Meenakshi, 'Bhojpuri stars spice up poll mix,' *Times of India*, 28 March 2009.

3. Interview conducted by the author at Tiwari's Mumbai office in March 2008.

4. Ibid.

5. Ibid.

6. Ibid.

7. Ibid.

8. Ibid.

9. Ibid.

10. Ibid.

11. Ibid.

12. Ibid.

13. From an interview conducted at his office in March 2008.

14. Ghosh, Avijit, 'Attacks can't dent Bhojpuri star Tiwari's mass appealm,' *Times of India*, 7 February 2008.

15. Interview conducted by the author at Alok Dubey's office in Benares in May 2008.

16. Jha, Giridhar, 'Nothing official about Dutch stamp on Manoj Tiwari,' *Mail Today*, 28 May 2008.

17. Interview conducted by the author at Pandey's Benares residence in May 2008.

18. Ghosh, 'Attacks can't dent Bhojpuri star Tiwari's mass appeal'.

19. Sinha, 'Bhojpuri stars spice up poll mix'.

20. Kumar, Anuj, 'A date with Dal Bhat', *Hindu*, 21 December 2006.

21. From an interview conducted by the author at Kishan's Mumbai residence in March 2008.

22. Ibid.

23. Ibid.

24. Ibid.

25. Ibid.

26. Ibid.

27. Ibid.

28. Ibid.

29. Ibid.

30. From Sharma, Parul, 'The shining star of Bhojpuri cinema,' *Hindu*, 26 March 2007.

31. Telephone interview with the author on 24 March 2009.

32. Ibid.

33. Ibid.

34. Ibid.

35. Ibid.

36. Ibid.

37. Ibid.

38. Ibid.

39. Interview with the author at Rajesh Kumar Singh's office in Naaz building, Mumbai, in March 2008.

40. Interviewed at the theatre by the author in May 2008.

41. Ibid.

42. Ibid.

43. From a telephone interview conducted by the author on 24 March 2009.

44. Ibid.

45. Ibid.

46. Ibid.

10. The Directors

1. Quoted from Bharati, Arun, '*Bhojpuri filmon ka bazaar hai aur rahega*,' *Lokpath*, 7 August 1965.

2. Information taken from S.N. Tripathi's profile on the website *downmelodylane.com*.

3. Quoted from '*Sita Maiya ek abhootpoorva darshaniya chitra*,' *Rambha*, 5 September 1964.

4. Quoted from '*Videshon ki nakal sharmnak*,' *Rambha*, 14 September 1965.

5. Quoted from an interview conducted by the author at his Mumbai residence in March 2008.

6. Ibid.

7. Quoted from 'Writers must present reality—Nazir Hussein recalls [sic] Netaji's advice,' *Screen*, 12 October 1973.

8. Ibid.

9. Ibid.

10. From an interview conducted by the author in March 2008.

11. Quoted from '*Bhojpuri doobi nahi, doob rahi hai*,' *Chitravani*, 4 July 1965.

12. Quoted from an interview conducted by the author at his residence in March 2008.

13. From an interview conducted by the author at his residence in March 2008.

14. From an interview with Dipankar Bose conducted by the author in Mumbai in March 2008.

15. Ibid.

16. From a telephonic interview conducted by the author on 30 May 2008.

17. Quoted from an interview conducted by the author at Kunal Singh's Mumbai residence in March 2008.

18. From a telephone interview conducted by the author in March 2009.

19. From a telephone interview conducted by the author on 26 January 2008.

20. Ibid.

21. Ibid.

22. Ibid.

23. Quoted from an interview conducted by the author at his Mumbai residence on 28 March 2008.

24. Ibid.

25. Ibid.

26. Ibid.

27. Ibid. Tiwari had first been signed up to act in the film.

28. Ibid.

29. Quoted from Ranjan, Prabhat, '*Darshak hi lagayenge ankush*,' *Hindustan*, 2 November 2007.

30. Quoted from a telephone interview conducted by the author on 7 August 2009.

31. Interviewed on the phone by the author on 8 February 2009.

32. Ibid.

33. Ibid.

34. Ibid.

35. Ibid.

36. From an interview conducted at his office in Mumbai in March 2008.

37. Ibid.

38. From article 'Bali seriously injured, in ICU,' *ndtvmovies.com*, accessed on 16 June 2009.

39. Ibid.

40. Information provided by Braj Bhooshan in the same interview.

41. Ibid.

42. Ibid.

43. Ibid.

44. From an interview conducted by the author on the phone on 6 August 2009.

45. Ibid.

11. The Heroines

1. Quoted from an e-mail response by Kumkum to a questionnaire sent by the author.

2. Ibid.

3. Kumkum made this point in an e-mail response to the author.

4. Ibid.

5. Ibid.

6. Quoted from Bachchan Bholanath, '*Naaz ki 18 varsh baad Bhojpuri mein punah wapsi*,' *Sanmarg*, 4 September 1983.

7. Ibid.

8. See Gangadhar, V., 'Bright as a star,' *rediff.com*, accessed on 12 November 2005.

9. Quoted from a telephonic interview conducted by the author on 3 June 2008.

10. Ibid.

11. Ibid.

12. Quoted from Bharti, Dinesh, '*Padma Khanna*', *Swatantra Bharat*, 12 April 1981.

13. From a telephone interview with the author on 8 March 2009.

14. Ibid.

15. From an interview conducted on the phone by the author on 10 March 2009.

16. Ibid.

17. Quoted from a telephonic interview with the author.

18. From an interview conducted on the phone by the author.

19. Quoted from a telephonic interview with the author.

20. From Jha, Giridhar, 'Miss Jammu Anara Gupta is Bhojpuri film queen,' *Mail Today*, 16 October 2008.

21. From an interview by the author at the music launch of *Baklol Dulha*.

22. Ibid.

23. Ibid.

24. From Kumar, Abhay, 'Bhojpuri cinema: UP, Bihar looted,' *Deccan Herald*, 21 October 2007.

25. Quoted from Olivera, Roshni, 'Hindi movies are overrated,' *Bombay Times*, 29 September 2005.

26. From Sinha, 'Bhojpuri stars spice up poll mix'.

27. From an interview conducted on phone by the author on 24 January 2009.

28. Ibid.

29. Ibid.

30. Ibid.

31. Ibid.

32. Ibid.

33. Interviewed on the phone by the author on 24 January 2009.

34. Interviewed on phone by the author on 16 March 2009.

35. Ibid.

36. From an interview conducted on the phone by the author on 26 June 2009. All the information included here on the actress has been provided by Pakhi herself.

37. Ibid.

38. Ibid.

39. Ibid.

40. Ibid.

41. Ibid.

42. Ibid.

43. Ibid.

12. People and Places

1. Quoted from an interview conducted by the author in May 2008 at Pandey's residence in Benares.

2. Ibid.

3. Ibid.

4. Quoted from a telephonic interview conducted by the author on 12 February 2009.

5. Ibid.

6. Ibid.

7. Ibid.

8. Ibid.

9. From a telephonic interview conducted by the author on 15 February 2009.

10. Ibid.

11. Ibid.

12. Information provided by Arti Bhattacharya in an interview with the author in Mumbai in March 2008.

13. Ibid.

14. Ibid.

15. Ibid.

16. From an interview conducted by the author in May 2008 at Dubey's office in Benares.

17. Ibid.

18. Ibid.

19. Information provided by Tiwari in a telephone interview conducted by the author on 8 March 2009.

20. Ibid.

21. Ibid.

22. Ibid.

23. Interviewed by the author in Mumbai in March 2008.

24. Ibid.

25. Ibid.

26. From a telephonic interview conducted by the author on 9 June 2009.

27. Ibid.

28. From Ghosh, Avijit, 'Dalits strive to make it in Hindi, Bhojpuri films,' *Times of India*, 6 April 2008.

29. Ibid.

30. From a telephonic interview conducted by the author on 11 June 2009.

31. Quoted from Mahurkar, Uday, 'Bhojpuri Plot,' *India Today*, 24 November 2008.

32. Ibid.

33. From a telephonic interview conducted by the author on 26 January 2008.

34. Ibid.

35. Ibid.

36. From a telephonic interview conducted by the author on 10 June 2009.

37. Ibid.

38. Ibid.

39. See Desai, Shweta, 'Gorakhpur, Maharashtra,' *Indian Express,* 7 February 2010.

13. Melody to Rhythm

1. Quoted from the interview conducted by the author at Pandey's residence in May 2008.

2. Quoted from a telephonic interview with him conducted for this book.

3. Mumtaz Hussain, son of Nazir Hussain, gave this information. Majrooh Sultanpuri had written the lyrics of their home production *Hamaar Sansar*.

4. A contemporary journalist also praised the music and lyrics of *Laagi Nahi Chhute Ram*. See Dubey, '*Bhojpuri filmein tab aur ab*'.

5. See the movie's advertisement in *Rambha* in 1965.

6. Quoted from Vijayakar, Rajiv, 'Chitragupta: Low-profile composer,' *Screen*, 8 February 2002.

7. Quoted from an interview conducted by the author in March 2008.

8. Ibid.

9. Ibid.

10. Quoted from an interview conducted at his residence in March 2008.

11. Ibid.

12. Quoted from an interview conducted by the author in Mumbai in March 2008.

13. Ibid.

14. See by Shankar Dutt Dubey in *Rambha*, 12 July 1965.

15. See '*Pandit Rammurti Chaturvedi ki ek jhalak*,' *Rambha*, 5 April 1965.

16. See '*Ayeel Basant Bahar ki apaar safalta se*,' *Rambha*, 29 March 1965.

17. Quoted from an interview conducted by the author at Kunal Singh's residence in March 2008.

18. From an interview conducted by the author in Mumbai in March 2008.

19. Quoted from a telephonic interview with Aslam Sheikh on 8 February 2009.

14. The New Kings and Queens of Music

1. Quoted from an interview conducted by the author in Mumbai in March 2008.

2. Ibid. Gulshan Kumar was shot dead by assassins outside a temple in Mumbai's Andheri area in August 1997.

3. Ibid.

4. Ibid.

5. Ibid.

6. Ibid.

7. Ibid.

8. Ibid.

9. Quoted from an interview conducted by the author in Mumbai in March 2008.

10. Ibid. Sameer is a well-known Bollywood lyricist.

11. Ibid.

12. Ibid.

13. Ibid.

14. Ibid.

15. Ibid.

16. Ibid.

17. Ibid.

18. Quoted from a telephonic interview conducted by the author in 24 March 2009.

19. Quoted from a telephonic interview conducted by the author in 9 June 2009.

20. Ibid.

21. Quoted from an interview conducted by the author at Andheri's Trio Studio on 28 March 2008. Other information for this profile also from the same interview.

22. These awards are conducted by Vinod Gupta, who runs the website *bhojpurifilmaward.com*.

23. Ibid.

24. Ibid.

25. Ibid.

Filmography

Note

Collating a list of all Bhojpuri films released between 1962 and 2007 was a difficult task. I have checked various sources to put it all together. I tried to cross check and verify the information put on the list here, yet there remains a small margin of error. The information on several films is incomplete, and waiting to be filled, and I have also included an unverified list of 2008 films. I have translated every film's name, the idea being to provide a general sense of what they mean. This part of the book remains a work in progress. But I hope it will be of some value to those want to work further on the subject.

The number in parenthesis next to the years indicates the number of Bhojpuri films released that year.

1962 (1)

Ganga Maiya Tohe Piyari Chadhaibo (O Mother Ganga, I'll offer you the yellow cloth)—Producer: Bishwanath Prasad Shahabadi. Director: Kundan Kumar. Music: Chitragupta. Lyrics: Shailendra. Cast: Kumkum, Ashim Kumar, Nazir Hussain, Tiwari, Bhagwan Sinha, Helen, Leela Mishra and introducing Kumari Padma (later Padma Khanna).

1963 (2)

1. *Bidesiya* (One who has gone to a foreign land, metaphorically, a deserter)—Producer: Bachubhai Shah. Director: S.N. Tripathi. Music: S.N. Tripathi. Lyrics: Rammurti Chaturvedi. Cast: Naaz, Sujit Kumar, Jeevan, Kumari Padma, S.N. Tripathi, Helen and Bhikhari Thakur.

2. *Laagi Nahin Chhute Ram* (Love never goes away)—Producer: Tiwari. Director: Kundan Kumar. Music: Chitragupta. Lyrics: Majrooh. Cast: Kumkum, Ashim Kumar, Tiwari, Nazir Hussain.

1964 (7)

1. *Balma Baḍa Nadaan* (My lover is very innocent)—Director: Baldev Jhingan. Music: Chitragupta. Cast: Kumkum, Ashim Kumar.

2. *Naihar Chhutal Jaye* (Leaving my parent's home)—Director: Devendra. Music: Jaidev. Cast: Kumkum, Deven Verma, Asit Sen.

3. *Kab Hoihain Gawanwa Hamaar* (When will my *gawna* happen)—Music: Iqbal Qureshi.

4. *Naag Panchami*—Producer: SS Dhanuka. Director: Shantilal Soni. Music: Jamal Sen. Cast: Preetibala, Sheel Kumar, Mohan Choti and 1001 *nag* (snakes).

5. *Jekra Charanwa Mein Lagle Paranwa* (At whose feet lies my heart)—Director: Adarsh. Music: S.N. Tripathi. Cast: Jagdeep, Jaimala, Helen, Rajendranath.

6. *Sita Maiya* (Mother Sita)—Director: S.N. Tripathi. Music: S.N. Tripathi. Cast: Sheel Kumar, Kanu Roy, Bela Bose, S.N. Tripathi, Chandrima Bhaduri, Hari Shukla, Bhagwan Sinha.

7. *Jogin* (Ascetic woman): Music: S.N. Tripathi.

1965 (7)

1. *Ayeel Basant Bahar* (The spring has come)—Producer: Shakti Samant. Director: Devendra. Music: Hemant Kumar. Cast: Naaz, Sujit Kumar, Jeevan and Chandrashekhar.

2. *Bhauji* (Elder brother's wife)—Producer-director: Kundan Kumar. Music: Chitragupta. Lyrics: Majrooh. Cast: Kumkum, Sujit Kumar, Sabita Chatterjee, Leela Mishra, Hari Shukla, Bhagwan Sinha, Tuntun, Bela Bose and Helen.

3. *Ganga*—Producer: Kumkum's home production. Director: Kundan Kumar. Music: Chitragupta. Lyrics: Shailendra. Cast: Kumkum, Sujit Kumar, Anwar Hussain, Nana Palsikar, Leela Mishra.

4. *Hamaar Sansar* (My/Our world)—Producer-writer: Nazir Hussain. Director: Naseem. Music: Shyam Sharma. Lyrics; Majrooh. Cast: Ashim Kumar, Lily Chakraborty, Helen, Leela Mishra, Indrani Mukherjee, Nazir Hussain.

5. *Saiyan Se Bhaile Milanwa* (When I met my lover)—Director: P.L. Santoshi. Music: Robin Chatterjee. Cast: Sujit Kumar, Saeeda Khan, Sabita Chatterjee, Jahar Roy.

6. *Saiyan Se Neha Lagaibe* (I will love my darling)—Director: SM Abbas. Music: Ghulam Mohammed. Cast: Naaz, Sujit Kumar, Jagirdar, Yunus Parvez, Bela Bose and King Kong.

7. *Solaho Singaar Kare Dulhiniya* (The bride decks up)—Producer: Bishwanath Prasad Shahabadi. Director: Romni De. Music: Babu Singh. Cast: Motilal, Anita Guha, Naaz, Leela Mishra, Bhagwan Sinha, Tridip Kumar, Helen.

1966 (2)

1. *Loha Singh*—Producer: Mohan Rai Khaitan. Director: Kundan Kumar. Music: S.N. Tripathi. Cast: Sujit Kumar, Vijaya Chowdhury, Prof Rameshwar Singh Kashyap, Tiwary, Helen.

2. *Mitwa* (Lover)—Producer: Jagmohan Mattu. Director: Govind Moonis. Music: C Ramchandra. Lyrics: Shailendra. Cast: Amita, Shekhar, Jeevan, Leela Mishra, Bhagwan Sinha and Bela Bose.

1968 (1)

Vidhana Naach Nachave (Fate makes you dance)—Music: Dattaram. Lyrics: Shailendra. Cast: Sujit Kumar, Mumtaz.

1971 (1)

Dher Chalaaki Jin Kara (Don't act too smart)—Producer: Lalchand Tejwan Chug. Director: Datta Keshav. Music: Shankar Rao Kulkarni. Cast: Raj Gosavi, Agha, Bhagwan (also made as *Ati Shahana Tyachya* in Marathi).

1977 (2)

1. *Dangal* (The Bout)—Producer: Bachubhai Shah. Director: Rati Kumar. Music: Nadeem-Shravan. Cast: Sujit Kumar, Prema Narayan, Ram Singh, Iftekar.
2. *Daku Rani Ganga*—Director: Krishna Kant. Music: Dilip Dholakia. Cast: Rajiv, Ragini, Arvind Pandya, Helen, Padma Khanna.

1978 (1)

Amar Suhagin (Eternally married)—Director: Babubhai Mistry. Music: S.N. Tripathi. Cast: Snehlata, Amjad Khan.

1979 (2)

1. *Balam Pardesia* (The lover from a foreign land)—Producer: Mumtaz Hussain. Director: Nazir Hussain. Music: Chitragupta. Cast: Rakesh Pandey, Padma Khanna, Vijaya Chowdhury and Nazir Hussain.
2. *Mai K Lal* (Apple of mom's eye)—Producer: GL Chadha. Director-lyricist: Rajpati. Music: Nadeem Shravan. Cast: Sujit Kumar, Prema Narayan, Hari Shukla, Ram Singh, Jaishree T., Yunus Pervez.

1980 (3)

1. *Baaje Shehnaai Hamaar Anganaa* (The shehnai plays in my courtyard)—Producer: A Khan. Director: Javed Rehman.

Music: Zakir Hussain (not the famous tabla player). Cast: Bharat Bhushan, Devendra, Naaz, Abha Dhuliya, Jaishree T., Lalitesh.

2. *Jaagal Bhag Hamaar* (My stars are rising)—Director: S.N. Tripathi. Music: S.N. Tripathi. Cast: Sujit Kumar, Prema Narayan, Ram Singh, Hina Kausar, Hari Shukla, Bhagwan Sinha, Leela Mishra, S.N. Tripathi.

3. *Roos Gayeele Saiyan Hamaar* (My lover is sulking)—Director: Nazir Hussain. Music: Chitragupta. Cast: Rakesh Pandey, Padma Khanna, Nazir Hussain, Vijaya Chowdhury, Leela Mishra, Tuntun, Bhagwan Sinha.

1981 (5)

1. *Chanwa Ke Taake Chakor* (The chakor bird looks at the moon)—Producer: Devnath Singh. Director: Nazir Hussain. Music: Chitragupta. Cast: Rakesh Pandey, Hina Kausar, Nazir Hussain.

2. *Dharti Maiya* (Mother Earth)—Producer: Ashokchand Jain. Director: Qamar Narvi. Music: Chitragupta. Lyrics: Laxman Shahabadi. Cast: Padma Khanna, Srigopal, Kunal Singh, Gouri Khurana, Hari Shukla, J. Mohan and Rakesh Pandey.

3. *Ganga Ghat*—Director-lyricist: Rajpati. Music: Nadeem-Shravan. Cast: Sujit Kumar, Prema Narayan and Yunus Parvez.

4. *Ganga Aur Sarju* (Ganga and Sarju)—Director: Akbar Balam. Music: Shyam Sagar. Cast: Rakesh Pandey, Dilip Sinha, Madhu Malini.

5. *Saiyan Tohre Karan* (For you my love)—Producer: Dhaneshwar Singh. Director: Radhakant. Music: Chitragupta. Cast: Rakesh Pandey, Padma Khanna and Kumud Chhugani.

1982 (3)

1. *Balma Nadaan* (Naïve lover)—Director: Akbar Balam. Cast: Rakesh Pandey, Madhu Malini.

2. *Bitiya Bhayeel Sayaan* (My daughter has grown up)—Producer:

Dhaneshwar Singh. Director: Radhakant. Music: Chitragupta. Cast: Sujit Kumar, Jaishree T.

3. *Ganga Maiya Bhar De Acharwa Hamaar* (O Mother Ganga bless me)—Producer: Lalji Gupta. Director: Dilip Bose. Music: Ravindra Jain. Cast: Madhu Mishra and Narayan Bhandari.

1983 (11)

1. *Chutki Bhar Senur* (A pinch of vermilion)—Director: Nasir Hussain. Music: Chitragupt. Lyrics: Majrooh. Cast: Kunal Singh.
2. *Hamaar Bhauji* (My elder brother's wife)—Producer: Mohanji Prasad. Director: Kalpataru. Music: Chitragupta. Cast: Tanuja, Sachin, Padma Khanna.
3. *Ganga Kinare Mora Gaon* (My village is on the banks of the Ganga)—Producer: Ashokchand Jain. Director-story: Dilip Bose. Music: Chitragupta. Lyrics: Laxman Shahabadi. Cast: Naaz, Kunal Singh, Gouri Khurana, Hari Shukla, Dev Malhotra and J. Mohan.
4. *Jai Bhawani*—Cast: Kunal Singh, Rekha Sahay.
5. *Jahan Bahe Ganga Dhar* (Where the Ganga flows)—Director: Shyam Kaushal. Music: S.N. Tripathi. Cast: Dharmesh Tiwari, Hina Kausar, Padma Khanna.
6. *Phulwari* (Garden): Music: Ravindra Jain.
7. *Piya Nirmohiya* (Cruel lover)—Producer: Jagdish Singh. Director: Prem Singh. Cast: Jai Tilak, Ram Singh and Madhu Malini.
8. *Sajai Da Maang Hamaar* (Marry me)—Producers: Sarju Prasad and K.S. Singh. Director: Rati Kumar. Lyrics: Maya Govind, Laxman Shahabadi, K.K. Shahi. Music: Nadeem-Shravan. Cast: Sujit Kumar, Padma Khanna, Kanhaiyalal, Leela Mishra, Nana Palsikar.
9. *Sampoorna Tirtha Yatra* (The complete pilgrimage)—Director: Rajpati. Cast: Sujit Kumar.
10. *Senur* (Vermilion)—Director: Amar Gupta. Music: Ravindra Jain. Cast: Rakesh Pandey, Padma Khanna, Hina Kausar, Abhi Bhattacharya.

11. *Sonva Ke Pinjra* (The golden cage)—Director: Lalji Yadav. Cast: Rakesh Pandey, Prema Narayan, Jaishree T.

1984 (9)

1. *Bansuriya Baaje Ganga Teer* (The flute plays on the banks of the Ganga)—Director: Rakesh Pandey. Music: Chitragupta. Cast: Padma Khanna, Prema Narayan, Abhi Bhattacharya.
2. *Bairi Saawan* (Cruel month of Saawan)—Director: Prem Singh. Music: Shyam Sagar. Cast: Sujit Kumar, Rajni Sharma, Brijesh Tripathi.
3. *Bhaiya Dooj*—Director: Qamar Narvi. Music: Chitragupta. Cast: Sujit Kumar, Padma Khanna, Rakesh Pandey, Gouri Khurana.
4. *Gajab Bhaile Rama* (What a strange thing has happened)—Director: K.P. Shukla.
5. *Kishen Kanhaiya*.
6. *Maibha Mahtari* (The stepmother)—Producer: J.S. Mehta. Director-actor: Man Singh.
7. *Paan Khaye Saiyan Hamaar* (My lover chews paan)—Director: Sujit Kumar. Music: Naushad. Cast: Amitabh Bachchan, Rekha, Ranjit, Bandini Mishra, S.N. Tripathi.
8. *Saiyan Magan Pahelwani Mein* (My lover is busy wrestling)—Director: Radhakant. Music: Chitragupt. Cast: Rakesh Pandey, Sujit Kumar, Padma Khanna and Jaishree T.
9. *Thakurayeen* (The thakur's wife)—Director: Bhagwant Thakur. Cast: Sujit Kumar, Padma Khanna, Brijesh Tripathi.

1985 (6)

1. *Bihari Babu* (The Bihari)—Producer: Shatrughan Sinha. Director: Dilip Bose. Music: Chitragupta. Lyrics: Brijkishore Dubey. Cast: Shatrughan Sinha, Kunal Singh, Alpana Goswani, Pyaremohan Sahay, Rekha Sahay and two item girls: Tina Munim and Anita Raaj.
2. *Ganga Maiya Tohar Kiriya* (I swear on you Mother Ganga)—

Producer: B.N. Daga and Naresh Kumar. Director: Naresh Kumar. Music: Chitragupta. Cast: Sujit Kumar, Padma Khanna, Bandini Mishra, Manoj Verma, Shobha Khote, Mohan Choti.

3. *Naihar Ki Chunri* (The stole from my parents' home)— Producer: Lalji Gupta. Director: Hasmukh Rajput. Music: Shankar. Cast: Lalitesh, Meera Madhuri, Kewal Krishna, Dev Malhotra, Madhuri Mishra.

4. *Piya Ke Gaon* (My lover's village)—Producer: Muktinarayan Pathak. Director: Dilip Bose. Music: Chitragupta. Lyrics: Dr Ramnath Pathak 'Pranayi'. Cast: Meera Madhuri, Danish, Ajitesh, Jaishree T., Aruna Irani.

5. *Pritam More Ganga Teere* (My lover is on the banks of Ganga)—Producer: Bharat Rawal. Director-writer: Rajkumar Pardesi. Music: Shankar.

1986 (19)

1. *Aangan Ke Lakshmi* (The courtyard's Lakshmi)—Producer: Lalji Gupta. Director: Tejesh Akhauri. Music: Chander-Rafiq. Cast: Meera Madhuri and Lalitesh.

2. *Babua Hamaar* (My son): Director: K.K. Verma. Music: Dilip Dutta.

3. *Bahina Tohre Khatir* (For you my sister)—Producer: Gyanendra Shrivastava. Director: Hasmukh Rajput. Music: Rajesh Raj. Cast: Meera Madhuri, Madhuri Mishra and Sunil Pandey.

4. *Bitiya Chalal Sasural* (My daughter goes to her in-laws')— Director: Dilip Bhatt. Cast: Kiran Kumar, Sheila David, Madhuri Mishra.

5. *Dharti Ki Aawaz* (The voice of the earth)—Producer: Bhubaneshwar and Jawaharlal Jha. Director: K.D. Singh. Music: Onkar. Cast: Sujit Kumar, Padma Khanna, Kunal Singh, Bandini Mishra, Manoj Verma.

6. *Dulha Ganga Paar Ke* (The groom from across the Ganga)— Producer: Rani Shree. Director: Rajkumar Sharma. Music-lyrics: Laxman Shahabadi. Cast: Kunal Singh and Gouri Khurana.

7. *Dulhin* (Bride)—Producer-Director: Ashok Chand Jain. Music: Chitragupta. Cast: Kanan Kaushal, J. Mohan, Jaishree T.

8. *Ganga Hamaar Mai* (Ganga my mother)—Director: Dilip Bose. Cast: Sujit Kumar, Manoj Verma.

9. *Ganga Jaisan Bhauji Hamaar* (My elder brother's wife is like the Ganga)—Producer: Mohan Sehgal. Director: Dilip Bose. Lyrics: Sameer. Music: Chitragupta. Cast: Sujit Kumar.

10. *Ganga Ke Teere Teere* (By the banks of the Ganga)—Director: Rajpati. Cast: Ram Singh, Madhu Malini, Yunus Parvez, Bharat Kapoor.

11. *Ganga Ki Beti* (The daughter of the Ganga)—Writer-director: K.D. Singh. Lyricist: Sameer. Music: Onkar. Cast: Padma Khanna, Sujit Kumar, Kunal Singh, Bandini Mishra.

12. *Ghar Grihasti* (The household)—Director: Dilip Bose. Cast: Sujit Kumar, Rakesh Pandey, Bandini Mishra, Jai Tilak.

13. *Gorakhnath Baba Tohe Khichdi Chadhaibo* (O Gorakhnath Baba, I'll offer you *khichdi*)—Director: Surendra.

14. *Paijaniya* (Anklet)—Producer: Ram B. Sharma. Director: Aslam Sheikh. Music: Dilip Dutta. Cast: Sujit Kumar, Hina Kausar, Seema Vaz.

15. *Parbatiya Banal Panditayeen* (Parbatiya turns into a panditayeen)—Producer: Sheetla Prasad Agrahari. Director: Ramnath Rai. Music: Pratima Dutta.

16. *Ram Jaisan Bhaiya Hamaar* (My brother is like Ram)—Producer: Trilok Chand Jain. Director: Adarsh Jain. Music-lyrics: Laxman Shahabadi. Cast: Kunal Singh, Meera Madhuri, Hari Shukla, Prithvi Singh, Pyare Mohan Sahay, Sandhya, Huma Khan.

17. *Senurwa Bhayeel Mohal* (Vermilion has become rare)—Director: Gyan Kumar. Cast: Kunal Singh, Kalpana Iyer, Amjad Khan, Bharat Bhushan, Pradeep Kumar and Sonia Sahni.

18. *Sohag Bindiya* (The *bindi* of marriage)—Director: Paramjit Singh Sangha. Cast: Kunal Singh, Rajni Sharma.

19. *Tulsi Sohe Hamaar Angna* (The tulsi plant adorns my courtyard)—Producer: Raj Kumar. Director: Rakesh Pandey. Music Director: Chitragupta. Cast: Sujit Kumar, Rakesh Pandey, Padma Khanna, Aruna Irani.

1987 (14)

1. *Bahuriya* (Daughter-in-law)—Director: Tejesh Akhauri. Cast: Padma Khanna, Rakesh Pandey, Sangeeta Naik, Madhuri Mishra.
2. *Champa Chameli*—Producer: Sarju Singh. Director: B. Thakur. Cast: Sujit Kumar, Padma Khanna, Jagdeep, Yunus Parvez.
3. *Ganga Jwala*—Producer: Harish Gupta and others. Director: Ashwini Kumar. Music: Laxman Shahabadi. Cast: Kunal Singh, Rekha Sahay, Lalitesh, Shiela David, Aruna Irani.
4. *Ganga Tulsi*—Producer-director: Ram Singh.
5. *Ganga Aabad Rakhiha Sajanwa Ke* (O Ganga please protect my love)—Director: Rajeev Ranjan.
6. *Godana* (Tattoo)—Director: Vinay Shukla.
7. *Hamri Dulhaniya* (Our bride)—Director: Shri Gopal.
8. *Pia Ke Pyaari* (The lover's favourite)—Producer: Mukti Narayan Pathak. Director: Prem Singh. Music: Nirmal Pathak.
9. *Piritiya Ke Khel* (The game of love)—Director: Jagdish Sinha.
10. *Piya Rakhiha Senurwa Ke Laaj* (Please protect my vermilion's honour)—Producer: V.P. Vishwakarma. Director: K. Vinod. Music: Usha Khanna. Cast: Kunal Singh, Meera Madhuri, Bandini Mishra, Hari Shukla.
11. *Saiyan Bina Ghar Soona* (The home feels empty without you)—Director: Lalji Yadav.
12. *Sajanwa Bairi Bhaile Hamaar* (My lover has become my enemy)—Director: Dilip Bose. Music: Chitragupta. Cast: Sujit Kumar, Deepika.

1988 (8)

1. *Birha Ke Raat* (The night of separation)—Director-writer: Lalji Yadav. Cast: Ram Singh.
2. *Dagabaaz Balma* (Cheater-lover)—Producer: Rajiv Singh. Director: Arti Bhattacharya. Music: Laxman Shahabadi. Cast: Kunal Singh, Sahila Chadha, Dev Malhotra, Prabha Mishra and Shetty.

3. *Ganga Aur Gouri*—Director: Jagdish Singh. Cast: Jai Tilak and Meera Madhuri.
4. *Ganga Maiya Kara Da Milanwa Hamaar* (O Mother Ganga, unite us)—Director: Prem Singh.
5. *Lagal Chunri Mein Daag* (A blemish on my stole)—Producer: Sita Ram. Director: B.L. Kashyap. Music: Sumitra Lahiri. Cast: Lalitesh, Kunal Singh, Seema Vaz.
6. *Pyari Dulhiniya* (Charming bride)—Director: Pandit Ramnath Shukla. Music: Sapan Jagmohan. Cast: Meera Madhuri, Arun Govil.
7. *Tikuli Ke Laaj* (Tikuli's honour).

1989 (10)

1. *Anchara Ke Laaj* (The honour of my aanchal).
2. *Bhag Ke Lekha* (Destiny)—Director: Navin Joshi. Music: Chander Rafiq Sagar.
3. *Chhutki Bahu* (Younger daughter-in-law)—Producer: Sanjay Rai. Director: Dilip Bose.
4. *Hamaar Dulha* (Our groom).
5. *Kaisan Banaul Sansar* (What kind of world have you made?).
6. *Kajri*—Director: K.K. Verma. Music: Sapan Jagmohan.
7. *Mai* (Mother)—Producer: Sachidanand Yadav. Director: Rajkumar Sharma. Music: Ram Babu. Cast: Padma Khanna, Pankaj Sharma, Sheila David, Vijay Khare.
8. *Patoh Bitiya* (A daughter-in-law-like daughter)—Producer: Shyam Jethwani. Director: Aslam Sheikh. Music: Jitin-Shyam. Cast: Sujit Kumar, Ulhas, Bandini Misra, Seema Vaz.

1990 (5)

1. *Beti Udhar Ke* (Borrowed daughter)—Director: Chandrabhushan Mani. Cast: Kunal Singh, Sona.
2. *Hamaar Betwa* (Our son). Producer: Jude D'Mello. Director: Kishore Kumar Singh. Music: Chitragupta. Cast: Sujit Kumar, Kunal Singh, Jamuna.

3. *Toote Na Piritiya Hamaar* (Our love won't break)—Producer: Bhubaneshwar Jha and Jawaharlal Jha. Director: K.D. Singh. Music: Onkar. Cast: Sujit Kumar, Padma Khanna, Kunal Singh, Huma Khan, Bandini Mishra.

4. *Toote Na Piritiya Ke Dor* (May the string of love not break)— Director: Akbar Balam. Cast: Bandini Mishra, Anjana Mumtaz, Rakesh Pandey.

5. *Kasam Ganga Jal Ke* (I swear over holy Ganga water)— Producer: K.C. Bokadia. Director: Dilip Bose. Cast: Kunal Singh.

1991 (8)

1. *Bhaiya Bhauji Ke Dular* (The affection of my elder brother and his wife)—Producer and director: A.B. Tiwari. Music: Ram Laxman. Cast: Rakesh Pandey, Nandita Thakur, Meera Madhuri and Seema Vaz.

2. *Dhania Munia*—Director: A.A. Darpan. Cast: Bandini Mishra.

3. *Dulha* (Groom)—Producer: Kanchan Sharma. Director: Adarsh Jain. Music: Dilip Dutta. Cast: Atlee Brar, Jamuna.

4. *Ganga Maiya Bhar Da Godiya Hamaar* (O Mother Ganga, make me a mother)—Producer: Mahendra Prasad Singh. Director: Jagdish Singh.

5. *Ganga Se Nata Ba Hamaar* (I have a bond with Ganga)— Producer: Nisha Jain. Director-story-screenplay: Dilip Bose. Music: Ravindra Jain. Cast: Rita Bhaduri, Pankaj Sharma.

6. *Ganga Kahe Pukaar Ke* (Ganga beckons)—Director: Sri Gopal. Music: Chitragupta. Cast: Sujit Kumar.

7. *Jug Jug Jiya More Laal* (May you live forever my child)— Director: S.K. Srivastava. Music: Uttam Singh. Cast: Vijay Khare, Dev Malhotra.

8. *Piya Bina Nahi Chain* (Restless without my love)—Producer: K.C. Singhal. Director: K Vinod. Music: Usha Khanna. Cast: Kunal Singh, Seema Vaz, Neelam Mehra.

9. *Saanchi Piritiya Hamaar* (My love is true)—Producer and

director: Pramod Kumar Singh. Music: Chander Rafiq Saagar. Cast: Dinesh Kaushik, Anuradha Sawant.

1992 (8)

1. *Baba Ke Dulari* (Father's favourite girl).
2. *Bairi Kangna* (Enemy bracelet)—Director: Nihal Singh. Cast: Kunal Singh, Meera Madhuri.
3. *Birhin Janam Janam Ke* (A pitiful woman over several lives)—Director: Radhakant. Cast: Rakesh Pandey, Padma Khanna.
4. *Chhute Na Sangatiya* (Unbreakable partnership)—Producer: J. Singh. Music: T. Mohan. Cast: Jaya Prabha, Satish Kaul, Bandini Mishra.
5. *Gawna*—Director: Tejesh Akhauri. Music: Ajay Swami. Cast: Manoj Verma, Meera Madhuri, Madhuri Mishra.
6. *Kab Aihein Dulha Hamaar* (When will my groom come)—Music: Surendra Kohli. Cast: Kunal Singh.

1993 (2)

1. *Ghar Angna* (The home and courtyard)—Director: Arti Bhattacharya. Music: Ajay Swami. Cast: Kunal Singh, Vidyashree, Aanchal.
2. *Palna Mein Jhoole Lalna Hamaar* (On the cot swings my lovely baby)—Cast: Padma Khanna, Rakesh Pandey, Bandini Mishra.

1994 (4)

1. *Chala Sakhi Dulha Dekhe* (Let's go to see the groom, friend)—Director: Raju Singh. Music: Surendra Kohli. Cast: Kunal Singh, Lalitesh, Sunaina.
2. *Hamaar Sajna* (My lover): Director: Aslam Sheikh.
3. *Langari Anhari* (Lame and blind girl).
4. *Rakhiha Laaj Ancharva Ke* (Keep the honour of the aanchal).

1995 (6)

1. *Dulha Dulhin* (Bride and groom).
2. *Ghar Mandir* (The house is a temple)—Music: Sukhwinder Singh.
3. *Ho Jaye Da Naina Chaar* (Let our eyes meet)—Producer: Sanjay Rai. Director: Rajkumar Sharma. Music: Uttam-Jagdish. Cast: Pankaj Sharma and Indrani Banerjee.
4. *Ma Qasam* (I swear by my mother).
5. *Naag Devta* (Snake God)—Producer-director: Ram Narayan. Music: Raam-Laxman. Cast: Lalitesh, Rooplata, Vijay Khare (This film was made in three languages).

1996 (6)

1. *Haq Ke Ladai* (The fight for justice)—Producer: Meera. Director: Kiran Kant. Music: Arun Baijnath. Cast: Padma Khanna, Rakesh Pandey, Kunal Singh, Vijay Khare.
2. *Jhumkee* (Earrings).
3. *Palkan Ke Mehman* (The favoured guest)—Producer: S.S. Naeem. Director: Rajpati. Music: Surendra Kohli.
4. *Piritiya ke Dushman* (The enemy of love).
5. *Saat Phere* (Marriage)—Director: Nihal Singh. Music: Surinder Kohli. Cast: Kunal Singh, Shoma Anand, Lalitesh, Sunaina.
6. *Saath Hamaar Tohar* (Our togetherness).

1997 (2)

1. *Bhaile Piya Guleri Ke Phool* (My love has become like the *guleri* flower)—Producer: Sanjay Singh Thakur. Director: Prem Singh. Music: Uttam Singh.
2. *Hum Na Jaibo Sasur Ghar* (I won't go to my in-laws' place)—Producer: Mohanji Prasad, S.K. Jain. Director: Kalpataru. Cast: Sachin, Raj Kiran, Sriram Lagoo, Tanuja.

1998 (6)

1. *Bairi Sajna* (Enemy lover)—Director: Raju Singh. Cast: Kunal Singh, Kirti Singh, Shoma Anand, Rakesh Pandey.
2. *Batohiya* (Traveller)—Producer: B.R. Choubey. Director: Ashim Paul. Music: Ram Laxman. Cast: Sujit Kumar, Rakesh Pandey, Meera Madhuri.
3. *Ganga Maiya Tohri Mamta Mahan* (O Mother Ganga, your generosity knows no bounds)—Music Director: Ravindra Jain.
4. *Mahua*—Producer: Rana Anil Singh. Director: Akash Yogi. Music: R.K. Khanna.
5. *Neha Lagauni Saiyan Se* (I love my sweetheart)—Producer: Kamtanath Dube and Mithilesh Kumar. Director: Jagdish Singh. Music: Surendra Kohli. Cast: Rashmi Anand, Yusuf Khan.
6. *Sapna Ke Angna Mein* (In the courtyard of dreams).

1999 (2)

1. *Biyah* (Marriage)—Director: Shriman Mishra. Music: Vijay Shrivastava. Cast: Brij Kishore, Vijay Khare, Vazir Khan, Parnita Jaiswal, Sushma Seth.
2. *Dilwa Pe Kehu Ke Jor Nahi* (Love knows no coercion)—Director: Zulfikar Ali. Music: Rishi Raj.

2000 (2)

1. *Dulhin Bani More Bahiniya* (My sister will be a bride)—Producer: Satshri Bihari. Director: Pramod Bharadwaj. Music: S. Bavre. Cast: Lalitesh, Satnam Kaur.
2. *Hey Tulsi Maiya* (O mother tulsi [plant])—Producer: Mohan Tiwary. Director: Padma Khanna. Music: Uttam Singh. Cast: Rakesh Pandey, Rita Bhaduri, Lalitesh, Neeta Puri.

2001 (3)

1. *Lagal Karejwa Mein Teer* (An arrow has pierced my heart)—Music: Satyanarayan Mishra.
2. *Maai Ke Dulaar* (Mother's love)—Producer: Deep Shresth. Director: S. Sinha. Music: Dheeraj Kumar. Cast: Kunal, Sonashree and Deep Shresth.
3. *Sohaagan* (The married woman).

2002 (7)

1. *Balma Anadi* (Inexperienced lover)—Producer: Yugal Kumar Mishra. Director: Prabir Ganguly. Music: Bulu-Papa.
2. *Guru Dakshina* (Tutor's fee)—Producer: Mahesh Verma. Director: Lalji Yadav. Music: Vedpal Verma and Vijay Ajit. Cast: Vijay Behl, Saraswati Chatterjee.
3. *Jingi Bairi Bhail Hamaar* (Life's become my enemy)—Music: Aziz Ali.
4. *Saajan Pardesiya* (Foreigner-lover).
5. *Saiyan Bedardi* (Unfeeling lover)—Producer: Jagat Kishore. Writer-director: Lalji Yadav. Music: Baba Jagirdar. Cast: Amit Kapoor, Rajni Singh, Satnam Kaur, Rajesh Tomar and Bharat Kapoor.
6. *Saiyan Hamaar* (My lover)—Producer-director-writer: Mohanji Prasad. Music: Tabun and Sujit Kumar. Cast: Ravi Kishan, Arpita Paul.
7. *Sajna Ke Angna* (The courtyard of my love)—Music: Dilip Sen-Sameer Sen. Cast: Kunal Singh, Ajay Sinha.

2003 (10)

1. *Chalin Aaj Deswa Ki Ore* (Let's go towards our native place)—Producer-writer: Manoj Verma. Director: Prabhat Prabhakar. Music: Aziz Ali Zaveri. Cast: Manoj Verma, Mona Parekh, Rajesh Mishra, Ratan Varshney.

2. *Ehi Kaisan Kanyadan* (What kind of *kanyadaan* is this)—Producer: Vakil Ahmed Khan. Director: Raju Singh. Music: Shikhar Sharma.

3. *Jaibey Sajanwa Ke Des* (Will go to my lover's country).

4. *Kahia Doli Leke Aiboo* (When will you bring the palanquin).

5. *Kanyadaan*—Producer: Marina Upadhyay. Director: Sushil Upadhyay. Music: Amod Bhatt and Manoj Tiwari. Cast: Kunal Singh, Ravi Kishan, Kirti Gaekwad.

6. *Mai Tohre Khatir* (For you my mother)—Producer: Harish Chand Jain. Director: Prem Singh. Music: M. Anand. Cast: Upasana Singh, Dev Joshan.

7. *Najariya Kahe Se Ladavla* (Why did you let our eyes meet).

8. *Nadi Ke Lahariya Bole* (The waves of the river speak)—Director: Diwakar and Dipankar Bose.

9. *Piya Ke Ghar Pyaara Lage* (My lover/husband's home is great)—Producer: Baiju Pandey. Director: Braj Bhooshan. Music: Pappu Srivastava. Cast: Uday Srivastava, Madhuri Mishra, Gopal Rai, Rajesh Singh, Asne and Gaurav.

10. *Saiyan Se Kar Da Milanwa He Ram* (O God, please unite me with my love)—Producer: Daga. Director: Mohanji Prasad. Music: Tabun. Cast: Ravi Kishan, Rupa Ganguly, Rakesh Bedi, Rekha Sahay.

2004 (21)

1. *Balma Bada Nadaan* (My lover is naïve)—Producer: Dr Dushyant Tyagi and others. Director: Sujit Kumar. Music: Dhananjay Mishra. Cast: Samarth Chaturvedi, Divya Desai, Madhuri Mishra and Sujit Kumar.

2. *Balma Mora Banka* (My love is brave)—Director: Triloknath Bhatia. Cast: Seema Vaz, Abhishek, Sujit, Mehnaz.

3. *Devar Bhabhi* (Husband's brother and brother's wife)—Music: Surendra Kohli.

4. *Durga Banli Kali* (Durga has become Kali)—Producer: Mohan Dubey, Onkar Singh Mawa. Director: Narendra Tiwary. Music: Bimal-Pravesh.

5. *Ganga Jaisan Mai Hamaar* (Ganga is like my mother)—Producer: Mohanji Prasad, Kishan Khagadia, Kamal Nayan. Director-writer: Mohanji Prasad. Music: Rajesh Gupta. Cast: Kunal Singh, Ravi Kishan, Sikander, Chandni Chopra, Jagdeep, Upasna Singh.

6. *Ganga Jaisan Paawan Piritiyaa Hamaar* (My love is sacred like the Ganga)—Producer: Rajkumar Shahabadi. Director: Govind Moonis. Music: Omkaar. Cast: Ravi Kishan, Sadhna Singh, Divya Dwivedi, Rajesh Singh.

7. *Ganga Ke Paar Saiyan Hamaar* (My lover is on the other side of Ganga): Producer: Ashok Chand Jain. Director: Braj Bhooshan. Music: Surendra Kohli and Dhananjay Mishra. Cast: Kunal, Gaurav, Maansi, Gouri Khurana, Sahila Chadha, Vijay Khare.

8. *Humke Maafi Daee Da* (Forgive me)—Producer: Jyoti Vinay Joshi, Shailesh Patil and Yogesh Kulkarni. Director: Dipankar and Diwakar Bose. Music: Bapi-Salim. Cast: Manoj Tiwari, Hemakshi.

9. *Laagi Chhute Na* (You cannot cast off love).

10. *Mai Ke Maryada* (Mother's honour).

11. *Manva Ke Meet* (Love of the heart)—Music: Sidhant Madhav.

12. *Mohe Bhool Gaye Saanwariya* (My lover has forgotten me).

13. *Naihar Ke Mado Piya ki Chunri* (The wedding seat of the natal home, the stole given by the husband): Cast: Manoj Tiwari, Jayabharti.

14. *Nayanva Ke Baan* (Arrow of the eyes).

15. *Piparwa Paar Ke Brahm* (The ghost beyond the peepul tree). Cast: Kunal Singh

16. *Saanchi Piritiya Hamaar* (My love is true)—Producer-director: Anand Girdhar. Music: Ajay Swami.

17. *Sasura Bada Paisewala* (Father-in law has pots of money)—Producer: Ajay Sinha and Sudhakar Pandey. Director: Ajay Sinha. Music: Lal Sinha. Cast: Manoj Tiwari, Rani Chatterjee.

18. *Senur Tohar Naam Ke* (The vermilion of your name).

19. *Sohagan Bana Da Sajna Hamaar* (Marry me my lover)—Producer: Sunil Boobna. Director-story: Sunil Sinha. Music: Nikhil-Vinay. Cast: Ravi Kishan, Rinku Ghosh, Divya Desai, Avinash Wadhavan.

20. *Suhagin* (The married woman)—Producer: Ahmed Ali Sheikh and Pawan Verma. Director: Nihal Singh. Music: Shekhar Sharma.
21. *Vidhana Tohre Des Mein*—Producer: Kashinath Mishra. Director: Shailesh Srivastava. Music: Younis Qureshi. Cast: Sujit Kumar, Swati Anand, Sarvesh Dube.

2005 (45)

1. *Aashish Ganga Maiyaa Ke* (The blessings of Mother Ganga).
2. *Bandhan Toote Na* (The ties shouldn't break)—Producers: Abhay Sinha and Chandru Bhaktiani. Director: Aslam Sheikh. Music: Dhananjay Mishra. Cast: Manoj Tiwari, Madhumita Sarkar, Mahesh Raja, Rani Chatterjee, Upasana Singh, Arvind Pandey, Kunal Singh and Shakti Kapoor, Meera.
3. *Damaadji* (Son-in-law)—Producer: Sudhir Kumar and Meenaxi Sinha. Director: Bobby Singh. Music: Lal Sinha. Cast: Manoj Tiwari, Rani Chatterji, Anjan Srivastava, Pushpa Verma, Brijesh Tiwari.
4. *Daroga Babu I Love You*—Producer: Sudhakar Pandey and Vijay Shukla. Director: Bali. Music: Lal Sinha. Lyrics: Vinay Bihari. Cast: Manoj Tiwari, Rinku Ghosh, Akhilesh Singh.
5. *Dhartiputra* (Son of the earth)—Producer: Tinu Verma. Director: Bali. Music: Lal Sinha. Cast: Manoj Tiwari, Lovy Rohatgi, Tinu Verma, Bali.
6. *Doli* (Palanquin)—Music: Shekhar Sharma.
7. *Doli Aayee Tohar Angna* (Palanquin comes to your home)— Director: Kanhaiya Ramlal.
8. *Dulha Aisan Chahi* (I want a groom like this).
9. *Dulha Milal Dildaar* (I got a generous groom)—Producer: Avinash Kashid and Sudhir Kumar. Director: Sunil Prasad. Music: Rajesh Gupta. Cast: Ravi Kishan, Kunal Singh, Nagma, Dilip Sinha, Namrata Thapa, Pravin Sisodia.
10. *Dulhin Hoye To Aisan* (I need a bride like this)—Producer: Naresh Namdev. Director: Manoj Bharadwaj. Music: Bubli. Cast: Barkha Khandelwal, Achint Nag, Kanisha Khan, Vinod Tripathi, Liliput.

11. *Dulhaniya Naach Nachaye* (The bride makes you dance)—Producer-director: Ajay Sinha. Music: Lal Sinha. Lyrics: Bipin Bahar. Cast: Vikrant Singh, Mansii, Ajay Sinha.

12. *Dushmani* (Enimity)—Music: Dheeraj Sen.

13. *Firangi Dulhaniya* (Foreigner-bride)—Producer: Jyoti Premi, Preeti Singh and Pooja Khandpur. Director: Ranjan Kumar Singh. Music: Satish-Ajay. Cast: Taniya, Surendra Pal, Siraj Mustafa, Manoj Verma, Shamim Sheikh, Prakash Jais.

14. *Ganga Mile Sagar Se* (Ganga meets the sea)—Producer: Shailendra Goel. Director: Braj Bhooshan. Music: Rakesh Trivedi. Cast: Gaurav, Gunjan Kapoor, Sona Batra, Sahila Chadha, Vijay Khare.

15. *Ganga Tohaar Pani Amrit* (O Ganga your water is like nectar)—Producer: Arvind Kumar and Renu Jaiswal. Director-writer: K.K. Singh. Music and lyrics: Ravindra Jain. Cast: Mahesh Raja, Mansii Shah, Arvind Kumar.

16. *Ganga Maiya Tohe Chunri Chadhaibo* (Mother Ganga, I'll offer you a stole)—Producer: Pradeep Bharadwaj. Director-writer: Chandrabhushan Mani. Music and lyrics: Ashok Ghayal. Cast: Rani Chatterjee, Samarth Chaturvedi, Seema Pandey.

17. *Gawna*—Producer-director: Sunil Mukesh. Music: Gurnaam Singh Mann. Cast: Brijesh Tripathi, Anuradha Dubey.

18. *Ghar Duar* (Home)—Producer-director-writer: Mahesh Pandey. Music: Suresh Anand. Cast: Gautam Chaturvedi, Suchita Tripathi, Deepak Qazir, Rinku Dhawan.

19. *Hamaar Bahiniya* (Our sister)—Director: Diwakar and Dipankar Bose.

20. *Hamaar Ghar, Hamaar Parivar* (My home, my family)—Producer: Aftab Hussain. Director: Sona. Music: Sona-Nasir. Cast: Sona, Kunal Singh, Upasna Singh.

21. *Hamaar Bhoomi* (Our land)—Producer: A. Darpan. Music: Sujit Choubey. Cast: Madhuri Mishra, Seema Pandey.

22. *Hum Ta Ho Gaini Tohaar* (I have become yours)—Producer: Shobha Bhatia and Kamla Devi. Director: Jatin Kumar. Music: Mukesh Singh. Lyrics: Chacha Chaudhary. Cast: Ravi Kishan,

Paresh Rawal, Kiran Kumar, Sreeprada, Kunal Singh, Shakti Kapoor, Aparijita.

23. *Jaane Tohara Hirday Hamre Jiyara Ke Haal* (Your heart knows the state of my heart)—Producer: Bharat Singh, Suryakant Tamradaman. Director: Diwakar and Dipankar Bose. Music: Bapi-Salim. Cast: Karan, Surya Dwivedi, Mansi Pandey, Roshan Khan and Sapna who appeared in an item number.

24. *Kab Hoi Gawna Hamaar* (When will my *gawna* happen)—Producer: Deipa Narayan Jha. Director: Anand D. Ghatraj. Music: Nikhil Vinay. Cast: Kunal Singh, Ravi Kishan, Divya Desai, Mahesh Raja, Paintal, Madhuri Mishra, Dinesh Hingoo, Yunus Pervez.

25. *Kab Hoi Milanwa Hamaar* (When shall we meet?).

26. *Mai Jaisan Bhauji Hamaar* (My elder brother's wife is like my mother)—Producer: Uday Lal Maurya. Director: Sona Diljag. Music: Ashok Ghayal. Cast: Prithvi, Neelam Singh, Sona, Ali Khan, Minakshi Tiwari.

27. *Mai Re Kar Da Bidai Hamaar* (Mother, send me to my husband's place)—Producer: Ankur Joshi. Director-writer: Sunil Prasad. Music: Rajesh Prasad. Cast: Ravi Kishan, Kunal Singh, Divya Desai, Namrata Thapa.

28. *Mai Ke Bitua* (Mother's son)—Producer: Champak Jain and Kanchan Kotwani. Director: Manoj Sharma. Music: Altaf Raja. Cast: Inder Kumar, Sangeeta Roy, Ashok Saraf, Upasana Singh, Sadashiv Amrapurkar.

29. *Mandir Jaisan Ghar Hamaar* (My home is like a temple)—Producer: Sushil Kumar Agarwal. Director: Kalpataru. Music: Rajesh Roshan. Cast: Vivek Mushran, Parikshit Sahni.

30. *Nadia Ke Teer* (Bank of the river).

31. *Nehia Ke Dorr* (Strings of love).

32. *Panditji Bataeen Na Biyah Kab Hoee* (Tell me panditji, when will we get married?)—Producer: Mohanji Prasad, Kishan Khagadiya and Kamal Nayan. Director: Mohanji Prasad. Music: Rajesh Gupta. Cast: Ravi Kishan, Sikander, Nagma, Rita Joshi, Kunal Singh, Brijesh Tripathi, Paintal.

33. *Piya Piya Bole Jiya* (My heart calls out to my love)—Producer: Piyush Chakravarty. Director-writer: Jeetendra Suman. Music: Dhruvajit Gogoi. Cast: Samarth Chaturvedi, Seema Pandey, Priya Mallik, Madhuri Mishra, Santosh Tandon.

34. *Piya Tohre Kaaran* (Because of you my love).

35. *Preet Na Jaane Reet* (Love knows no tradition)—Producer: Kavita Tiwari. Director: Ranjan Kumar Singh. Music: Sujit Choubey. Cast: Ravi Kishan, Chandni Chopra, Surendra Pal.

36. *Raja Bhojpuriya*—Producer: Alok Kumar and Ajit Srivastava. Writer-director: Ajit Srivastava. Music: Dhananjay Mishra. Cast: Ravi Kishan, Sangeeta, Kunal Singh, Prakash Jais, Sona Batra.

37. *Ram Lakhan Jaisa Betwa Hamaar* (My sons are like Ram and Laxman).

38. *Sach Bhaeel Sapanwa Hamaar* (My dreams have come true)—Producer-director: Madhuvrat Rai. Music: Prem-Kokila. Cast: Dev Joshan, Kashish Duggal, Dilip Sinha, Madhurima Tiwari.

39. *Saiyan Tohare Pe Naaz Ba* (My love, I am proud of you)—Producer-director: Gulshan R. Ali. Music: Bimal Raj. Cast: Aditya Vishwakarma, Sanjana, Raza Murad, Kunal Singh.

40. *Sakhi Hum Na Jaibe Sasur Ghar Mein* (Friend, I won't go to my in-laws' place): Producer: Rajesh Sinha and Shashikant Sharma. Director: Khalid S. Akhlaque. Music: Palash. Lyrics: Fanindra Rao. Cast: Nitu Singh, Mansi Shah, Pyare Mohan Sahay, Liliput.

41. *Satla Ta Gaila* (You are doomed if you get too close)—Producer: Shashank Srivastava. Director: Shailendra Srivastava. Music: Ajay Prasanna. Cast: Guddu Rangeela, Deepali, Sarvesh Dube, Mehfooz, Sona Batra, Maya Yadav.

42. *Shubh Vivah* (Happy marriage)—Producer: Gauhar-Amreen Khan. Director: Parvez Khan. Music: Palash Choudhary. Cast: Kunal Singh, Vijay Khare, Arvind Sharma, Yunus Parvez and Prema Kiran.

43. *Senura Ke Laaj* (The honour of vermilion)—Producer: Parmanand Agarwal. Director: Nihal Singh. Music: Manoj Negi. Cast: Surendra Pal, Reza Murad, Sheetal Suvarna, Umesh Singh.

44. *Yashoda Mai Jaisan Bhauji Hamaar* (My elder brother's wife is like Yashoda Mai [Lord Krishna's mother])—Producer: Umesh, Manoj and Bihari Kushwaha. Director; Devendra Kapoor. Music: Vijay K. Bihari. Cast: Abhilasa, Seema Pandey, Paras Raj.

2006 (76)

1. *Ab Ta Ban Ja Sajanwa Hamaar* (At least now become my lover)—Producer: Saira Banu and Sultan Ahmed. Director: Arshad Khan. Music: Gunwant Sen-Raj Sen. Cast: Ravi Kishan, Nagma, Mona Thiba, Tej Sapru and Saahil Jaffrey.

2. *Aisan Pyaar Kahan* (Where can one get love like this?!)—Producer: Sadiq Ali, Dinesh Gupta, Ravi Chaurasia and Dinesh Chakravarty. Director: Mithilesh Avinash. Music: Shekhar Sharma. Lyrics: Dinesh Chakravarty 'Shayar'. Cast: Mahesh Raja, Surjeet Kumar, Gajendra Chauhan, Mehnaaz and Madhuri Mishra.

3. *Babul Pyaare* (Loving father)—Director: Rajesh Bhatt. Music: Gunwant Sen-Raj Sen. Cast: Ravi Kishan, Hrishita Bhatt, Jessica Bath, Arun Govil, Raj Babbar and Sachin.

4. *Bairi Piya* (Enemy-lover)—Producer: Vivek Shankar and M. Hakim. Director: Gyan Sahay. Music: Amar Haldipur. Cast: Mohit Daga, Pakhi, Shashi Puri, Dayashankar Pandey, Reema Lagoo.

5. *Balma 420* (Lover 420 [420 is the section in the Indian Penal Code dealing with petty crime])—Producer: Tanmay Sengupta. Director: Aslam Sheikh. Music: Dhananjay Mishra. Cast: Manoj Tiwari, Urvashi Chaudhari, Dilip Sinha, Shabnam Kapoor, Yunus Parvez, Shakti Kapoor, Jagdeep.

6. *Bambai Ke Laila Chhapra Ke Chhaila* (Bombay girl, Chhapra dude)—Producer: Punya Rana. Director: Mukesh Singh. Music: Satish-Ajay. Cast: Sikander Kharbanda, Divya Desai, Vivek Rawat, Prakash Jais, Rakesh Shahi.

7. *Beti Bhaeel Pardesi* (My sister has become a foreigner)—Producer: Manjubala, Archana, Suraj, Madho. Director-writer:

Amit Munna. Music: Sunil Chhaila Bihari. Cast: Sunil Chhaila Bihari, Siju Katariya, Kunika, Anjan Srivastava, K.K. Goswami.

8. *Bhagykar Laxmi* (also made in Jharkhandi).

9. *Bhaiya Anadi Bhauji Khiladi* (Brother inexperienced, his wife skilled)—Producer: Marina Upadhyay. Director: Sushil Upapdhyay. Music: Sapan Gum. Cast: Raghuveer Yadav, Sushil Singh, Swati Chhabra, Neha Kapoor.

10. *Bhakla* (made in the Bhojpuri dialect spoken in Chhattisgarh).

11. *Bhojpur Ke Chhaila Mumbai Ke Laila* (Bhojpur's dude, Mumbai's girl)—Producer: Sunil Kumar. Director: Bali. Music: Dhananjay Mishra. Cast: Ravi, Neha, Gyan Singh.

12. *Biahuti Chunri* (The wedding stole)—Producer: Yadu Nandan Mondal. Director-writer: Chandra Bhushan Mani. Music: Ajay Prasanna and Dilip Dutta. Cast: Neetu Singh, Sanjay Sharma, Sunil Mishra, Mukul Mani.

13. *Chacha Bhatija* (Uncle-nephew)—Producer: Sunil Kumar. Director: Bali. Music: Dhananjay Mishra. Cast: Vinay Anand, Gurline Chopra, Bali, Ranjiv Verma.

14. *Chalat Musafir Moh Liyo Re* (The traveller has been ensnared)—Producer: Sadhna and Sudhakar Pandey. Director-writer: Manoj Ojha. Music: Rajesh Gupta. Cast: Dinesh Lal Yadav 'Nirahua', Sunil Chhaila Bihari, Kalpana, Sushil Singh, Asrani.

15. *Charwaha Babu* (The cowherd)—Producer: Vidya Gandhi and Jagnarayan Pandey. Director-writer: Vidya Shankar. Music: A.K. Upadhyay. Cast: Gehna, Prithvi, Virendra, Suresh Chatwal, Sudipta Saxena.

16. *Chhaila Babu* (The dude)—Producer: Raj Kumar Pandey and G.D. Singh Chauhan. Director-writer: Raj Kumar Pandey. Music: Shekhar Sharma. Cast: Ayub Khan, Rani Chatterjee, Gaurav Ghai, Gunjan Kapoor, Seema Pandey, Himani Shivpuri, Kanu Mukherjee, Akshita Arora, Bandini Mishra.

17. *Coolie* (Porter)—Director: Sapan Saha. Music: Rajesh Gupta and Ashok Badr. Cast: Mithun Chakraborty, Meghna Naidu (Dubbed into Bhojpuri from the Hindi original).

18. *Dehati Babu* (The rustic)—Producer: N.R. Pachisia. Director:

Bali. Music: Lal Sinha. Cast: Manoj Tiwari, Shilpi Sharma, Bali, Brijesh Tiwari, Raza Murad.

19. *Devarjee* (Husband's brother)—Producer: Shravan Agarwal. Director: Ravi Sinha. Music: Rajesh Gupta. Lyrics: Nawab Arzoo. Cast: Krishna Abhishek, Sangeeta Tiwari.

20. *Dharti Kahe Pukaar Ke* (The earth calls out)—Producer: Nirmal Jani. Director-writer: Aslam Sheikh. Music: Dhananjay Mishra. Cast: Ajay Devgan, Manoj Tiwari, Sharbani Mukherjee, Shiv Baba, Aiyaz Khan.

21. *Didi Tor Devar Deewana* (Sister your husband's brother is crazy)—Producer: Kumari Mai Movies. Director-editor: Guddu Jaffri. Music: Shams Jameel. Cast: Sikander Kharbanda, Jharna, Sushil Chhetri, Vijay Khare.

22. *Driver Babu* (The driver)—Producer-director: Satyarth Sinha. Music: Master Shubarth. Cast: Yogesh Mahajan, Pragya Jadhav, Brij Gopal, Asha Tiwari, Ganga Verma.

23. *Dulhiniya Leke Jaib Hum* (I will take the bride away)— Producer: Ajit Kumar Singh. Director: Sanjay Sinha. Music: Rajesh Gupta. Cast: Mahesh Raja, Rashmi Shaw, Rakesh Pandey, Prithvi Singh.

24. *Gaon Ki Dulhiniya* (The village bride).

25. *Gaon Ki Ore* (Towards the village)—Producer: Amarendar Singh and Bhupender Singh. Director: Ramashrya Gupta. Music: Murlidhar. Cast: G.M. Singh (who was a Bahujan Samaj Party MLA), Namrata, Virender Singh.

26. *Gajab Bhail Rama* (A strange thing has happened)—Producer: Naushad A. Siddiqui. Director: Ahmed H. Siddqui. Music: Sayed Ali. Cast: Rahul Roy, Divya Desai, Yunus Parvez, Surendra Pal.

27. *Ganga*—Producer: Deepak Sawant. Writer-director: Abhishek Chadha. Music-lyrics: Ashok Ghayal. Choreographer: Saroj Khan, James Anthony and Ganesh Acharya. Cast: Amitabh Bachchan, Hema Malini, Manoj Tiwari, Ravi Kishan, Nagma, Vijay Khare.

28. *Ganga Jamuna*—Director: Suresh Jain. Cast: Gulshan, Aniket, Pratap Priya Singh.

29. *Godhan* (The wealth of cows)—Producer: Dhananjay Prasad. Director-writer: Jhunnu Srivastava. Music: Hemant Acharya. Cast: Samarth Chaturvedi, Seema Pandey, Aparna Agaskar, Pyare Mohan Sahay.

30. *Hum Bal Brahmachari Tu Kanya Kunwari* (I am a celibate and you are a virgin)—Producer: Shobha Kapoor, Ekta Kapoor and Mahesh Pande. Writer-director: Mahesh Pande. Cast: Kunal Singh, Sikander Kharbanda, Divya Desai.

31. *Hamaar Biyah Tohre Se Hoi* (I'll get married only to you)—Producer-Director: Salim Khan. Music: Durga-Natraj. Cast: Irfan Khan, Vidisha, Pyare Mohan Sahay, Mona Roy, Monika Patel.

32. *Hamaar Goriya* (My fair lady)—Producer: Anil Tripathi. Director: Lalji Yadav. Music: Baba Jagirdar. Cast: Shakti Arora, Priyanka Chhabra, Sonia Mishra, Ali Khan.

33. *Hamaar Gharwali* (My wife)—Producer: Sumesh Singh. Director: Dhananjay. Music: Ashok Ghayal. Cast: Ravi Kishan, Kunal Singh, Rinku Ghosh, Pankaj Kesri, Prakash Jaish.

34. *Hamka Aisa Waisa Na Samjha* (Don't think I am riff-raff)—Producer: Amita Srivastava, Shashiraj and Geetashree. Director-writer: Dr Sanjay Srivastava. Music: Ajay Prasanna. Cast: Dinesh Lal Yadav 'Nirahua', Supriya Chitransi, Jugal Kishore and Zafar Khan.

35. *Hamra Se Biyah Karba* (Will you marry me?)—Producer: Shridhar Shetty. Director: Braj Bhooshan. Music: Dhananjay Mishra. Choreographer: Ganesh Acharya. Cast: Ravi Kishan, Pratibha Pandey, Kunal Singh, Gunjan Kapoor.

36. *Hamri Bhi Aawegi Baraat* (Even my wedding procession will come)—Producer: Rajesh Tripathi. Director: B.N. Tiwari. Music: Nikhil-Vinay. Cast: Gaurav Dixit, Mukesh Tiwari, Pushpa Verma, Gita Mishra.

37. *Ho Gayeel Ba Pyaar Odhaniya Wali Se* (I have fallen in love with a girl wearing a stole)—Producer: Alok Kumar. Director: Ashok Kumar Deep and Rajeev Ranjan Das. Music-lyrics: Ashok Kumar Deep. Cast: Sunil Chaila Bihari, Dinesh Lal Yadav 'Nirahua', Ruby Singh and Poonam Saagar.

38. *Jai Jagannath*.
39. *Jhulaniya Lai Da Rajaji* (Rajaji, get me a swing)—Producer: Shakuntala Sengar. Director-writer: Devendra Pathik. Music: Rakesh Trivedi. Cast: Mahesh Raja, Neetu Singh, Uday Srivastava, Anuradha Singh.
40. *Julmi Sang Ankhiya Ladi* (I have fallen for a heartless person)— Producer: Ravi Ujjain. Director: Shatru. Music: Vinay Panwari. Cast: Ravi Ujjain and Himakshi.
41. *Kab Le Aayee Bahar* (When will the spring come?)—Producer: Dhananjay Pandey. Director: Aminesh Parvat. Music: Rajesh Gupta. Cast: Prithvi, Shalini Kapoor, Karan Anand, Dev Malhotra.
42. *Kangna Khanke Piya Ke Angna* (The braclet tinkles in my love's courtyard)—Producer: Anil Sisodia. Director-writer: Rajkumar Pandey. Music: K. Ratnesh. Cast: Vinay Anand, Rani Chatterjee, Divya Desai, Yunus Pervez, Brijesh Tripathi, Sona Batra.
43. *Kanhaiya*—Producer: Manish and Ajay Patadiya. Director-writer: Arti Bhattacharya. Music-lyrics: Ashok Ghayal. Cast: Ravi Kishan, Kunal Singh, Upasana Singh, Rati Agnihotri, Mona Thiba, Sheetal Bedi.
44. *Lagana*.
45. *Mai Baap* (Father-mother)—Producer: Sagoon Wagh. Director: Mohanji Prasad. Music: Rajesh Gupta. Cast: Ravi Kishan, Kunal Singh, Rati Agnihotri, Mahima Mukherjee, Reshmi Bhattacharya.
46. *Mai Ke Ancharwa Mein Charo Dham* (In my mother's anchal are the four holy pilgrimage spots)—Producer: Narendra Singh Lal. Director: Khalid S. Akhlaque. Music: Suresh Anand. Cast: Amresh Kumar, Lata, Anjan Shrivastava, Tiku Talsania, Pushpa Verma and Anup Jalota.
47. *Maiya Rakhiha Senurwa Aabaad* (O mother, protect my husband)—Producer: Ravi Bhushan and Ranjeet Kumar. Director: Ravi-Sanjay. Music: Durga-Natraj. Cast: Neeraj Bharadwaj, Kashish, Rakesh Pandey, Sriprada, Lalitesh, Dilip Sinha and Jasbir Jassi.

48. *Mangalsutra* (Sacred thread/chain symbolizing marriage)—
Producer: Gopi Mallya. Director: Bobby Singh. Music: Lal
Sinha. Cast: Manoj Tiwari, Shalini Kapoor, Ranjeev Verma,
Surendra Pal and Anjana Mumtaz.

49. *Mor Karejwa Ke Tukra* (Apple of my eye)—Producer: Narayan
Bhandari. Director: Narayan-Abhishek. Music: Ashok Ghayal.
Cast: Kunal Singh, Vijay Khare, Dev Joshan, Sweety Chhabra,
K.K. Goswami.

50. *Najariya Kahe Ke Ladavla* (Why did you fall in love?).

51. *Pandit* (The priest)—Producer-director: Tinu Verma. Music:
Dhananjay Mishra. Cast: Ravi Kishan, Nagma, Kunal Singh,
Tinu Verma.

52. *Pati Parmeshwar* (Husband-God).

53. *Piya Tohse Naina Laage* (I have fallen in love with you)—
Producer: Rishi Prakash Mishra. Director: Bal Krishna. Music:
K. Ratnesh. Music: Akhilesh Pandey, Priya Gill, Kashish
Duggal, Vibhuti Tripathi.

54. *Pujiha Charan Mai Baap Ke* (Worship your parents' feet)—
Producer: Hema Shahi. Director: Sunil Sinha. Music: R.K. Arun
and Suresh Anand. Cast: Kunal Singh, Rama Vij, Krishna
Abhishek, Rani Chatterjee, Vijay Khare.

55. *Pyaar Ke Bandhan* (The bonds of love)—Producer: Abhay
Sinha and Pradeep Bharadwaj. Director: Aslam Sheikh. Music:
Dhananjay Mishra. Cast: Manoj Tiwari, Sadhika Randhawa,
Raza Murad, Shabnam Kapoor, Brijesh Tripathi, Anand Mohan.

56. *Raja Thakur*—Producer-director: Tinu Verma. Music: Lal Sinha
and Dhananjay Mishra. Cast: Shatrughan Sinha, Manoj Tiwari,
Tinu Verma, Nagma.

57. *Raghupati Raghav Raja Ram*—Director: Diwakar and
Dipankar Bose. Cast: Vikrant Singh, Charu Sharma, Monalisa.

58. *Raksha Bandhan-Aego Bachan* (Raksha Bandhan—a
promise)—Producer: Nasir Jamal. Director-story: Tufail
Ahmed. Music: Dhananjay Mishra. Cast: Vikrant Singh,
Deepali, Samarth Chaturvedi, Seema Mallik, Ranjiv Verma.

59. *Rangli Chunariya Tohre Naam* (I painted the stole in your
name)—Producer: Prem Prakash Shah, Rajesh Upadhyay,

Mandar Muranjan. Director-writer: Vikash Mitra. Music: Ghunghroo. Cast: Pawan Singh, Sonali Joshi, Rakesh Pandey, Gaurav Ghai.

60. *Rasili Tohre Khatir* (For you, o sexy one)—Producer: Ravi Kishan. Lyrics: Bimal Kashyap. Music: Baiju Vansi. Cast: Ravi Kishan, Sonia Tiwari.

61. *Ravi Kishan*—Director: Anmol Shetge. Music: Satish-Ajay. Cast: Ravi Kishan, Zarina Wahab, Mona Thiba, Avedesh Mishra, Sneha Ahuja.

62. *Sathi Sanghaati* (Friend and companion)—Producer: N. Jain, M. Sharma, V. Desai and P. Lunavat. Director: Prabhat Prabhakar. Music: Rajesh Gupta. Cast: Krishna Abhishek, Daksh Sethi, Sweety Chhabra, Divya Desai, Anupam Shyam.

63. *Saiyan Se Solah Singaar*—Producer: Aditya Narain Singh. Director: Ramnesh Puri. Music: Pramod Tripathi. Cast: Ravi Kishan, Nagma, Pakhi Hegde, Sheetal Bedi, Roshan Khan and Deep Raj Rana.

64. *Saiyan Sipahia* (My cop-lover): Producer: Vimal Jha and Menka Ojha. Director-writer: Devendra.

65. *Pathik* (The traveller)—Music: Sanjeev Rana. Cast: Abhay Kumar, Rajesh Singh, Gunjan Kapoor, Uday Srivastava, Janardan Rajbhar and Brijesh Tripathi.

66. *Sasurari Zindabad* (The in-laws' home, zindabad)—Producer: Shivkumar Damani. Director: Ravi Sinha. Music: Rajesh Gupta. Lyrics: Vinay Bihari and Pushpa Verma. Cast: Ravi Kishan, Swati Verma, Damini, Rajesh Puri, Raza Murad and Himani Shivpuri.

67. *Saugandh* (The promise)—Producer: Sunil Boobna. Director: Alok Kushwaha. Music: Rajesh Gupta. Cast: Manoj Tiwari, Rinku Ghosh, Sweety Chhabra, Surendra Pal Singh, Upasna Singh, Madhuri Mishra, Harsh Jain.

68. *Sindoorwa Badaa Anmol Sajanwa* (The vermilion is priceless my love)—Producer-writer: M. Singh. Director: Santosh Badal. Music: Jayant Aaryan. Cast: Vijay Khare, Yogesh Mahajan, Seema Pandey, Pradip Sharma, Avdesh Mishra and Nagendra Yadav.

69. *Sitapur Ki Geeta* (Sitapur's Geeta).
70. *Suhaag* (Spouse/Marriage)—Producer: Jyotsna Gupta. Director: Ravi Sinha. Lyrics: Vinay Bihari Music: Rajesh Gupta. Cast: Krishna Abhishek, Rinku Ghosh, Gajendra Chauhan, Dilip Sinha and Anand Mohan.
71. *Suraj Bihari*—Director: Bakul Soni. Music: Pawan Kumar.
72. *Tohar Kiriya* (I swear by you)—Producer: Deepak and Harish Punjabi. Director: Rajesh Babbar. Music: Satish-Ajay. Cast: Ravi Kishan, Mona Thiba, Rakhi Malhotra and Kunal Singh.
73. *Tohar Pyaar Chahi* (I want your love)—Producer: Dinesh, Kinnari and Ujjawal Somani. Director-writer: Jagdish C. Pandey. Music: Vishnudhar Mishra and Devendra Bharti. Cast: Krishna Abhishek, Seema Mallik, Madhurima Tiwari.
74. *Tohse Pyar Ba* (I love you)—Producer: Naveen and Rajendra Agarwal. Director: Ranjan Kumar Singh. Music: Rajdhar Suresh. Lyrics: Virendra Singh Vatsa. Cast: Vinay Anand, Divya Desai, Nilesh Kumar, Malini Kapoor, Guddi Maruti, Roshan Khan and Surendra Pal Singh.
75. *Uthaila Ghoongta Chand Dekh Le* (Raise the veil and see the moon)—Producer: Satyan J. Sharma. Director: Jagdish Sharma. Music: Rajesh Gupta. Cast: Ravi Kishan, Bhagyashree, Kunal Singh, Brijesh, Upasana Singh and Pushpa Verma.

2007 (67)

1. *Ae Babuni* (Hey girl)—Producer: Virendra Kumar Mishra. Director: Umesh Srivastava. Music: Shashikant Mishra. Cast: Sadhna Singh, Dev Joshan, Divya Dwivedi.
2. *Ankiya Ladiye Gayeel* (The eyes met at last)—Producer: Sushil Singh and Satish Kumar. Director: Sunil Sinha. Music: Satish Munna. Lyrics: Vinay Bihari. Cast: Vinay Anand, Rinku Ghosh, Sweety Chhabra, Vijay Khare, Upasna Singh, Shakti Kapoor and Sambhavna Seth.
3. *Badki Mai* (Elder mother)—Producer: Ashok Chand Jain. Director-writer: Dularchand. Music: Surendra Kohli. Cast: Sumeet Baba, Kalpana Shah, Dev Malhotra.

4. *Baklol Dulha* (Stupid groom)—Producer; Arvind Srivastava. Director: Oman Khan. Music: Gunwant Sen-Raj Sen. Cast: Pankaj Kesri, Rani Chatterjee, Namrata Thapa.

5. *Banke Bihari MLA*—Producer: Ramesh Rao. Director-writer: Babloo Soni. Music: Gunwant Sen-Raj Sen. Choerography: Rekha Chinni Prakash. Cast: Ravi Kishan, Rambha, Kunal Singh, Vijay Khare.

6. *Bedardi Balma* (Cruel lover)—Director: K. Bhushan. Music: Pravin Kumar. Cast: Amit Pachori, Aman Sagar, Amisha, Reena.

7. *Bhaai Hokhe To Bharat Niyan* (A brother should be like Bharat)—Producer: Shashidhar Singh. Director: Abhishek. Music: Ashok Ghayal. Cast: Rani Chatterji, Bharat Sharma, Lalitesh, Sweety Chhabra, Dev Joshan.

8. *Bhaeel Pyaar Nachaniya Se* (Have fallen in love with a dancing girl)—Producer: Ram Hriday Soni. Director: Maninder Bhandari. Music: Pravin Kumar. Cast: Samarth Chaturvedi, Chandni Chopra.

9. *Bhojpuriya Bhaiya*—Producer: Sudip Pandey. Director-writer: Harry Fernandes. Music: Gunwant Sen-Raj Sen. Cast: Sudip Pandey, Bali, Rakesh Pandey, Roshan Khan.

10. *Chhotki Dulhin* (Younger bride)—Director: Abhay Aditya Singh. Music: Ganesh Pathak. Cast: Sikander Kharbanda, Rani Chatterjee, Nirmal Pandey, Sudhir Kumar.

11. *De Da Piritiya Udhar* (Give me love on loan)—Producer: Anil Samrat. Director: Ajit Srivastava. Music: Pappu Srivastava. Cast: Krishna Abhishek, Rinku Ghosh, Sweety Chhabra, Saurabh Sharma and Chhotu Chhalia.

12. *Des Mein Lawtal Pardesi* (The deserter has returned home)— Producer: K.C. Sharma. Director-story-screenplay: Prem Singh. Music: Madhukar Anand. Cast: Upasana Singh, Dinesh Bagri, Seema Azmi.

13. *Devaa*—Producer: Satyan J Sharma. Director: Jagdish Sharma. Music: Lal Sinha. Cast: Manoj Tiwari, Bhagyashree, Mushtaq Khan, Upasna Singh, Brijesh Tripathi.

14. *Gangotri*—Producer: Deepak Sawant. Writer-director: Abhishek. Music director: Ashok Ghayal. Cast: Amitabh

Bachchan, Hema Malini, Manoj Tiwari, Bhumika Chawla, Kunal Singh, Aruna Irani.

15. *Gawanva Le Ja Rajaji*—Producer: Alok Kumar. Director: Ajit Srivastava. Music and lyrics: Ashok Kumar Deep. Cast: Krishna Abhishek, Sweety Chhabra, Pakhi Hegde and Sambhavna Seth.

16. *Hamaar Dulhaniya Badi Paisewali* (My bride is a moneybag)— Director: Raja Ejaz Khan. Music: Rajesh Gupta. Cast: Vikrant, Deepali.

17. *Hamaar Izzat* (My/Our honour)—Producer: Manoj Gupta. Director-writer: Vijay Solanki. Music: Babu Kishan and Nirmal Pawar. Cast: Krishna Abhishek, Rani Chatterjee, Gajendra Chauhan, Jaishree T., Dev Malhotra and Ajay Anand.

18. *Hamaar Sainya Hindustani* (My lover is an Indian)—Producer: Raja Chaudhary, Nandlal Nandvani and Rajiv Singh. Director: Mohanji Prasad. Music: Rakesh Trivedi. Cast: Ravi Kishan, Shweta Tiwari, Raja Chaudhary, Surendra Pal, Rakesh Bedi, Upasna Singh, Raza Murad, Yunus Pervez.

19. *Hanuman Bhakt Havaldar* (The havaldar who worships Hanuman)—Producer and director: B.N. Tiwari. Music: Rajendra Salil. Cast: Manoj Tiwari 'Mridul', Nagma, Mukesh Tiwary, Sambhavna Seth, Ehsaan Qureshi.

20. *Ho Gayeel To Ho Gayeel* (If it has happened, it has happened)—Producer: Sanjeev Agarwal and Sunita Kumari. Director: Manoj Giri. Music: Pappu Srivastava. Cast: Vinay Anand, Gaurav Ghai, Farhana, Meena Nathani.

21. *Hoi Pyaar Ke Jeet* (Love will triumph)—Producer: Chandra Prakash Bhatia. Director: Maninder Bhandari. Music: Aman Shlok. Lyrics: Badar Asharfi. Cast: Samarth Chaturvedi, Chandni Chopra, Anup Arora.

22. *Hoke Tu Rahbu Hamaar* (You will become mine)—Director: Gopal Srivastava. Music: Sujeet Choubey. Cast: Vinay Anand, Sonali Joshi, Vijay Khare, Lalitesh, Sambhavna Seth.

23. *Hum Hayeen Ganwar* (I am uncouth)—Director: Raj Kumar Sharma. Music director: Sujit Chaubey. Cast: Vinay Anand, Divya Desai.

24. *Janam Janam Ke Saath* (Together for many lives)—Producer: Abhay Sinha. Director: Aslam Sheikh. Music: Dhananjay Mishra. Cast: Manoj Tiwari, Ravi Kishan, Bhagyashree, Rambha, Shakti Kapoor, Kiran Kumar and Mohan Joshi.

25. *Kab Aibu Aganwa Hamaar* (When will you come to my courtyard)—Producer: Pulse Media. Director-writer: Sanjay Tripathi. Music: Dhananjay Mishra. Cast: Manoj Tiwari, Shweta Tiwari.

26. *Kab Kahbu Tu I Love You* (When will you say I love you)—Producer; Deipa Narayan Jha. Director: Anand D Ghatraj. Music: Rajesh Gupta. Lyrics: Vinay Bihari. Cast: Amar Upadhyay, Gul, Mahesh Raja, Shivam Tiwari, Yunus Pervez, Pravin Sisodia, Sambhavna Seth and Yukta Mookhey.

27. *Kable Aihen Sajanva Hamaar* (When will my lover come?)—Producer: Lal Bahadur. Director: Vijay Borwanker. Music: Gunwant Sen-Raj Sen. Cast: Karan Anand, Namrata, Madhuri Mishra.

28. *Kahan Jaiba Najariya Churaike* (Where will you go to avoid me)—Producer: Suresh Maurya. Director: Mohammed Hanif. Music: Rajesh Prasad. Cast: Krishna Abhishek, Sikander Kharbanda, Kashish Duggal and Seema Mallik.

29. *Kahan Jaiba Raja Najariya Ladaike* (Where will you after stealing my heart)—Producer: Sunil Boobna. Director: Bali. Music and lyrics: Vinay Bihari. Cast: Dinesh Lal Yadav 'Nirahua', Monalisa, Gunjan Kapoor, Avdhesh Mishra, Bali.

30. *Kaise Kahin Tohara Se Pyar Ho Gayeel* (How do I say I have fallen in love with you?)—Producer: Nasir Jamal. Director-writer: G. Subbarao. Music: Dhananjay Mishra. Cast: Dinesh Lal Yadav 'Nirahua', Pakhi Hegde, Riaz Khan.

31. *Kasam Dharti Maiya Ki* (I swear on Mother Earth)—Producer: Pappu Bhai and Rajesh Singh. Director: Ajay Sinha. Music: Shashikant Sharma. Cast: Dinesh Lal Yadav 'Nirahua', Arti Patel, Rupam Kishore, Ritu Pandey.

32. *Lal Chunariya Wali* (The girl with the red stole)—Producer-director: Sanjeev Tony. Music: Ashok Ghayal. Cast: Rakesh Pandey, Vinay Anand, Rinku Ghosh, Vijay Khare, Lalitesh.

33. *Lage Raho Yadav Bhaiya* (Carry on brother Yadav).
34. *Londonwali Se Neha Lagauli* (I have fallen for a girl from London)—Producer: Rajendra Patel. Director: Devendra Pathik. Music: Sanjeev Rana. Cast: Krishna Abhishek, Rani Chatterji, Chandni Chopra, Ketaki Dave.
35. *Maati* (Earth)—Producer: Kunika Lal. Director: Sunil Prasad. Music: Rajesh Gupta. Cast: Ravi Kishan, Vijay Khare, Namrata Thapa, Kunika, Kunal Singh, Hiten Kumar, Pankaj Dheer.
36. *Manoj Bhaiya*.
37. *Mumbaiwali Muniya* (The girl from Mumbai)—Cast: Sumit Baba, Kalpana, Raza Murad, Vijay Khare.
38. *Munna Pandey Berojgar* (Unemployed Munna Pandey)—Director: Manish Jain. Music: Lal Sinha. Cast: Manoj Tiwari, Rani Chatterji, Abha Parmar, Ranjeet.
39. *Nachaniya: Ek Tamasha* (Dancing girl: An amusement)—Producer: Sanjeev Mehta and Dharampal Singh. Director-writer: Arvind Tripathi. Music: Pravin Kunwar. Cast: Samarth Chatruvedi, Gunjan Kapoor, Anupam Shyam.
40. *Nautanki* (Play).
41. *Nirahua Rickshawala* (Nirahua Rickshaw-puller)—Producer: Ashok K. Kotwani. Director: K.D. Music: Rajesh-Rajnish. Lyrics: Shyam Dehati. Cast: Dinesh Lal Yadav 'Nirahua', Pakhi Hegde, Sushil Singh, Manoj Tiger and Sambhavna Seth.
42. *Pandav*—Producer: Ajai, Roli and Pragna Jaiswal. Director: Jai Prakash. Music: Dhananjay Mishra. Cast: Ravi Kishan, Kunal Singh, Sikander Kharbanda, Sadhika Randhawa, Brijesh Tripathi.
43. *Pammy Se Pyar Ho Gayeel* (I am in love with Pammy).
44. *Pappu Ke Pyar Ho Gayeel* (Pappu has fallen in love)—Producer: Vinod Bachchan. Director: Aslam Sheikh. Music: Lal Sinha. Cast: Manoj Tiwari, Divya Desai, Brijesh Tripathi, Roshan Khan, Mushtaq Khan.
45. *Phoolva Se Mahke Angna Hamaar* (My courtyard smells of flowers)—Producer: Anil Gajraj. Director: Braj Bhooshan. Music: Amresh Shahabadi. Cast: Rohit Choudhary, Gunjan Kapoor, Jai Tilka, Dilip Sinha, Vijay Khare.

46. *Pinjrewali Muniya* (The girl in the cage)—Producer: Shailesh Patil and Yogesh Kulkarni. Director: Kanchan Nayak. Music: Manoj Vinay. Cast: Ravi Kishan, Rinku Ghosh, Mohan Joshi, Ashish Vidyarthi.

47. *Purab* (East)—Producer: Murtaza Jafri. Director: Aslam Sheikh and Abhay Aditya Singh. Music: Lal Sinha. Cast: Manoj Tiwari, Sadhika Randhawa, Nirmal Pandey, Upasna Singh.

48. *Piritiya Tohaar* (Your love)—Producer: Dr Balwant Shastri. Director: Manoj Sharma. Music: Rajan Guruji. Cast: Krishna Abhishek, Lovy Rohatgi, Upasna Singh, Priya Subba, Rajesh Vivek, Madhuri Mishra.

49. *Purab Aur Paschim* (East and west)—Producer: Manoj Bhatnagar. Director-writer: Jayprakash. Music: Gunwant Sen-Raj Sen. Cast: Ravi Kishan, Suman Ranganath, Smita Jayakar, Sheela Sharma.

50. *Qasam Dharti Maiya Ke* (I swear by Mother Earth).

51. *Ram Balram*—Producer: Pradeep Bharadwaj and Chandan Singh. Director-writer: Mohanji Prasad. Music: Rajesh Gupta. Cast: Ravi Kishan, Rambha, Vidisha, Sikander, Aruna Irani, Kunal Singh, Rakhi Sawant, Brijesh Tripathi.

52. *Rang Barse Ganga Kinaar* (Colour rains by the banks of the Ganga)—Producer: Santosh, Animesh and Neeraj. Director: Shriram Dubey. Music: Surendra Kohli. Cast: Krishna Abhishek, Kashmira Shah, Kashish Duggal, Sambhavna Seth.

53. *Rasik Balma* (Sexy lover)—Producer: Mohan Rayana and Venkatesh Rayana. Director: Mohanji Prasad. Music: Rajesh Gupta. Cast: Ravi Kishan, Rambha, Tiku Talsania, Anjan Shrivastava, Brijesh Tripathi, Sunil Pal, Vivek Shauq, Upasna Singh, Sambhavna Seth.

54. *Saas Nanad Bhauji* (Mother-in-law, husband's sister and his brother's wife)—Writer-director: Manoj Narayan.

55. *Saas Rani Bahu Naukrani* (Mother-in-law is queen and the daughter-in-law is the servant)—Producer: Manatee Productions. Director: Braj Bhooshan. Music: Sujit Chaube. Cast: Gaurav Ghai, Urvashi Dholakia, Sahila Chadha, Kunal Singh.

56. *Sab Golmaal Ha* (Everything's improper)—Producer: Inder Kumar and Ashok Thakeriya. Director: Johny. Cast: Ravi Kishan, Sunil Chaila, Sweety Chabria, Pakhi Hegde.

57. *Sajanwa Anadi, Sajania Khiladi* (The boy/lover is inexperienced, the girl is skilful)—Director-writer: Kishore Rana 'Magar'. Music: Baba Jagirdar. Cast: Krishna Abhishek, Vijay Khare, Nikhil Upreti.

58. *Sajanwa Sath Nibhaiha* (My love, always be my companion).

59. *Sajanwa Tohre Khatir* (For you my love)—Producer: Rajesh Gupta, Puneet and Vineet Bhatia. Director: Fateh Masoom. Music: Dhananjay Mishra. Cast: Ravi Kishan, Rinku Ghosh and Kunal Singh.

60. *Shammi Bhaiya*—Producer: Sandeep and Nilabh Tiwari. Director: Sanjeev Boharpi. Music: Aman Shlok. Cast: Shammi Tiwari, Arti Patel, Kunal Singh.

61. *Shreeman Driver Babu* (Mr Driver)—Producer: Anita and Raj Israni. Director: K.D. (Dinkar Kapoor). Music: Dhananjay Mishra. Lyrics: Vinay Bihari. Cast: Dinesh Lal Yadav 'Nirahua', Mona Lisa, Manoj Tiger, Akshita Arora, Manmoujee and Birbal.

62. *Teej*—Writer-director: Ashutosh Prabhakar. Music: Santosh Sharma. Cast: Avinash Shahi, Komal Dhillon, Manoranjan Jha.

63. *Toote Na Sanehia Hamaar* (Hope our love doesn't break)—Producer: R.C. Verma. Director: Nihal Singh. Music: Phoolchand Kokate. Cast: Sangram Singh, Smriti Singh, Babloo Dubey, Rani Mishra.

64. *Toote Na Sanehiya Ke Dor* (Hope the strings of our love don't break)—Producer: Arun Kumar Singh. Director: Vinod Kumar Singh. Music: Madhumay. Cast: Ketan Singh, Shivam Tiwari, Vaishali Shroff, Reza Murad, Kunal Singh, Manish Kabya.

65. *Tu Hamaar Haoo* (You are mine)—Producer: Kamal Rashid. Director: Jai Prakash. Lyrics: Bipin Bahar and Fanindra Rao. Music: Nikhil Vinay Cast: Ravi Kishan, Nagma, Manoj Tiwari, Upasna Singh.

66. *Tujhse Laagi Lagan* (I am in love with you)—Producer: Ashok Srivastava. Director: Mohan Hari. Music: Rampravesh. Cast: Subrat Dutta, Vishal Vijay, Poonam Bharti, Guddu Rangeela.
67. *Tulsi*—Producer: Anil Achrekar. Director: Bhagirath Swain. Music: Baba Jagirdar. Cast: Kunal Singh, Sidhant, Divya Desai, Amit Rai.
68. *Uga Ho Suraj Deo Arag Ke Bhail Ber* (Rise O sun god, it's time for an offering)—Producer: Jai Shanker. Director: Chandra Bhushan Mani. Music: Premji Lataji. Cast: Vinay Anand, Rinku Ghosh, Gunjan Kapoor, Yunus Pervez, Birbal.
69. *UP Bihar Bambai Express*—Producer: Abhishek and Harsh Tiwari. Director-writer: Rajkumar Pandey. Music: Aman Shlok. Lyrics: Shyam Sahni. Cast: Mohit Ghai, Rani Chatterjee, Rekha Sahay, Viju Khote, Kunal Singh, Poonam Sagar, Bandini Mishra.
70. *Vihulaa*.

2008 (unconfirmed list of 69 titles of films)

1. *Ae Balamji*.
2. *Ae Balam Pardesi*—Producer: J.C. Sharma. Director: Mohanji Prasad. Music: Rakesh Trivedi. Cast: Ravi Kishan, Sangita Tiwari, Priyanka Moitra, Rakesh Bedi.
3. *Aa Gaini Devi Maiyya Hamre Aanganwa*.
4. *Aapan Maati Aapan Desh*—Producer: Jai Kishen and Aashish Kedia. Director: M.I. Raj. Music: R.P. Thakur. Cast: Ravi Kishan, Sikander, Sudesh Berry, Sweety Chhabra, Megha Ghosh, Milind Gunaji.
5. *Ae Bhauji Ke Sister*—Producer: Barkha S. Singh. Director: Surendra Pal. Music: Dhananjay Mishra. Cast: Manoj Tiwari, Shweta Tiwari, Mukesh Khanna, Raza Murad.
6. *Aaya Pardesi More Gaon Re*—Producer: A. Ahmed, Abu Taib, Subhash Maurya. Director: Roshan Azmi. Music: Kshitij Anand. Cast: Akash Tripathi, Seema Sen, Vishnu Kunwar.
7. *BA Pass Bahuriya*.

8. *Betwa Bahubali*—Director: Sujit Puri. Music: Lal Sinha Cast: Ajay Dixit, Lovy Rohtagi.

9. *Bhai Hokhe To Aisan.*

10. *Bhaiya Ke Saali.*

11. *Bhojpuriya Daroga*—Producer: Sudip Pandey, Shikha Chidambare. Director: Manjul Thakur. Music: Gunwant Sen-Raj Sen. Cast: Sudip Pandey, Shikha Chidambare, Madhurima Tiwary, Ranjeev Verma.

12. *Bhole Shankar*—Producer: Gulshan Bhatia. Director: Pankaj Shukla. Music: Dhananjay Mishra. Cast: Mithun Chakraborty, Manoj Tiwari, Monalisa, Shabnam Kapoor, Lovy Rohatgi.

13. *Bidai*—Producer: Chandrashekhar Rao and Ishtiyak Sheikh. Director: Aslam Sheikh. Music: Dhananjay Mishra. Cast: Ravi Kishan, Rinku Ghosh, Brijesh Tripathi, Mohan Joshi.

14. *Chahee Maal Pani.*

15. *Chanda*—Music: Dhananjay Mishra.

16. *Chhodab Na Sang Tohar*—Music: Dipesh Bajpai.

17. *Dharam Veer*—Producer: Mukesh Pande. Director: Mohanji Prasad. Music: Dhananjay Mishra Cast: Ravi Kishan, Amar Upadhyay, Sadhika Randhawa, Brijesh Tripathi, Raza Murad.

18. *Dulha Albela*—Director: K.D. Cast: Monalisa, Vikrant, Sushil Singh, Priya Sharma, Prakash Jais.

19. *Ego Chumma De Da Rajaji*—Producer: Srishi Entertainment. Director: Javed Sayyed. Music: Jatin-Pandit. Cast: Manoj Tiwari, Ravi Kishan, Bhagyashree, Sweety Chhabra, Deep Shikha, Upasana Singh.

20. *Ee Mitte Me Sabch Kuchh Bate*—Music: Jayanti Mala.

21. *Gabbar Singh*—Producer: Shobha Kapoor, Ekta Kapoor, Mahesh Pandey. Director: Mahesh Pandey. Music: Satish-Ajay. Cast: Jeetendra, Dinesh Lal Yadav 'Nirahua', Ravi Kishan, Sikander, Mona Thiba, Seema Mallik, Sujit Kumar, Sambhavna Seth.

22. *Ganga Kinare Pyar Pukare*—Music: Akhilesh Kumar.

23. *Ganga Tohre Desh Mein*—Director: Amit Chauhan. Music: Aman Shlok. Cast: Dinesh Lal Yadav 'Nirahua', Gunjan Kapoor.

24. *Gorki Patarki Re*—Director: Amit Kumar Munna. Cast: Uttam Kumar, E. Ravi Shankar, Rani Chaturvedi.

25. *Hum Bahubali*—Director: Anil Ajitabh. Music: Dhananjay Mishra. Cast: Ravi Kishan, Dinesh Lal Yadav 'Nirahua', Amar Upadhyay, Rinku Ghosh, Sonal Jha, Dayashankar Pandey.

26. *Jaan De Deb Tohre Khatir*.

27. *Jab Lahu Pukarela*—Music: Rajesh Gupta.

28. *Jai Maiya Ambe Bhawani*—Music: Rajesh Gupta.

29. *Jogi Ji Dheere Dheere*—Producer: Anil Agarwal and Tarique Ejaaz. Director: Tarique Ejaaz. Music: Rajesh Gupta Cast: Pawan Singh, Sikandar Kharbanda, Kalpana Shah, Priyanka Moitra.

30. *Ka Kari Ka Na Kari*.

31. *Kahe Gaye Pardes Piya*.

32. *Kahawan Ke Bandhan Kahan Jud Jala*—Music: Santosh-Subhash.

33. *Karni Ke Phal Aaj Na Ta Kal*—Music: Vimal Raj.

34. *Khatailal Mithailal*—Producer: Chunnu Mehra. Director: Deo Pandey. Music: Dhananjay Mishra. Cast: Ravi Kishan, Vinay Anand, Monalisa, Lovy Rohatgi, Brijesh Tripathi, Sushil Singh.

35. *Khiladi No 1*—Music: Dhananjay Mishra.

36. *Kishan Arjun*—Producer-director: Sunil Boobna. Cast: Anuj Sharma, Gaurav Ghai, Rinku Ghosh.

37. *Lagal Raha Ae Rajaji*—Director: Rajkumar Pandey. Music: Ashok Kumar Deep. Cast: Dinesh Lal Yadav 'Nirahua', Rani Chatterjee, Manoj Singh Tiger.

38. *Lakhon Mein Ek Hamaar Bhauji*—Music: Babli.

39. *Lakshmi Aisan Dulhin Hamaar*—Music: Pappu Shrivastava.

40. *Maati Ke Saugandh*—Music: Dilip Verma.

41. *Maha Maya*—Music: Lalit Sen.

42. *Mai Ta Bas Mai Baadi*—Producer: Shiv-Hari Films and Vithal Vora. Director: Dayanand Rajan. Music: Anand-Milind. Cast: Rita Bhaduri, Ravi Kishan, Kunal Singh, Rati Agnihotri.

43. *Maare Karejwa Mein Teer*.

44. *Mera Piya Ghar Aaayo O Ramji*.

45. *Munna Bajrangi*—Producer: Reena Pasi. Director: K.D. Music: Rajesh Gupta. Cast: Vikrant Singh, Sushil Singh.
46. *My Name Is Sheikh Chilli.*
47. *Naag Nagin*—Producer; Dharma Ramani. Writer-director: Rajkumar R. Pandey. Music: Dhananjay Mishra. Cast: Krishna Abhishek, Kashmira Shah, Rekha Sahay, Gopal Rai, Madhuri Misha, Sambhavna Seth.
48. *Nehiya Sanehiya.*
49. *Nirahua Chalal Sasural*—Producer: Ashok K. Kotwani. Director: K.D. Music: Rajesh-Rajnish. Cast: Dinesh Lal Yadav 'Nirahua', Pakhi Hegde, Vijaylal Yadav, Sushil Singh and Sambhavna Seth.
50. *Pratigya*—Producer: Anil Samrat and Sanjay Sinha. Director: Sushil Kumar Upadhyay. Cast: Dinesh Lal Yadav 'Nirahua', Pawan Singh, Pakhi, Kunal Singh, Manoj Singh Tiger.
51. *Pyar Jab Kehu Se Hoi Jala*—Director: Umar Khan. Music: Gunwant Sen–Raj Sen. Cast: Jeet, Divya Desai, Kunal Singh.
52. *Rang De Basanti Chola*—Producer: Sudhakar Pandey. Director: Vishal Verma. Music: Vinay Bihari Cast: Dinesh Lal Yadav 'Nirahua', Pankaj Kesari, Pakhi Hegde, Sweety Chhabra, Daya Shankar Pandey, Anand Mohan.
53. *Rangeela Babu*—Music: Babloo Mahendra.
54. *Saat Bijliyan.*
55. *Sabse Bada Rupaiya.*
56. *Saiyan Anadi Ba Hamaar*—Music: Amresh Shahabadi.
57. *Saiyan Bane Thanedar*—Music: Laxmi-Vasant.
58. *Sajan Pardesiya*—Music: Sanjeev Rana.
59. *Sajan Sang Laagi Laganiya Re*—Producer: Kamlesh Kumar. Director: Braj Bhooshan. Music: Anand Milind. Cast: Kunal Singh, Gaurav Ghai, Gunjan Kapoor, Rachna Maurya, Anil Dhavan.
60. *Sajna Sajai Da Maang*—Producer-director: Shreedhar Shetty. Music: Dhananjay Mishra. Cast: Ravi Kishan, Pratibha Pandey, Pakhi Hegde, Bandini Mishra and Kunal Singh.
61. *Senurwa Ke Rang Hazaar.*
62. *Suratiya Arajiya Hamaar.*

63. *Swarg Jaisan Ghar Sansar*—Producer: B. Mandal. Director: Umesh Srivastava. Music: Prasenjit Chakraborty. Cast: Priya, Dhiraj Pandit.
64. *Thela No 501*—Producer: Robert D'Mello. Director: Anirudh Tiwari. Music: Dhananjay Mishra. Cast: Manoj Tiwari, Nagma, Johny Lever, Sadashiv Amrapurkar, Raza Murad.
65. *Tohre Se Biyah Karab Memsaheb*—Director: Sanjay Mukherjee and Parthasarthy. Music: Aseem Chatterjee and Santosh Aneesabadi. Cast: Rachna Banerjee and Jishu.
66. *Tu Babuaa Hamaar*—Producer: Hetal Upadhyay and Dr Dev Dutt Kapadia. Director: Anand D. Ghataraj. Music: Dhananjay Mishra. Cast: Amar Upadhyay, Monalisa, Vijay Khare, Shivam Tiwari.
67. *Umariya Kailin Tohre Naam*.
68. *Vidhata*—Producer: Pratibha Singh. Director: Harry Fernandes. Music: Gunwant Sen-Lal Sinha. Cast: Ravi Kishan, Dinesh Lal Yadav 'Nirahua', Anara Gupta, Pakhi Hegde.
69. *Yaad Rakhiha Bachan Dada Ke*.

* * *

The following films were also made, but the years when they were censored and released remain unknown: *Nautanki*, *Patna Ke Babu*, *Sach Bhaile Sapanwa Hamaar*, *Kahe Roothle Vidhata*, *Ghayal Piyawa*, *Ganga Ke Gaon*, *Biyah Kar La Lagi Na Dahej*, *Saiyan Tohre Pe Naaj Ba*, and *Rang Barse*. Another film *Mai Ke Anchra*, produced by a person from Holland, was made in 1986.

Sources

Brochures of Bhojpuri films; film trade magazines such as *Film Information*; a list published by Hindustan newspaper on 23 November 1993; a list published in Manoj Kumar Bhavuk's *Bhojpuri Cinema ke Vikas Yatra*; Har Mandir Singh 'Hamraaz', *Hindi Film Geet Kosh* (Vol. IV), and Bishwanath Chatterjee, *Hindi Film Geet Kosh* (Vol. V).

I have also taken information from various internet sites such as *ciwf.com*. The information on the number of Bhojpuri films censored every year from 1962–94 is from the *Encyclopaedia of Indian Cinema* by Ashish Rajadhyaksha and Paul Willemen. Some statistics have also been taken from the poorly maintained and occasionally dysfunctional website of the Indian Censor Board.

Sources

This book includes material taken from original interviews conducted by the author with the following individuals. They were carried out in person, on phone and via emails.

Abha Dhuliya (Actress); Abhay Sinha (Producer, 2008); Adarsh Jain (Director, 2008); Ajay Sinha (Director, 2006 and 2009); Alok Dubey (Anand Mandir, Benares); Anand D. Ghatraj (Director, 2008); Anand–Milind (Music composer duo, 2008); Anirudh Tiwary (Writer, 2008); Anjani Tiwary (Art director, 2009); Arti Bhattacharya (Actress, 2008); Aslam Sheikh (Director, 2009); Babloo Soni (Director, 2008); Bandini Mishra (Actress, 2009); Bhagtu Motwani (VCD producer, 2009); Braj Bhooshan (Director, 2009); Brijesh Tripathi (Actor, 2009); Cinema goers at Milan Chitra Mandir, Raja ki Talab and Kanhaiya Talkies, Mughalsarai; Dev Malhotra (Actor); Dhananjay Mishra (Music composer, 2008); Dinesh Lal Yadav 'Nirahua' (Actor-singer, 2009); Dipankar Bose (Director, 2008); Divya Desai (Actress, 2009); Govind Moonis (Director, 2009); Hasmukh Rajput (Director, 2008); Himalaya Dassani (Producer, 2008); J. Mohan (Producer-actor, 2008); Jaidev Karmakar (Gatekeeper, Kanhaiya Talkies, Mughalsarai); Jaishree T. (Actress); Joginder Mahajan (Distributor); K.D. [Dinkar Kapoor] (2009); Kalpana (Singer, 2009); Kamal Kumar Shukla (Small-time film exhibitor, 2008); Kirit Desai (Moti Cinema, Delhi, 2009); Kumkum (Actress); Kumud Chhugani (Actress, 2008); Kunal Singh (Actor, 2008); Lal Sinha (Music composer, 2008);

Lalitesh (Actor, 2009); Lalji Gupta (Producer, 2008); Lily Chakraborty (Actress);

Madhuri Mishra (Actress, 2009); Manoj Tiwari (Actor-singer, 2008); Mohanji Prasad (Director, 2008); Monalisa (Actress, 2009); Mukhtar Khan (Usher, Milan Chitra Mandir, Raja ki Talab); Mumtaz Hussain (Writer, 2008); Munnu Prasad Pandey (Journalist, 2008); Pakhi Hegde (Actress, 2009); Pandit Radhakant (Director, 2008); Pooja Vora (representative of T-series); Pushpa Verma (Actress, 2008); Raghubir Singh Gohil of Raj Pipla (2009); Rajesh Kumar Singh (Distributor, 2008); Rajkumar Shahabadi (son of Bishwanath Prasad Shahabadi); Rajkumar Sharma (Director, 2008); Rakesh Pandey (Actor, 2008); Rana Bhattacharya (son of actor Ashim Kumar, 2008); Rani Chatterjee (Actress); Ravi Kishan (Actor, 2008); Rinku Ghosh (Actress, 2009); Sambhavna Seth (Actress, 2009); Seema Vaz (Actress, 2009); Shakti Samanta (Producer, 2008); Sheela Sahtoe (Holland-based academic); Sudhakar Pandey (Producer, 2006); Sudhir Singh (Gatekeeper, Milan Talkies, Raja Ki Talab, 2008); Suresh Prasad Pandey (Journalist, 2008); Vanaja T. Thekkat (Ministry of Overseas Indian Affairs); Vijay Khare (Actor, 2009); Vinay Bihari (Lyricist, 2008); Birendra Paswan (Actor, 2008); Visham Bhimull (Trinidad-based Bhojpuri cinema lover)

Select References

Books

Rajadhyaksha, Ashish and Paul Willemen, *Encyclopaedia of Indian Cinema* (New Delhi: Oxford University Press, 1999).

Rangoonwalla, Firoze, *A Pictorial History of Indian Cinema* (London: Hamlyn, 1979).

Tiwary, Mukteshwar, 'Besudh,' *Bhojpuri Lokotiyan Aur Muhavare* (Baliya: Hindi Parishad, 1971).

Articles

Bharadwaj, Ajay, 'In Punjab, Bhojpuri Films Doing Great Business,' *DNA*, August 2007.

Bharati, Arun, '*Bhojpuri Filmon Ka Bazaar Hai Aur Rahega*,' *Lokpath*, 7 August 1965.

Borpujari, Utpal, 'Bhojpuri film with Marathi-speaking villains a big hit,' *Sakal Times*, 24 September 2008.

Chopra, Anupama, 'Bye-bye Bharat,' *India Today*, 1 December 1997.

Dubey, Shankar Dutt, '*Bhojpuri Filmein Tab Aur Ab*,' *Rambha*, 12 July 1965.

Ghosh, Avijit, 'Attacks Can't Dent Bhojpuri Star Tiwari's Mass Appeal,' *Times of India*, 17 February 2008.

———. 'Bhojpuri Flicks like Oxygen for Ludhiana Cinema Halls,' *Times of India*, 16 October 2007.

———. 'Bhojwood Dreams Big,' *Times of India*, 27 May 2007.

———. 'Cinema Halls Attacks Reveal Envy, Resentment,' *Times of India*, 5 February 2008.

———. 'Dalits Strive to Make it in Hindi, Bhojpuri films,' *Times of India*, 6 April 2008.

———. 'Father-in-law Has Pots of Money,' in *First Proof, The Penguin Book Of New Writing From India 3* (New Delhi: Penguin, 2007).

———. 'The Lost Village,' *Pioneer*, 4 January 1998.

———. 'The Mofussil's Revenge,' *Times of India*, 1 November 2005.

———. 'Western UP Carves its Own Bollywood,' *Times of India*, 26 May 2006.

Gupta, Trisha, 'High Culture,' *Tehelka*, 1 August 2009.

Jha, Girdhar, 'Bhojpuri Films Oust Bollywood from Bihar Halls,' *Mail Today*, 23 December 2007.

———. 'Nothing Official about Dutch Stamp on Manoj Tiwari,' *Mail Today*, 28 May 2008.

Jha, Kumar Vinay, '*Bhojpuri Ki 70 Phisdi Filmein Aundhein Mooh Girin*,' *Hindustan*, 20 December 2007.

Joshi, Namrata, '*Ab Hamaar Film Hit Hoi*,' *Outlook* (3 October 2005).

Kumar, Abhay, 'Bhojpuri Cinema: UP, Bihar Looted,' *Deccan Herald*, 21 October 2007.

Kumar, Anuj, Manoj Tiwari, 'A Date with Dal Bhat,' *Hindu*, 21 December 2006.

Mahapatra, Anirban Das, 'Cowbelt Calls,' *Telegraph*, 16 November 2008.

Mahurkar, Uday, 'Bhojpuri Plot,' *India Today* (24 November 2008).

Mane, Anuradha, 'Bhojpuri Film wins Silver Bear at Berlin Festival,' *Times of India*, 14 February 2008.

Nivas, Namia, 'In the Name of the Father: Raj Kumar Shahabadi,' *Screen* (6 February 2009).

Prabhat, Ranjan, '*Darshak Hi Lagayenge Ankush: Mohanji Prasad*,' *Hindustan*, 2 November 2007.

Press Trust of India, 'Anil Kapoor, Raveena to Debut in Bhojpuri Films,' *DNA*, 9 November 2008.

———. 'Bihar to Have a Studio for Bhojpuri Films,' *Hindu*, 8 November 2008.

———. 'MNS Fear: Bhojpuri Film Industry May Shift Out of Mumbai,' 2 November 2008.

———. 'Now Corporate Funding for Bhojpuri Films,' *DNA*, 17 July 2008.

Raman, Anuradha, 'Bollywood's Trying to Read Bhojpuri,' *Indian Express*, 5 June 2005.

Sahi, Ajit, 'The Revenge of the Bhojpuria,' *Tehelka*, 15 March 2008.

Salam, Ziya Us, 'Feast from the East,' *Hindu*, 7 October 2005.

Sawhney-Joshi, Anubha, 'I Have Offers from Three Bollywood Filmmakers,' *Times of India*, 15 June 2008.

Shankar, A., 'The Rise and Rise of Bhojpuri Cinema,' *Business Standard* (21 February 2007).

Sharma, Parul, 'The Shining Star of Bhojpuri Cinema,' *Hindu*, 26 March 2007.

Shukla, Shruti, 'Bihar's First Hero,' *Youth Times*, 16–30 June 1980.

Singh, Manoj Kumar, 'Bhavuk,' '*Bhojpuri Cinema ke Vikas Yatra*,' *Bhojpuri Varta* (July–September 2000 and January–March 2001).

Sinha, Meenakshi, 'Bhojpuri Stars Spice Up Poll Mix,' *Times of India*, 28 March 2009.

Uncredited, 'Bachchan Bholanath,' *Sanmarg* (4 September 1983).

Uncredited, '*Bhojpuri Doobi Nahi, Doob Rahi Hai*,' *Chitravani* (4 July 1965).

Uncredited, 'No Final View till UPSC Language Policy is Finalized,' *Tribune*, 5 May 2008.

Uncredited, *'Sita Maiya Ek Abhootpoorva Darshaniya Chitra,'* *Rambha* (5 September 1964).

Uncredited, *'Videshon Ki Nakal sharmnak,'* *Rambha* (14 September 1965).

Uncredited, 'Writers Must Present Reality—Nazir Hussein Recalls Netaji's Advice,' *Screen* (12 Oct 1973).

Other source material includes back issues since 1964 of *Rambha*, a weekly Hindi film newspaper published from Benares; trade magazines such as *Film Information*, *Super Box Office* and *Complete Cinema*; publicity brochures of Bhojpuri films, websites such has *bhojpuria.com*, *bhojpurifilmaward.com*, *citwf.com*, *downmelodylane.com*; and census data from the 2001 Census of India.

Index